Augmented Security Operations

AI, Automation and Guardrails for Cybersecurity Leader

Table of Contents

Acknowledgement 24

About the Author 24

Why "Augmented Security Operations"? 25

Who This Book Is For 26

What This Book Will Help You Do 27

How to Read (and Use) This Book 28

When One Login Changes Everything 29

The Reality of Modern Security Operations 30

The AI Promise and Why It's Not Enough 31

Augmentation, Not Replacement 32

The Need for Guardrails 33

Data: The Unavoidable Foundation 35

People at the Center 36

Ethics, Bias, and Surveillance Temptations 37

From Concept to Roadmap 38

What You Should Expect to Walk Away With 39

A Final Word Before We Begin 40

Chapter 1 – Why Classical SOCs Are Failing 41

    1. **The Volume, Velocity, and Variety Problem** 42
        1.1. Volume: More Data Than Humans Can Reason About 42
        1.2. Velocity: Everything, Everywhere, All at Once 42
        1.3. Variety: Heterogeneous, Noisy, and Incomplete 43

    2. **Alert Fatigue and Analyst Burnout** 43
        2.1. The Growing Pile of "Unloved" Alerts 43
        2.2. The Human Cost: Burnout and Turnover 44
        2.3. Quality Degrades as Quantity Grows 44

    3. **Skill Shortages and the Talent Gap** 45
        3.1. Limited Supply, Growing Demand 45
        3.2. Complexity of the Modern Stack 45
        3.3. The Experience Gap in Critical Moments 46

    4. **Fragmented Tools, Siloed Data** 46
        4.1. The "Tool Zoo" Problem 46
        4.2. Siloed Data, Siloed Context 47
        4.3. Integration Fatigue 47

    5. **Why Incremental Tuning Is No Longer Enough** 48
        5.1. Diminishing Returns from Rule Tuning 48

    5.2. Process Improvements Can't Keep Up with Complexity 48
    5.3. Automation Without Intelligence Is Shallow 48

6. **What "Autonomous Defense" Actually Means** 49
    6.1. Autonomy Is a Spectrum, not a Switch 49
    6.2. What Autonomous Defense Is Not 50
    6.3. What Autonomous Defense Is 50

Key Takeaways from Chapter 1 51

Chapter 2 – AI Building Blocks for Security Leaders (No Hype) 52

1. **Types of AI Relevant to SOCs** 53
    1.1. Supervised Learning 53
    1.2. Unsupervised Learning & Anomaly Detection 54
    1.3. Reinforcement & Decision Models 54
    1.4. Generative AI and Large Language Models (LLMs) 55

2. **Detection vs. Decision vs. Generation – Three Roles of AI** 56
    2.1. AI for Detection 56
    2.2. AI for Decision 56
    2.3. AI for Generation 57

3. **Data Foundations: Logs, Telemetry, Context, and Labels** 57
    3.1. Raw Logs and Events 58
    3.2. Telemetry and Metrics 58
    3.3. Context and Enrichment 58
    3.4. Labels and Outcomes 59

4. **Where AI Fits in the Existing SIEM/SOAR Stack** 59
    4.1. In the Data & Analytics Layer 60
    4.2. In the Automation & Orchestration Layer 60
    4.3. In the Analyst Interaction Layer 60
    4.4. In the Reporting & Governance Layer 61

5. **Limitations, Hallucinations, and Common Failure Modes** 61
    5.1. Data Quality and Bias 61
    5.2. Model Drift 62
    5.3. Overfitting to the Past 62
    5.4. Hallucinations in Generative AI 62
    5.5. Over-Automation and Loss of Human Intuition 63

6. **Principles for Safe and Controlled AI Adoption in Security** 63
    6.1. Start with Clear, Bounded Use Cases 63
    6.2. Keep a Human in the Loop for High-Impact Actions 64
    6.3. Design for Transparency and Explainability 64
    6.4. Build Feedback Loops by Design 64
    6.5. Separate Experimentation from Production 65
    6.6. Align AI Use with Ethics, Compliance, and Privacy 65

Key Takeaways from Chapter 2 66

Chapter 3 – Reference Architectures: From SOC to Autonomous SOC 67

1. **The Baseline: What a "Good" Modern SOC Looks Like Today** 67
    1.1. Core Components of the Baseline SOC 67
    1.2. Characteristics of a "Healthy Enough" SOC for AI 68

2. **Introducing the AI Augmentation Layers** 68
   - 2.1. Enrichment & Understanding Layer 69
   - 2.2. Triage & Prioritization Layer... 69
   - 2.3. Analyst AI assistant Layer 70
   - 2.4. Automation & Autonomous Action Layer 70

3. **Example Architecture: AI Sitting on Top of SIEM + SOAR** 71
   - 3.1. Data Flow: From Events to Action 71
   - 3.2. AI Analytics Service: Under the Hood 72
   - 3.3. AI Assistant Service: The Analyst's Interface 72
   - 3.4. AI Content & Documentation Service 72

4. **Multi-Tenant / MSSP Considerations** 73
   - 4.1. Data Separation and Security 73
   - 4.2. Shared vs. Per-Tenant Models 74
   - 4.3. Multi-Tenant Views and Experiences 74

5. **Integrating CTI, Deception, and External Telemetry** 74
   - 5.1. Threat Intelligence (CTI) Integration 75
   - 5.2. Deception and Honeypot Telemetry 75
   - 5.3. External Surface and Exposure Data 75

6. **Selecting Platforms vs. Building Your Own Components** 76
   - 6.1. Where Platforms Make Sense 76
   - 6.2. Where Customization Is Critical 77
   - 6.3. "AI in the Platform" vs. "AI Beside the Platform" 77
   - 6.4. Architectural Principles for Maintainability 77

Key Takeaways from Chapter 3 78

Chapter 4 – Data Strategy: Fuel for Your AI-Driven SOC 79

1. **Identifying Your "Golden Sources" of Security Data** 79
   - 1.1. Golden Sources vs. Nice-to-Have Sources 79
   - 1.2. Mapping Your Current Data Landscape 80
   - 1.3. Prioritizing Sources for AI 81

2. **Normalization, Enrichment & Context** 81
   - 2.1. Normalization: Agreeing on What Things Mean 81
   - 2.2. Enrichment: Filling the Gaps 82
   - 2.3. Context: Connecting to Business Reality 83

3. **Data Quality & Coverage: Are You Actually Ready for AI?** 83
   - 3.1. Coverage: Where Are the Blind Spots? 84
   - 3.2. Quality: Is the Data Clean Enough to Trust? 84
   - 3.3. A Simple Readiness Checklist 85

4. **Building Feedback Loops from Analysts to Models** 85
   - 4.1. From "Case Notes" to Structured Feedback 85
   - 4.2. Incorporating Feedback into Models 86
   - 4.3. Human-in-the-Loop as a Design Principle 86

5. **Retention, Privacy & Regulatory Constraints** 87
   - 5.1. Retention: Balancing History & Cost 87
   - 5.2. Privacy & PII in an AI-Augmented SOC 88
   - 5.3. Transparency and Explainability for Regulators & Customers 88

- 6. Metrics for Data Readiness and Improvement 88
  - 6.1. Coverage Metrics 89
  - 6.2. Quality Metrics 89
  - 6.3. Enrichment & Context Metrics 89
  - 6.4. Feedback & Learning Metrics 89
  - 6.5. Governance & Compliance Metrics 90

Key Takeaways from Chapter 4 90

Chapter 5 – AI for Alert Triage & Noise Reduction 91

- 1. Prioritization Models: From Flat Lists to Risk-Aware Queues 91
  - 1.1. Dimensions of Risk-Aware Prioritization 92
  - 1.2. Risk-Based vs. Asset-Based vs. Behavior-Based Models 92
  - 1.3. Combining Models into a Score 93
- 2. AI-Driven Deduplication & Correlation of Alerts 94
  - 2.1. The Duplication Problem 94
  - 2.2. Correlation and "Episode" Grouping 94
  - 2.3. AI Techniques for Deduplication & Correlation 95
- 3. Example Workflows: From Raw Alerts to Prioritized Queues 95
  - 3.1. Before AI: Traditional Triage 95
  - 3.2. After AI: Tiered, AI-Augmented Triage 96
- 4. Using LLMs to Summarize Complex Alerts into Plain Language 98
  - 4.1. From Fields to Narrative 98
  - 4.2. Use Cases for Summarization 98
  - 4.3. Guardrails for Summarization 99
- 5. Reducing MTTA and MTTD – What "Good" Looks Like 99
  - 5.1. Measuring Before and After 99
  - 5.2. What "Good" Might Look Like in Practice 100
- 6. Pitfalls: Over-Reliance, Missed Edge Cases, and Blind Spots 100
  - 6.1. Over-Reliance on Scores 100
  - 6.2. Blind Spots from Missing Data 100
  - 6.3. Misconfigured or Misaligned Models 101
  - 6.4. Model Drift as the Environment Changes 101
  - 6.5. Analyst Disengagement 101

Key Takeaways from Chapter 5 102

Chapter 6 – AI assistant for Analysts & Threat Hunters 103

- 1. Natural Language Querying: "Google for Your SOC" 103
  - 1.1. Why Natural Language Matters 104
  - 1.2. How It Works Under the Hood (At a High Level) 104
  - 1.3. Design Principles for Natural Language Querying 104
- 2. Enrichment Assistants: Pulling Context Automatically 105
  - 2.1. What Good Enrichment Feels Like to Analysts 105
  - 2.2. Typical Enrichment Sources 106
  - 2.3. Automation Patterns for Enrichment 106
- 3. Hypothesis Generation for Threat Hunting 107
  - 3.1. From Alert to Hunt: Asking "What Else Should I Check?" 107
  - 3.2. Hunt Libraries and Pattern Sharing 108

- 3.3. Proactive Hunting Campaigns 108
- 4. **Assisted Investigation Timelines & Root-Cause Summaries** 108
  - 4.1. From Raw Events to a Coherent Timeline 109
  - 4.2. Root-Cause Analysis Assistance 109
  - 4.3. Multi-Audience Reporting 110
- 5. **Training the AI assistant on Your SOC's Environment & Playbooks** 110
  - 5.1. Data & Knowledge to Feed the AI assistant 110
  - 5.2. SOC-Specific "Skills" for the AI assistant 111
  - 5.3. Continuous Tuning & Localization 112
- 6. **Keeping a Human in the Loop: Review, Approval, and Escalation** 112
  - 6.1. Where Human Oversight Is Essential 112
  - 6.2. Approval Flows and Guardrails 113
  - 6.3. Escalation and "I'm Not Sure" Cases 113
  - 6.4. Building and Maintaining Trust 113

Key Takeaways from Chapter 6 114

Chapter 7 – AI-Generated Playbooks, Runbooks & Reports 115

- 1. **Turning Tribal Knowledge into Standardized Playbooks** 115
  - 1.1. Interviewing Your SOC Through AI 116
  - 1.2. Structuring a Playbook for AI and Humans 116
  - 1.3. Keeping Playbooks Alive 117
- 2. **Using AI to Draft and Refine SOAR Workflows** 118
  - 2.1. From Playbook Text to SOAR Workflow Draft 118
  - 2.2. AI as a Workflow Reviewer 119
  - 2.3. Guardrails for Automated Workflows 119
- 3. **Automated Incident Reports for Executives and Customers** 119
  - 3.1. Input: What the AI Needs 120
  - 3.2. Output: Multi-Audience Reports 120
  - 3.3. Best Practices for AI-Generated Reports 121
- 4. **Generating Post-Incident Reviews and Lessons Learned** 121
  - 4.1. Drafting the Post-Incident Review 121
  - 4.2. Feeding Lessons Back into Playbooks and Models 122
- 5. **Template Library: Common Incident Types** 122
  - 5.1. Phishing & Business Email Compromise (BEC) 123
  - 5.2. Endpoint Malware & Ransomware 123
  - 5.3. Suspicious Authentication & Account Compromise 123
  - 5.4. Data Exfiltration & Insider Threat 123
  - 5.5. Cloud Security Incidents 124
- 6. **Governance Over AI-Authored Artifacts** 124
  - 6.1. Content Ownership and Approval 125
  - 6.2. Versioning and Change History 125
  - 6.3. Validation and Testing 125
  - 6.4. Policy for AI Usage in Documentation 126

Key Takeaways from Chapter 7 126

Chapter 8 – Pre-emptive Security with AI: CTI, Deception & Honeypots 127

1. **From Reactive to Pre-emptive Security – Mindset Shift** 127
   1.1. Reactive, Proactive, Pre-emptive – Not the Same Thing 128
   1.2. Why AI Matters Specifically for Pre-emptive Work 128
   1.3. Pre-emptive Security as a Feedback Function 128
2. **Leveraging AI for External CTI Processing and Clustering** 129
   2.1. From PDFs and Feeds to Structured Threat Records 129
   2.2. Clustering and Prioritizing Relevant Threats 130
   2.3. CTI Summaries for Executives and Engineers 130
3. **Honeypots and Deception: What to Collect, How to Analyze It** 131
   3.1. What Deception & Honeypots Are (and Are Not) 131
   3.2. What to Collect from Deception Systems 132
   3.3. AI's Role in Deception Analytics 132
4. **Using AI to Detect Emerging Attacker TTP Patterns** 133
   4.1. From IOCs to TTPs 133
   4.2. Pattern Discovery Across Multiple Data Sources 133
   4.3. Early-Warning Use Cases 134
5. **Feeding Pre-emptive Insights Back into Detection and Response** 134
   5.1. Detection Engineering: Turning Intel into Content 134
   5.2. Risk Scoring & Prioritization Adjustments 135
   5.3. Playbook & Workflow Updates 135
   5.4. Training & Awareness 135
6. **Example: Building a Continuous Threat Hunting & Deception Loop** 136
   6.1. Step 1 – Ingest & Analyze External CTI 136
   6.2. Step 2 – Deploy or Adjust Deception Assets 136
   6.3. Step 3 – Observe Attacker Behavior in Deception 136
   6.4. Step 4 – Hunt Internally Using Deception-Driven Hypotheses 137
   6.5. Step 5 – Update Detection, Playbooks, and Controls 137
   6.6. Step 6 – Close the Loop with Lessons Learned 137

Key Takeaways from Chapter 8 138

Chapter 9 – People, Skills & Operating Model in an Autonomous SOC 139

1. **New Roles in an AI-Augmented SOC** 139
   1.1. AI Engineer / ML Engineer for Security 140
   1.2. Automation Architect / SOAR Engineer 140
   1.3. SOC Product Owner 141
   1.4. Detection Engineer / Content Engineer (Evolved) 141
   1.5. Analysts & Hunters (Evolved, Not Removed) 141
2. **Upskilling Existing Analysts to Work with AI Tools** 142
   2.1. Core Mindset Shift for Analysts 142
   2.2. Practical Training Themes 143
   2.3. Training Formats That Work 143
3. **From Ticket Processors to Security "Product" Teams** 144
   3.1. Capability-Aligned Teams 144
   3.2. Outcomes vs. Activity Metrics 144
   3.3. Cross-Functional Collaboration 145
4. **Designing AI-Assisted Workflows & RACI Models** 145
   4.1. RACI in an AI-Driven Context 145

- 4.2. Levels of AI Involvement 146
- 4.3. Workflow Design Principles 146

5. Measuring Analyst Productivity & Satisfaction Post-AI 147
- 5.1. Productivity Metrics That Actually Matter 147
- 5.2. Measuring Analyst Experience and Satisfaction 148
- 5.3. Avoiding Metric Misuse 148

6. Change Management: Bringing the Team Along 148
- 6.1. Clear Narrative and Intent 148
- 6.2. Involving Practitioners Early 149
- 6.3. Phased Rollout 149
- 6.4. Addressing Fears & Misconceptions 150
- 6.5. Leadership Behaviors That Matter 150

Key Takeaways from Chapter 9 150

Chapter 10 – Risk, Governance & Compliance for AI in the SOC 152

1. The Risk Landscape of AI in Security Operations 152
- 1.1. Technical Risks 153
- 1.2. Operational Risks 153
- 1.3. Legal, Regulatory & Ethical Risks 153

2. Defining an AI Governance Model for the SOC 154
- 2.1. Ownership: Who Owns AI in the SOC? 154
- 2.2. Policy: What Is AI Allowed (and Not Allowed) to Do? 155
- 2.3. AI Use Case Lifecycle 155

3. Data Protection, Privacy & Jurisdiction 156
- 3.1. Data Classification and AI 156
- 3.2. Jurisdiction & Data Residency 156
- 3.3. Privacy by Design in SOC AI 157

4. Controls: Testing, Validation & Monitoring of AI 157
- 4.1. Pre-Deployment Testing 157
- 4.2. Performance Monitoring & Model Drift 158
- 4.3. LLM-Specific Controls 158

5. Third-Party / Vendor AI Risk Management 159
- 5.1. Due Diligence Questions to Ask Vendors 159
- 5.2. Contracts and SLAs 160
- 5.3. Vendor Lock-In & Portability 160

6. Handling AI-Related Failures and Incidents 161
- 6.1. Defining "AI Incidents" 161
- 6.2. Investigation & Root Cause for AI Issues 161
- 6.3. Learning and Transparency 162

7. Documentation, Evidence & Audit Readiness 162
- 7.1. What to Document 162
- 7.2. Audit-Friendly AI 163

Key Takeaways from Chapter 10 163

Chapter 11 – AI Guardrails & Safe Autonomy in the SOC 165

1. What AI Guardrails Really Are 165

2. **Design Principles for Safe Autonomy** 166
    2.1. Least Autonomy Principle 166
    2.2. Defense in Depth 166
    2.3. Reversibility 166
    2.4. Observability & Explainability 167
    2.5. Simplicity Over Cleverness 167
3. **Guardrails Across the Four Layers** 167
    3.1. Data Layer Guardrails 168
    3.2. Model Layer Guardrails 168
    3.3. Workflow Layer Guardrails 169
    3.4. Enforcement Layer Guardrails 170
4. **Guardrails for LLM-Based AI Assistants** 171
    4.1. Input Guardrails 172
    4.2. Output Guardrails 172
    4.3. Integration Guardrails 172
5. **Guardrails for Automation & Level 2 Autonomy** 173
    5.1. Scoping Autonomy by Use Case 173
    5.2. Escalation & Fallback Paths 174
    5.3. Separation of "Decide" vs "Do" 174
6. **Testing & Validating Guardrails** 174
    6.1. Pre-Deployment Testing 174
    6.2. Ongoing Validation 175
7. **Knowing When Guardrails Are Too Tight—or Too Loose** 176
    7.1. Signs Guardrails Are Too Loose 176
    7.2. Signs Guardrails Are Too Tight 176

Key Takeaways from Chapter 11 177

Chapter 12 – Measuring Value: Metrics, ROI & the Business Case for AI 178

1. **What "Value" Means for AI in the SOC** 178
2. **Core Metrics: What to Actually Measure** 179
    2.1. Operational Metrics 179
    2.1.1. Alert Volume & Triage Load 179
    2.1.2. Time to Triage and Investigate 179
    2.1.3. MTTA, MTTD, MTTR 179
    2.2. Detection & Risk Metrics 180
    2.2.1. True Positive / False Positive Balance 180
    2.2.2. Dwell Time for Confirmed Incidents 180
    2.2.3. Coverage of Key Threat Scenarios 180
    2.3. Human & Organizational Metrics 181
    2.3.1. Time Allocation of Analysts 181
    2.3.2. Onboarding & Skill Growth 181
    2.3.3. Analyst Satisfaction & Burnout Signals 181
3. **Establishing Baselines (Before AI)** 182
    3.1. Pick a 30–90 Day Baseline Window 182
    3.2. Use What You Already Have 182
4. **Linking AI Capabilities to Specific Metrics** 182
    4.1. Capability → Metric Mapping 183

4.2. Control vs Experiment Where Possible 183

5. Simple ROI Models & Worked Examples **184**
5.1. Time-Savings ROI 184
5.2. "Analysts Avoided" / Capacity ROI 185
5.3. Risk Reduction ROI (Simplified) 185

6. Building the Business Case for AI **186**
6.1. Structure of a Strong Business Case 186
6.2. Slide-Friendly Narrative 187

7. AI-Specific KPIs and Dashboards **187**
7.1. AI Triage & Scoring KPIs 187
7.2. AI Assistant Usage KPIs 187
7.3. Automation & Autonomy KPIs 188

8. Common Pitfalls in Measuring Value **188**

9. A 90-Day Measurement Plan **189**
Weeks 1–2: Decide What to Measure 189
Weeks 2–4: Establish Baselines 189
Weeks 4–8: Launch AI in Suggest-Only Mode 189
Weeks 8–12: Compare, Tune, and Tell the Story 189

Key Takeaways from Chapter 12 .... **190**

Chapter 13 – AI Tooling Buyer's Guide for the SOC **191**

1. Categories of AI in the SOC Tooling Landscape **191**
1.1. Native AI Features in Existing Platforms 191
1.2. AI Assistants / "Security Copilot"-Style Tools 192
1.3. AI-Powered Analytics / Data Platforms 192
1.4. SOAR / Automation Platforms with AI 192
1.5. CTI, Deception & Specialist AI Tools 193

2. Core Evaluation Principles (Beyond AI Hype) **193**
2.1. Use Cases First, Technology Second 193
2.2. Data & Integration Are King 193
2.3. Guardrails & Control Matter More Than Cleverness 194
2.4. Transparency & Observability 194
2.5. Avoid "One Giant Bet" 194

3. Key Evaluation Dimensions & Questions **194**
3.1. Use Cases & Capabilities 195
3.2. Data & Integration 195
3.3. Autonomy, Guardrails & Control 195
3.4. Model Transparency & Performance 196
3.5. Security, Privacy & Data Usage 197
3.6. Multi-Tenant & MSSP Features 197
3.7. Operations, UX & Adoption 198
3.8. Pricing & Licensing 198
3.9. Vendor Maturity & Roadmap 199

4. Buying SIEM/XDR vs AI Assistant vs SOAR vs Analytics **199**
4.1. SIEM/XDR with AI 199
4.2. AI Assistant (Cross-Tool) 199
4.3. SOAR & Automation Platforms 200

- 4.4. Analytics / Data Platforms & UEBA 200
5. **MSSP & Multi-Tenant Buyer Considerations** 200
6. **Red Flags & "Too Good to Be True" Patterns** 201
   - 6.1. Pure "Magic Box" Marketing 201
   - 6.2. No Clear Data Story 201
   - 6.3. No Metrics, No Benchmarks 202
   - 6.4. No Story on Guardrails & Autonomy 202
   - 6.5. Lock-In Without APIs 202
7. **Example Scorecard / Evaluation Template** 203

Key Takeaways from Chapter 13 203

Chapter 14 – Roadmap & Maturity Model for the Autonomous SOC 205

1. **Why You Need a Roadmap (Not a Big Bang)** 205
2. **A Simple 5-Level Maturity Model for the Autonomous SOC** 206
   - 2.1. Fragmented & Manual SOC 206
   - 2.2. Instrumented SOC 207
   - 2.3. Augmented SOC 207
   - 2.4. Semi-Autonomous SOC 208
   - 2.5. Selectively Autonomous SOC 209
3. **The First 90 Days: Foundations & Quick Wins** 210
   - 3.1. Baseline Assessment (Weeks 1–2) 210
   - 3.2. Choose 2–3 High-Impact Use Cases (Weeks 2–3) 210
   - 3.3. Data & Process Tune-Up for Those Use Cases (Weeks 3–6) 210
   - 3.4. Pilot AI in Shadow / Suggest Mode (Weeks 6–10) 211
   - 3.5. Decide What to Industrialize (Weeks 10–12) 211
4. **A 12–24 Month Roadmap to an AI-Augmented SOC** 211
   - 4.1. Phase 1 (Months 0–6): Consolidate & Augment 212
   - 4.2. Phase 2 (Months 6–12): Governed Automation & Pre-emptive Intelligence 212
   - 4.3. Phase 3 (Months 12–24): Toward Semi-Autonomous SOC 213
5. **Long-Term Target State: Selective Autonomy (3+ Years)** 214
   - 5.1. What "Good" Looks Like in 3+ Years 214
   - 5.2. Where Not to Automate (On Purpose) 215
6. **Adjusting the Roadmap for Different Organizations** 215
   - 6.1. Large Enterprise, Single-Organization SOC 215
   - 6.2. MSSP / Service Provider / Telco 216
   - 6.3. Highly Regulated or Critical Infrastructure 216
   - 6.4. Small / Mid-Market SOC or "SOC-of-One" 217
7. **Common Pitfalls & Anti-Patterns to Avoid** 217
   - 7.1. "AI First, Data Later" 217
   - 7.2. "Pilot Forever" 218
   - 7.3. "Automation Without Guardrails" 218
   - 7.4. "Magic Box Mentality" 218
   - 7.5. "Ignoring People and Org Design" 219

Key Takeaways from Chapter 14 219

Chapter 15 – Real-World Stories: Wins, Failures & Lessons Learned 220

1. Global Enterprise: Killing Alert Fatigue with AI Triage 220
   - Context 220
   - What They Did 221
   - What Worked 221
   - What Went Wrong 222
   - Lessons Learned 222

2. Automation Gone Wrong: When Containment Overreached 222
   - Context 222
   - What They Did 223
   - What Went Wrong 223
   - How They Detected the Issue 223
   - Response & Recovery 223
   - Metrics & Impact 224
   - Lessons Learned 224

3. MSSP: Scaling from 20 to 80 Customers with AI 225
   - Context 225
   - What They Did 225
   - What Worked 225
   - What Went Wrong 226
   - Metrics & Outcomes 226
   - Lessons Learned 226

4. Highly Regulated Org: AI Under the Microscope 227
   - Context 227
   - What They Did 227
   - What Worked 227
   - What Went Wrong 228
   - Metrics & Outcomes 228
   - Lessons Learned 228

5. The "SOC of One": Punching Above Its Weight with AI 229
   - Context 229
   - What They Did 229
   - What Worked 229
   - What Went Wrong 230
   - Metrics & Outcomes 230
   - Lessons Learned 230

6. Bringing It Back to Your SOC 231

Chapter 16 – Role-Based Guides: What This Journey Means for You 232

1. For CISOs / Heads of Security 232
   - How AI Changes Your World 232
   - Your Responsibilities 233
   - Your 90-Day Actions 233
   - Pitfalls to Avoid 233

2. For SOC Managers / Leads 234
   - How AI Changes Your World 234
   - Your Responsibilities 234
   - Your 90-Day Actions 234
   - Pitfalls to Avoid 234

3. For Detection / Content Engineers 235
    How AI Changes Your World 235
    Your Responsibilities 235
    Your 90-Day Actions 235
    Pitfalls to Avoid 235
4. For Automation / SOAR / Platform Engineers 236
    How AI Changes Your World 236
    Your Responsibilities 236
    Your 90-Day Actions 236
    Pitfalls to Avoid 237
5. For SOC Analysts – Tier 1 237
    How AI Changes Your World 237
    Your Responsibilities 237
    Your 90-Day Actions 238
    Pitfalls to Avoid 238
6. For SOC Analysts – Tier 2 / Incident Responders 238
    How AI Changes Your World 238
    Your Responsibilities 238
    Your 90-Day Actions 239
    Pitfalls to Avoid 239
7. For Threat Hunters 239
    How AI Changes Your World 239
    Your Responsibilities 239
    Your 90-Day Actions 240
    Pitfalls to Avoid 240
8. For CTI Analysts 240
    How AI Changes Your World 240
    Your Responsibilities 241
    Your 90-Day Actions 241
    Pitfalls to Avoid 241
9. For IT / Cloud / Application Owners (Your Partners) 241
    How AI Changes Your World 241
    Your Responsibilities 242
    Your 90-Day Actions 242
    Pitfalls to Avoid 242
10. For Risk, Compliance & Audit 242
    How AI Changes Your World 242
    Your Responsibilities 243
    Your 90-Day Actions 243
    Pitfalls to Avoid 243

Key Takeaways from Chapter 16 243

Chapter 17 – Patterns & Anti-Patterns for AI in the SOC 245

1. Why Patterns & Anti-Patterns Matter 245
2. Core Patterns for AI in the SOC 245
    2.1. Pattern 1 – "Suggest First, Then Automate" 245
    2.2. Pattern 2 – "Decisions in AI, Actions in SOAR" 246

2.3.	Pattern 3 – "Guardrails by Design, Not by Accident"	247
2.4.	Pattern 4 – "Standardize First, Then Scale with AI"	247
2.5.	Pattern 5 – "Data-First AI"	248
2.6.	Pattern 6 – "Human Feedback Loops"	249
2.7.	Pattern 7 – "Safe Early Wins"	249
2.8.	Pattern 8 – "Multi-Tenant and Context-Aware by Design"	250
2.9.	Pattern 9 – "Metrics-Driven AI Adoption"	250

3. Common Anti-Patterns (and How to Fix Them) 251
   - 3.1. Anti-Pattern 1 – "AI First, Data Later" 251
   - 3.2. Anti-Pattern 2 – "Big Bang Automation" 252
   - 3.3. Anti-Pattern 3 – "Magic Box Vendor" 252
   - 3.4. Anti-Pattern 4 – "Pilot Forever" 253
   - 3.5. Anti-Pattern 5 – "Alert Washing with AI" 254
   - 3.6. Anti-Pattern 6 – "Shadow AI & Shadow Automations" 254
   - 3.7. Anti-Pattern 7 – "Ownerless AI" 255
   - 3.8. Anti-Pattern 8 – "Humans Not in the Loop (Culturally)" 255
   - 3.9. Anti-Pattern 9 – "No Kill Switch, No Rollback" 256

4. Patterns vs Anti-Patterns – Quick Comparison 256

5. A Self-Check for Your AI-in-SOC Program 257

Key Takeaways from Chapter 17 257

Chapter 18 – Ethics, Bias & Human Impact of AI in Security Operations 259

1. Why Ethics & Human Impact Matter in the SOC 259

2. Bias in Data, Detections & AI Decisions 260
   - 2.1. Where Bias Comes From 260
   - 2.2. How Bias Shows Up in Practice 261
   - 2.3. Mitigating Bias in AI-Driven SOC Workflows 261

3. Privacy, Monitoring & Responsible Use of Employee Data 262
   - 3.1. What's at Stake 262
   - 3.2. Principles for Privacy-Respecting SOC AI 262
   - 3.3. AI Assistants & Privacy 263

4. Explainability & Accountability: Who Is Responsible? 263
   - 4.1. Human Responsibility Doesn't Go Away 263
   - 4.2. Explainability in the SOC Context 264
   - 4.3. AI as "Advisor," Not "Authority" 264

5. Human Impact on Analysts: Wellbeing, Skills & Culture 265
   - 5.1. Risk: Burnout by Acceleration 265
   - 5.2. Designing for a Healthy Analyst Experience 265
   - 5.3. Career Impact & Skills Evolution 266

6. Handling AI Errors & AI-Related Incidents Ethically 266
   - 6.1. Treat AI Failures as First-Class Incidents 267
   - 6.2. Fair Treatment of Individuals 267

7. Practical Principles & Checklists for Ethical AI in the SOC 268
   - 7.1. Five Ethical Principles for AI in the SOC 268
   - 7.2. Quick Ethical Readiness Checklist 268
   - 7.3. Questions to Ask Before Turning on a New AI Use Case 269

Key Takeaways from Chapter 18 270

Chapter 19 – The Next 3–5 Years: The Future of AI-Driven Security Operations 271

1. What Won't Change 271
   1.1. You Still Need Good Telemetry 271
   1.2. Human Judgment Still Decides Risk 272
   1.3. Governance & Documentation Will Still Matter 272
2. Tooling & Architecture: From Silos to Security Data Fabrics 273
   2.1. From SIEM + XDR + UEBA + SOAR → Integrated Platforms 273
   2.2. Security Data Fabrics & Open Schemas 273
   2.3. AI Everywhere, Not Just One "AI Product" 274
3. The Realistic Trajectory of Autonomy 274
   3.1. Where We Are Now 275
   3.2. Where We're Likely to Be in 3–5 Years 275
   3.3. Playbook Fragments as Autonomous Units 276
4. The Future Operating Model: SOC as Product & Platform 276
   4.1. SOC as Product 276
   4.2. Security Platform Teams 276
   4.3. Collaboration with IT, SRE & DevOps 277
5. Regulation, Assurance & "AI Risk Management" 277
   5.1. What Regulators Are Likely to Ask 278
   5.2. Internal Assurance & Second Lines of Defense 278
6. Skills & Careers: What Changes, What Becomes Valuable 278
   6.1. Skills That Rise in Value 279
   6.2. Roles That Will Become Commonplace 279
   6.3. What Won't Be Automated Away 280
7. How This Plays Out for Different Types of Organizations 280
   7.1. Large Enterprises 280
   7.2. MSSPs & MDR Providers 280
   7.3. Mid-Market & Traditional Organizations 281
   7.4. Cloud-Native & "SOC of Few" Teams 281
8. "No-Regret Moves" You Can Make Today 281
   8.1. Invest in Data Quality & Context 281
   8.2. Standardize Playbooks & Processes 281
   8.3. Introduce AI in Low-Risk, High-Annoyance Areas 282
   8.4. Define Autonomy Levels & Guardrails Now 282
   8.5. Build AI Literacy Across Roles 282
   8.6. Start Measuring AI's Impact Early 282
   8.7. Formalize AI Governance 283

Key Takeaways from Chapter 19 283

Chapter 20 – Your 90-Day, 1-Year and 3-Year Plan 284

1. Principles for Your Roadmap 284
2. Your First 90 Days – Foundations & Safe Wins 285
   2.1. Weeks 1–2: Baseline & Alignment 285
   2.2. Weeks 2–4: Data & Tooling Readiness 286
   2.3. Weeks 4–8: Pilot AI in Safe Workflows 286

- 2.4. Weeks 8–12: Measure, Tune, and Decide Next Steps 287
3. **Your 12-Month Plan – Scale AI Assistance & Selective Automation** 288
    - 3.1. Months 4–6: Expand AI Assistance Across the SOC 288
    - 3.2. Months 4–9: Build Guardrails & Governance into Concrete Practice 289
    - 3.3. Months 6–12: Introduce Carefully Bounded Level 2 Automation 290
    - 3.4. End of Year 1: Where You Should Be 291
4. **Your 3-Year Horizon – Mature, Metrics-Driven, AI-Augmented SOC** 291
    - 4.1. By Year 2: Consolidation & Platform Thinking 291
    - 4.2. By Year 3: Deep Integration & Continuous Improvement 292
    - 4.3. What "Good" Looks Like at 3 Years 293
5. **A Simple Roadmap Table You Can Adapt** 294
6. **Turning This Chapter into Action Tomorrow** 294

Appendix A – Example Prompts for Common SOC Workflows 296

1. A1. How to Use These Prompts 296
2. A2. Alert Triage & Enrichment Prompts 296
    - 2.1. Initial Alert Understanding 296
    - 2.1.1. Prompt – Quick alert summary (Tier 1) 296
    - 2.1.2. Prompt – Severity sanity-check 297
    - 2.2. Context & Enrichment Requests 297
    - 2.2.1. Prompt – Enrichment checklist for an alert 297
    - 2.2.2. Prompt – Consolidated enrichment summary 297
    - 2.3. Prioritization & Queue Management 298
    - 2.3.1. Prompt – Relative priority of multiple alerts 298
    - 2.3.2. Prompt – Mapping alerts to episodes/incidents 298
3. A3. Investigation & Timeline Prompts 299
    - 3.1. Building a Timeline 299
    - 3.1.1. Prompt – Turn raw events into a timeline 299
    - 3.1.2. Prompt – Highlight key milestones in a timeline 299
    - 3.2. Hypothesis Generation 300
    - 3.2.1. Prompt – "What might be happening?" 300
    - 3.2.2. Prompt – Next investigative steps 300
    - 3.3. Root Cause & Containment 300
    - 3.3.1. Prompt – Draft root-cause options 300
    - 3.3.2. Prompt – Containment options with pros/cons 301
4. A4. Threat Hunting Prompts 301
    - 4.1. Hunt Design from an Idea or TTP 301
    - 4.1.1. Prompt – Turn a TTP into a hunt plan 301
    - 4.1.2. Prompt – From CTI report to hunt tasks 301
    - 4.2. Hunt Execution Assistance 302
    - 4.2.1. Prompt – Generate SIEM queries from natural language 302
    - 4.2.2. Prompt – Hunt result triage help 302
    - 4.3. Hunt Documentation 302
    - 4.3.1. Prompt – Document a completed hunt 302
5. A5. CTI & Deception Prompts 303
    - 5.1. CTI Digest & Relevance 303
    - 5.1.1. Prompt – CTI technical + exec summary 303
    - 5.1.2. Prompt – Relevance scoring for our environment 303

- 5.2. Honeypot / Deception Analysis 304
  - 5.2.1. Prompt – Summarize attacker activity on honeypot 304
  - 5.2.2. Prompt – From honeypot logs to TTPs 304
6. **A6. Playbooks, Runbooks & Automation Prompts** 304
  - 6.1. Drafting Playbooks 304
    - 6.1.1. Prompt – Build a playbook from case history 304
    - 6.1.2. Prompt – Simplify an existing playbook 305
  - 6.2. Automation Design Help 305
    - 6.2.1. Prompt – Automation candidates from a playbook 305
    - 6.2.2. Prompt – Risk review for a proposed automation 305
7. **A7. Reporting & Communication Prompts** 306
  - 7.1. Incident Reporting 306
    - 7.1.1. Prompt – Technical incident summary 306
    - 7.1.2. Prompt – Executive-facing incident summary 306
  - 7.2. MSSP / Customer Communication 306
    - 7.2.1. Prompt – Client incident notification (MSSP) 306
    - 7.2.2. Prompt – Monthly SOC report highlights 307
8. **A8. Governance, Risk & Audit Prompts** 307
  - 8.1. AI Use Case Documentation 307
    - 8.1.1. Prompt – Document an AI capability for auditors 307
  - 8.2. AI Failure / Incident Documentation 308
    - 8.2.1. Prompt – AI-related incident summary 308
  - 8.3. Policy Drafting 308
    - 8.3.1. Prompt – Draft SOC AI usage policy 308
9. **A9. Training & Coaching Prompts** 308
  - 9.1. Coaching New Analysts 308
    - 9.1.1. Prompt – Explain an alert type to a junior analyst 308
    - 9.1.2. Prompt – Practice scenarios for juniors 309
  - 9.2. Post-Incident Training 309
    - 9.2.1. Prompt – Turn an incident into a training case 309
- **Next Steps** 309

Appendix B – AI-in-SOC Policy & Guideline Snippets 311

1. **B1. How to Use These Snippets** 311
2. **B2. Purpose & Scope Snippets** 311
   - 2.1. B2.1 – AI-in-SOC Policy Purpose 311
   - 2.2. B2.2 – Scope 311
   - 2.3. B2.3 – Policy Objectives 312
3. **B3. Definitions Snippets** 312
   - 3.1. B3.1 – Key Terms 312
4. **B4. Roles & Responsibilities Snippets** 312
   - 4.1. B4.1 – CISO / Head of Security Operations 312
   - 4.2. B4.2 – SOC Product Owner / SOC Lead 313
   - 4.3. B4.3 – AI / ML Engineer (Security) 313
   - 4.4. B4.4 – Automation / SOAR Engineer 313
   - 4.5. B4.5 – Detection Engineer 313
   - 4.6. B4.6 – SOC Analysts & Threat Hunters 313
   - 4.7. B4.7 – Data Protection / Privacy Officer 314

5. B5. AI Use Case Classification & Autonomy Levels 314
- 5.1. B5.1 – Use Case Categories 314
- 5.2. B5.2 – Autonomy Level Statement 314
- 5.3. B5.3 – Approval Requirement Snippet 314

6. B6. Data Handling & Privacy Snippets 315
- 6.1. B6.1 – Data Minimization 315
- 6.2. B6.2 – Data Classification & AI Access 315
- 6.3. B6.3 – External / Cloud AI Services 315

7. B7. Model Governance & Lifecycle Snippets 315
- 7.1. B7.1 – AI Use Case Lifecycle 315
- 7.2. B7.2 – Performance Monitoring 316
- 7.3. B7.3 – Testing & Shadow Mode 316

8. B8. Automation Guardrails Snippets 316
- 8.1. B8.1 – Guardrail Principles 316
- 8.2. B8.2 – Safe Domains for Early Autonomy 317
- 8.3. B8.3 – Human Override 317

9. B9. Third-Party / Vendor AI Snippets 317
- 9.1. B9.1 – Vendor AI Assessment 317
- 9.2. B9.2 – Contractual Requirements 317

10. B10. AI Incident Handling & Logging Snippets 318
- 10.1. B10.1 – AI Incident Definition 318
- 10.2. B10.2 – AI Incident Response 318
- 10.3. B10.3 – Logging Requirements 318

11. B11. Training & Culture Snippets 319
- 11.1. B11.1 – Analyst Training 319
- 11.2. B11.2 – Culture of Questioning AI 319

12. B12. Example: One-Page "AI in SOC" Policy Summary 319

Next Steps 320

Appendix C – Sample Runbooks & Report Templates 321

1. C1. How to Use This Appendix 321

2. C2. Generic Incident Runbook Template 321
- 2.1. C2.1 Runbook Header 321
- 2.2. C2.2 Scope & Preconditions 321
- 2.3. C2.3 Roles & Responsibilities 322
- 2.4. C2.4 High-Level Flow 322
- 2.5. C2.5 Step Table (Pattern) 322
- 2.6. C2.6 Exit Criteria 322

3. C3. Runbook #1 – Suspicious User Login (Potential Account Compromise) 323
- 3.1. C3.1 Header 323
- 3.2. C3.2 Scope 323
- 3.3. C3.3 Step Table 323
- 3.4. C3.4 Exit Criteria 324

4. C4. Runbook #2 – Phishing Email Reported by User 324
- 4.1. C4.1 Header 324
- 4.2. C4.2 Scope 324

- 4.3. C4.3 Step Table 324
- 4.4. C4.4 Exit Criteria 325

5. **C5. Runbook #3 – Endpoint Malware Alert (Single Host, Non-Critical) 325**
   - 5.1. C5.1 Header 325
   - 5.2. C5.2 Scope 325
   - 5.3. C5.3 Step Table 326
   - 5.4. C5.4 Exit Criteria 326

6. **C6. Runbook #4 – Early-Stage Ransomware on Single Endpoint 326**
   - 6.1. C6.1 Header 326
   - 6.2. C6.2 Scope 327
   - 6.3. C6.3 Step Table 327
   - 6.4. C6.4 Exit Criteria 327

7. **C7. Technical Incident Report Template 327**
   - 7.1. C7.1 Header 328
   - 7.2. C7.2 Summary 328
   - 7.3. C7.3 Environment & Scope 328
   - 7.4. C7.4 Detection & Triage 328
   - 7.5. C7.5 Investigation 328
   - 7.6. C7.6 Root Cause & Contributing Factors 329
   - 7.7. C7.7 Containment, Eradication & Recovery 329
   - 7.8. C7.8 Impact Assessment 329
   - 7.9. C7.9 Lessons Learned & Improvements 329
   - 7.10. C7.10 Attachments & References 330

8. **C8. Executive Incident Summary Template 330**
   - 8.1. C8.1 Basic Details 330
   - 8.2. C8.2 What Happened (Plain Language) 330
   - 8.3. C8.3 Impact 330
   - 8.4. C8.4 Response 330
   - 8.5. C8.5 Risk & Next Steps 331

9. **C9. MSSP / Multi-Tenant Customer Report Template 331**
   - 9.1. C9.1 Monthly/Quarterly SOC Report – Structure 331
   - 9.2. C9.2 Example Section Text 332

10. **C10. Post-Incident Review (PIR) Template 332**
    - 10.1. C10.1 Basic Info 332
    - 10.2. C10.2 Objectives 332
    - 10.3. C10.3 What Happened 333
    - 10.4. C10.4 What Worked Well 333
    - 10.5. C10.5 What Didn't Work / Pain Points 333
    - 10.6. C10.6 Improvements & Action Items 333
    - 10.7. C10.7 AI-Specific Reflection (Optional Section) 333

Appendix D – SOC Maturity & Readiness Checklists 335

1. **D1. High-Level SOC Maturity Checklist 335**
   - 1.1. D1.1 Strategy & Governance 335
   - 1.2. D1.2 Data & Visibility 336
   - 1.3. D1.3 Detection & Response 336
   - 1.4. D1.4 People & Operating Model 336
   - 1.5. D1.5 Tooling, SOAR & Automation 337

- 2. **D2. AI Readiness Checklist (Pre-Autonomous SOC)** 337
  - 2.1. D2.1 Data & Telemetry Readiness for AI 337
  - 2.2. D2.2 Process & Playbook Readiness 338
  - 2.3. D2.3 Governance & Risk for AI 338
  - 2.4. D2.4 People & Culture Readiness 338
  - 2.5. D2.5 Technology & Integration Readiness 338
- 3. **D3. SOC "Autonomy Readiness" Checklist** 339
  - 3.1. D3.1 Policy & Guardrails 339
  - 3.2. D3.2 Logging, Monitoring & Control 339
  - 3.3. D3.3 Testing & Validation 340
  - 3.4. D3.4 Impact & Risk Awareness 340
- 4. **D4. AI-in-SOC Maturity Grid (Condensed)** 341
- 5. **D5. Quick "Go / No-Go" Gate for AI Triage & AI assistant** 341
- 6. **D6. Quick "Go / No-Go" Gate for Level 2 Autonomy** 342
- 7. **D7. Turning Checklists into a Practical Plan** 342

Appendix E – Practical Checklists, Templates & Worksheets 344

- 1. **Quick Checklists** 344
  - 1.1. AI Readiness Checklist (SOC-Level) 344
  - 1.2. AI Use Case Selection Checklist 345
  - 1.3. Guardrails & Autonomy Checklist 346
  - 1.4. Ethics, Bias & Privacy Quick Check 347
  - 1.5. Metrics & ROI Checklist 347
- 2. **Design Templates** 348
  - 2.1. AI Use Case Design Canvas 348
  - 2.2. Playbook + Autonomy Template 349
  - 2.3. Prompt Template Sheet 350
  - 2.4. AI-In-SOC Policy Skeleton (Mini Outline) 351
  - 2.5. Incident Report Template (AI-Assisted) 352
- 3. **Operational Worksheets** 354
  - 3.1. AI Use Case Inventory Worksheet 354
  - 3.2. AI Pilot Evaluation Worksheet 354
  - 3.3. Detection & Automation Improvement Log (AI-Driven) 355
- 4. **Review & Governance Helpers** 355
  - 4.1. Quarterly AI-in-SOC Review Snapshot 355
  - 4.2. AI-Related Incident Addendum 356
  - 4.3. New AI Feature Review Checklist 357

Appendix F – AI Buyer's RFP Checklist & Vendor Questionnaire 359

- 1. **How to Use This Appendix** 359
  - 1.1. Decide What You're Buying 359
- 2. **RFP Requirement Checklist** 359
  - 2.1. Use Case Fit & Capabilities 360
  - 2.2. Data & Integration 360
  - 2.3. Autonomy, Guardrails & Control 361
  - 2.4. Model Transparency & Performance 361
  - 2.5. Security, Privacy & Data Usage 362

	2.6.	Multi-Tenant & MSSP Readiness (if applicable)	362
	2.7.	UX, Adoption & Training	363
	2.8.	Pricing & Licensing	363
	2.9.	Vendor Maturity & Roadmap	364
3.	**Vendor Questionnaire (Ready-to-Use Question Bank)**		**364**
	3.1.	Use Cases & Capabilities	364
	3.2.	Data & Integration	365
	3.3.	Autonomy & Guardrails	365
	3.4.	Model Transparency & Performance	365
	3.5.	Security, Privacy & Data Usage	366
	3.6.	Multi-Tenant & MSSP	366
	3.7.	UX, Adoption & Training	366
	3.8.	Pricing & Commercials	367
	3.9.	Vendor Maturity & Roadmap	367
4.	**Example Scoring & Comparison Template**		**367**
	Next Steps		368

Appendix G – Hands-On Labs & Exercises **369**

1. **How to Use This Appendix** **369**
    1.1. Lab 1 – AI-Assisted Alert Summarization 370
    1.2. Lab 2 – AI-Assisted Investigation Timelines 371
    1.3. Lab 3 – CTI to Hunts & Detections 373
    1.4. Lab 4 – Designing Autonomy Levels & Playbooks 375
    1.5. Lab 5 – Shadow-Mode AI Triage Scoring 376
    1.6. Lab 6 – Metrics & ROI Mini-Project 378
    1.7. Lab 7 – Ethics, Bias & Privacy Tabletop 379
    1.8. Lab 8 – AI-Related Incident Postmortem Simulation 380

Appendix H – 90-Day / 1-Year / 3-Year Action Worksheets **383**

1. **Current State Snapshot Worksheet** **383**
    1.1. SOC Profile 383
    1.2. Tooling & Data Overview 383
    1.3. Telemetry Coverage Snapshot 384
    1.4. Current Metrics Baseline 384
    1.5. AI Usage Today (If Any) 384

2. **90-Day Plan Worksheet** **385**
    2.1. 90-Day Objectives (Top 3–5) 385
    2.2. Initial AI Use Cases (90-Day Scope) 385
    2.3. 90-Day Guardrail Decisions 385
    2.4. 90-Day Workplan (By Month) 386
    2.5. 90-Day Risks & Mitigations 387

3. **1-Year Plan Worksheet** **387**
    3.1. 1-Year Themes (3–5) 387
    3.2. Year-1 Use Case Expansion Map 387
    3.3. Year-1 Autonomy & Guardrail Roadmap 388
    3.4. Year-1 Governance & Policy Checklist 388
    3.5. Year-1 Milestone Timeline (Quarterly) 388

4. **3-Year Vision Worksheet** **389**

4.1.	3-Year Vision Statement (1–2 Paragraphs)	389
4.2.	3-Year Capability Targets	389
4.3.	3-Year "Non-Negotiables"	390
4.4.	3-Year "Big Rocks"	390

5. **Roadmap & Backlog Worksheet** 390
    5.1. Initiative Backlog 390
    5.2. AI Use Case Backlog 390

6. **Stakeholder & Ownership Worksheet** 391
    6.1. RACI for AI-in-SOC Program 391
    6.2. Named Owners 391

7. **Review & Retrospective Checklists** 392
    7.1. 90-Day Review Checklist 392
    7.2. Year-1 Review Checklist 392
    7.3. Annual "Health Check" Snapshot 392

Appendix I – Glossary & Acronyms **394**

A. 394
B. 395
C. 395
D. 396
E. 396
F. 397
G. 397
H. 397
I. 397
K. 398
L. 398
M. 398
N. 399
O. 399
P. 399
R. 400
S. 400
T. 401
U. 402
W. 402
X. 402

Miscellaneous Terms Used in the Book 403

Acknowledgement

This book would not exist without the people who live the reality of security operations every day. I am deeply grateful to the analysts, incident responders, detection engineers, architects, platform teams and security leaders – both colleagues and customers – who have shared their war stories, frustrations and hard-won lessons over the years; your honesty shaped the patterns, guardrails and cautions in these pages far more than any theory or marketing ever could. I also want to thank the mentors and peers who challenged my assumptions, pushed me to think more critically about AI and automation, and reminded me that good security is ultimately about people, not tools. Finally, my deepest thanks go to my family and close friends for their patience and encouragement through the long hours of writing and revising; your support made it possible to turn scattered ideas from the SOC floor into a structured guide that I hope will make the work of defenders a little more effective – and a little more sustainable – for years to come.

About the Author

Jawed Ahmad is a cybersecurity leader and architect with extensive experience designing and operating Security Operations Centers, Managed Security Services and AI-augmented detection and response capabilities. Over his career, he has worked across enterprise, service provider and consulting environments, helping organizations move from ad hoc, tool-driven security toward integrated, data-centric and automation-enabled operating models.

His work spans the full spectrum of security operations: defining operating models and playbooks, building analyst workflows, shaping incident response practices, and aligning day-to-day SOC activity with governance, risk and business priorities. He has led initiatives to reduce alert fatigue, formalize runbooks, introduce automation safely, and embed AI assistance into investigations, threat hunting, reporting and operational decision-making. A recurring theme in his work is making advanced capabilities—like AI and automation—**explainable, auditable and proportionate** to the organization's risk appetite.

This book, *Augmented Security Operations* distills the frameworks, patterns and practical lessons he has refined with real-world teams who are under constant pressure to "do more with less" – without losing control of their risk.

Why "Augmented Security Operations"?

The core belief in this book is simple:

Security operations should be augmented, not automated away.

AI and automation are not here to replace analysts, incident responders, detection engineers, or SOC managers. They are here to:

- Remove repetitive, low-value work
- Turn overwhelming data into clearer, usable context
- Suggest better next steps, faster
- Help small or stretched teams achieve more than they could alone

But they must do that within guardrails: clear boundaries for where AI is allowed to help, how far automation is allowed to go, and how quickly you can stop or reverse it when things go wrong.

Without those guardrails, "intelligent automation" becomes just another way to create self-inflicted incidents.

Who This Book Is For

This book is written for people who carry responsibility for security operations in any form:

- CISOs and security executives
- SOC managers and MSSP leaders
- Detection, IR, and threat hunting leads
- Security architects and platform/automation owners
- Senior analysts and engineers who feel the daily pain and see where things could be better

You don't need to be a data scientist or AI researcher.

You *do* need to understand:

- How your SOC works day-to-day
- What your current constraints and risks are
- Where you want to be in 1–3 years

If you can speak "alerts, incidents, SLAs, runbooks and risk", this book is for you

What This Book Will Help You Do

This is not a generic "AI in cybersecurity" overview. It is a **field manual** for:

- Understanding **realistic AI capabilities** in triage, investigations, reporting, threat hunting, and CTI
- Designing **safe autonomy levels** for automation (suggest-only, human-in-the-loop, narrow conditional autonomy)
- Building **guardrails** – preconditions, rate limits, kill switches, logging and explainability
- Getting your **data and telemetry** into a state where AI can add value instead of amplifying noise
- **Embedding AI** into **existing workflows** instead of creating yet another disconnected console
- Measuring **time savings, quality improvements and risk reduction** in ways leadership will respect
- Handling AI-related incidents and ethical concerns around bias, privacy, and over-monitoring
- Planning your next **90 days, 1 year and 3 years** with an executable roadmap, not wishful thinking

It is opinionated. It will push you away from "big bang" automation and toward incremental, measurable progress.

It will repeatedly bring you back to three questions:

- What problem in security operations are we solving?
- How will AI and automation make this better in practice?
- What guardrails and metrics do we need in place before we trust it?

How to Read (and Use) This Book

You can read it end-to-end, but you don't have to.

Think of it as a set of layers:

- **Conceptual foundation** – what "augmented security operations" really means
- **Practical workflows** – how AI and automation help in triage, investigations, CTI, hunting and reporting
- **Architecture and guardrails** – how to structure your data, platforms, and autonomy levels
- **People and ethics** – how this change affects analysts, engineers, leaders and the organization
- **Roadmaps and toolkits** – checklists, templates, runbooks, labs, RFP questions, and planning worksheets

Different chapters will speak more directly to different roles, but the central message is consistent:

AI and automation can materially improve security operations, **if** you design them as augmentations to human judgment, backed by strong guardrails, data discipline and clear accountability.

If that's the kind of transformation you want, then this book is for you.

Let's get into **Augmented Security Operations**

When One Login Changes Everything

On any given weekday, somewhere in your organization or a managed organization, a login happens that shouldn't.

- Maybe it's a real user on a compromised device.
- Maybe it's stolen credentials being tested quietly at 3:17 a.m.
- Maybe it's a VPN connection from a country where you have no staff.

The logs know.
Your tools might even generate an alert.
But whether someone sees it, understands it and reacts in time, that's the work of security operations

The Reality of Modern Security Operations

Security operations today are a constant attempt to separate **signals from noise** in an environment that's only getting noisier:

- You run on overlapping platforms: on-prem, multiple clouds, SaaS, remote endpoints, OT, maybe even shadow IT.
- You collect logs and telemetry from dozens of systems - identity, endpoint, network, cloud, applications.
- You've deployed a SIEM, perhaps XDR, maybe UEBA and a SOAR tool.
- Alerts flood in: some meaningful, many repetitive, some outright wrong.

Your analysts – whether you have three or thirty – sit at the convergence point of all of this. Their job is brutally simple and brutally hard:

- Acknowledge alerts
- Decide which matters
- Investigate the ones that do
- Coordinate and execute response
- Document everything in a way that makes sense to leadership, audit and regulators

At the same time, your reality as a leader is its own kind of triage:

- Recruiting and retaining people in a tight talent market
- Managing SLAs, expectations, and budgets
- Justifying investments to executives who mostly hear "AI" from vendors

You are expected to be **faster**, **smarter**, and **more efficient**, without an endless hiring budget. Something has to give.

Enter AI and automation.

The AI Promise and Why It's Not Enough

The pitch is seductive:

- "Our AI will prioritize alerts for you."
- "Our AI assistant will write your investigations and reports."
- "Our autonomous response will isolate compromised devices in seconds."

And some of this is true.

Modern AI really can:

- Summarize long, messy alert histories into something a human can parse in seconds
- Propose investigation steps and hunt queries
- Draft readable incident reports from raw case data
- Help spot patterns across identity, endpoint, and cloud activity
- Trigger well-defined response actions faster than a human could click through a UI

The problem is not that the technology is useless. The problem is that, used carelessly, it is **indifferent to context and consequences**.

- It does not know which systems in your environment are quietly fragile or business critical.
- It does not understand the political reality of locking out an executive during quarter close.
- It does not feel the weight of regulatory scrutiny if a response goes wrong.

So, while vendors are busy selling "autonomous SOCs", you are left with a harder, more important question:

How do we use AI and automation to **augment** our security operations, without handing them the keys to the kingdom?

That question runs through every page of this book.

Augmentation, Not Replacement

At the core of this book is a mindset shift:

- AI is not here to replace your analysts.
- Automation is not here to eliminate human judgment.

They are here to:

- Handle the repetitive and time-consuming parts of work
- Make better use of the data you already have
- Give your team higher-quality starting points, better triage context, better timelines, better first drafts of reports and playbooks

This is what "augmented security operations" means:

- Analysts still make decisions about risk and escalation.
- Incident responders still choose containment strategies.
- Detection engineers still decide what becomes a rule.
- Leaders still own the risk.

But they do so with systems that:

- Highlight the right alerts sooner
- Lay out coherent timelines of suspicious activity
- Bring together identity, endpoint, and cloud signals without manual stitching
- Draft case summaries and communications so humans can refine, not write from scratch

When that works, the impact is tangible: less time on noise, more on real incidents; fewer manual clicks, more analysis; less burnout, more learning.

The Need for Guardrails

Of course, the moment you connect AI and automation to **real action,** isolating endpoints, disabling accounts, changing firewall rules, you move into a different risk category.

The same capability that can save you minutes in a ransomware outbreak can also take down the wrong systems if misconfigured, mis-scored or misunderstood.

That's why this book will lean so heavily on **guardrails**.

It proposes a simple autonomy model:

- **Level 0 – Suggest Only**
  AI summarizes, highlights, scores, drafts and proposes. But it does not take action. Humans still click the buttons.

- **Level 1 – Human-in-the-Loop**
  AI and automation can prepare specific actions. They may pre-fill tickets, stage endpoint isolations, or generate IAM changes. But nothing goes live until a human approves.

- **Level 2 – Conditional Autonomy**
  For a carefully chosen set of low-risk scenarios, automation can execute without waiting for a human, but only when strict preconditions are met—specific asset types, environments, detection sources, rate limits, and visibility are all enforced.

Anything beyond that—broad, open-ended autonomy with loose checks—is treated as out of scope for responsible operations today.

Around those autonomy levels, guardrails include:

- **Preconditions** – Only act automatically:

  - On non-critical endpoints or user devices
  - In specific environments (e.g., not production databases or OT)
  - For certain vetted detections with high confidence

- **Rate Limits** – Cap the number of auto-actions in a given window:

  - To prevent runaway cascades from misfiring logic

- **Kill Switches** – Tested, well-known ways to stop:

  - A specific playbook
  - A specific integration
  - Or all automations of a given type

- **Rollback** – Practical methods:

- To un-isolate hosts, restore access or revert configuration changes

- **Logging & Explainability** – Clear records of:
    - What was done
    - Why it was done
    - Which logic or AI component contributed

These are not "nice to have." They are what turns AI and automation from a liability into an asset.

Data: The Unavoidable Foundation

If AI and automation are the "mind and hands" of augmented operations, your **telemetry and context** are the senses.

No model—statistical, machine learning or language-based—can reason about traffic it cannot see.

The book emphasizes, repeatedly, that the value of AI in security operations is constrained by:

- **Telemetry coverage** – Identity, endpoint, cloud, network, and key applications
- **Normalization and correlation** – Bringing disparate logs into coherent structure
- **Enrichment** – Attaching asset criticality, environment tags, user roles, and business context
- **Data quality** – Detecting and fixing missing sources, parse failures, time skews and noise

This is unglamorous work. It does not appear in glossy AI marketing. But without it, you end up with "AI-enhanced confusion", more confident-sounding outputs, not better decisions.

Augmented Security Operations assumes you are willing to work on the plumbing, not just the dashboards.

People at the Center

Perhaps the most important through-line in this book is that **people** remain at the center of security operations.

AI and automation change what people do, but they do not remove the need for:

- Analysts who can recognize when a story feels "off"
- Responders who understand operational fragility and business impact
- Engineers who can design detections and playbooks that make sense
- Leaders who can balance risk, investment, and capacity

The book recognizes the daily reality:

- Analysts are often overloaded and under constant time pressure.
- SOC managers are caught between what leadership wants and what is realistically achievable.
- Security architects and platform teams must integrate new capabilities into already complex stacks.
- CISOs must answer to boards and regulators who increasingly ask pointed questions about how AI is used in critical functions.

Augmented Security Operations frames AI not as a threat to these roles, but as a chance to reshape them:

- Less time copying data between tools, more time understanding adversary behavior.
- Less time creating repetitive reports, more time clarifying lessons learned.
- Less time fighting with broken processes, more time improving how the SOC works.

But this only happens if you are intentional about **where** AI is introduced and **how** success is measured.

Ethics, Bias, and Surveillance Temptations

There is one more dimension that leaders cannot ignore: the ethical and human impact of how security data is used.

The same logs you use to detect threats can reveal intimate details about how people work: when they log in, where from, which systems they access, sometimes even what they say.

AI makes it easier to correlate and analyze that data at scale. That's powerful for defense. It is also dangerous if misapplied, for example, drifting from security monitoring into employee scoring or performance surveillance.

This book pushes for:

- **Purpose limitation** – Use AI on SOC data for security purposes, not as a backdoor into HR analytics.
- **Data minimization and masking** – Especially when sending data to external AI providers.
- **Bias awareness** – Regularly reviewing patterns of who gets flagged, locked out, or scrutinized, and why.
- **Correctability** – Building processes so that when AI-influenced logic harms or mislabels someone, you can explain it, correct it, and update the system.

Augmented operations must be not just efficient, but **defensible -** technically, legally and ethically.

From Concept to Roadmap

Concepts are useful only if they turn into execution.

The book therefore devotes substantial space to:

- **First 90 days** – Baseline reality, choose 2–4 low-risk AI use cases (triage summaries, report drafting, CTI digestion), implement at Level 0 with strong feedback, start defining autonomy and guardrails.
- **First 12 months** – Scale AI assistance across more workflows, formalize autonomy levels in playbooks, introduce a small number of Level 1 and narrow Level 2 automations, build governance, metrics, and reporting.
- **3-year horizon** – Move toward a mature, platform-driven model where data, AI, automation and workflows are integrated; AI is embedded in tools analysts already use; metrics and guardrails are well understood; and you can explain your operating model clearly to leadership and regulators.

This is where the appendices become crucial: they provide checklists, templates, labs, worksheets and examples so that you are not starting from a blank page.

What You Should Expect to Walk Away With

If you fully absorb and apply the ideas in this book, you should be able to:

- Explain to your leadership team what "augmented security operations" means in your context
- Identify 3–5 high-value, low-risk AI use cases for your SOC and plan them properly
- Define autonomy levels for your major playbooks and put guardrails around them
- Build a baseline of metrics for time, quality, and risk, and show progress over time
- Run pilots and shadow-mode experiments that actually de-risk, not increase, your exposure
- Establish clear roles and responsibilities for AI and automation across your security org
- Talk about AI in security operations with auditors and regulators in a structured, confident way

Not every organization will adopt AI and automation at the same pace. Not every SOC will have the same tooling or constraints. But the principles in Augmented Security Operations are designed to hold across different sizes, industries and maturity levels.

You're not being asked to build a "self-driving SOC."

You're being asked to build a **better one**, with help from AI and automation, and with your hands still on the wheel.

A Final Word Before We Begin

AI won't magically fix a broken SOC.

It won't instantly turn junior analysts into experts or bad data into great decisions.

But used well, with clear guardrails and honest expectations, it can:

- Cut out a lot of mind-numbing work
- Help you see patterns you were missing
- Make your best people more effective
- Give you better stories and evidence for leadership and regulators

Most importantly, it can help you **spend more time on real threats and less time wrestling with tools**.

That's what this book is about.

Let's get started.

Chapter 1 – Why Classical SOCs Are Failing

Modern security operations centers weren't designed for the world they're defending today.

Most SOCs still look and feel like evolved versions of what we built 10–15 years ago: a room (physical or virtual) full of screens, a SIEM collecting everything, analysts triaging endless alerts, a ticketing system, a few playbooks, and a set of dashboards that only a handful of people truly understand.

On paper, the model still "works." In practice, it is cracking under pressure.

Attackers are faster, more automated, and better resourced. Business environments are more complex and dynamic than at any point in the last two decades. Cloud, SaaS, remote work, APIs, OT, and IoT have exploded the attack surface. Meanwhile, boards and regulators expect near-perfect visibility and rapid, well-documented response.

This chapter explains *why* the traditional SOC model is struggling and sets the stage for why AI-augmented and eventually autonomous defense is not just a buzzword – but an operational necessity.

We'll walk through six core pressure points:

1. The volume, velocity, and variety problem
2. Alert fatigue and analyst burnout
3. Skill shortages and the talent gap
4. Fragmented tools, siloed data
5. Why incremental tuning is no longer enough
6. What "autonomous defense" means

1. The Volume, Velocity, and Variety Problem

The first and most obvious reality: there is simply *too much* of everything.

1.1. Volume: More Data Than Humans Can Reason About

A modern enterprise SOC might ingest:

- Firewall, proxy, and DNS logs
- Endpoint, EDR, and agent telemetry
- Identity events from AD, IdPs, and SSO platforms
- Cloud platform logs (multiple providers)
- Application logs and API gateway events
- SaaS audit logs
- OT/IoT telemetry

Even with aggressive filtering, we're talking **billions of events per day** in larger environments and millions per day even in mid-market organizations.

Traditional SIEMs were built to *index and search* this data, not to reason over it in real time at human scale. The idea was always: "We'll let the system collect everything, then analysts will query and investigate as needed."

That model breaks when:

- The number of events far exceeds what humans can manually search and correlate.
- The attack surface changes faster than content (rules, dashboards, reports) can be updated.

1.2. Velocity: Everything, Everywhere, All at Once

Events don't just arrive in large quantities—they arrive **continuously** and in **bursts**.

- A developer misconfiguration in the cloud can generate a spike in logs within minutes.
- A phishing campaign can trigger thousands of authentication failures and unusual login attempts in an hour.
- An automated scanner can hit exposed services at scale in seconds.

The SOC is expected to:

- Detect suspicious patterns across this streaming flow
- Correlate signals from different tools
- Decide what to ignore and what to respond to
- Do this 24×7, without missing meaningful signals

Humans are good at pattern recognition and judgment, but they are not built to maintain continuous vigilance over high-speed streams of structured and unstructured data.

1.3. Variety: Heterogeneous, Noisy, and Incomplete

SOCs aren't just drowning in more data—they're drowning in *different* kinds of data:

- Different log formats and schemas
- Different naming conventions and fields
- Different levels of detail and reliability
- Different time sync accuracy
- Different security semantics (what constitutes an "event" vs a "log line" vs an "alert")

In theory, normalization and parsing solve this. In practice:

- Normalization is inconsistent across sources.
- Parsers break when vendors update formats.
- Critical context (like asset importance or user role) is often missing or maintained elsewhere.

This variety creates friction at every step:

- Writing rules and detections is harder.
- Correlating events across tools is harder.
- Investigations take longer.

The result: either you simplify your view of reality to what you can standardize (and miss things), or you accept messy complexity (and overwhelm your analysts).

2. Alert Fatigue and Analyst Burnout

When volume, velocity, and variety exceed human capacity, the symptoms show up where it hurts most: in the analysts.

2.1. The Growing Pile of "Unloved" Alerts

In most SOCs, there is a **backlog**—alerts that were never properly triaged, cases that were "parked," and suspicious events that nobody ever had time to fully investigate.

Typical patterns:

- Thousands of low- to medium-severity alerts per day
- A subset escalated to incidents and tickets

- Many closed with generic dispositions ("no issue found," "accepted risk," "false positive")

Over time, analysts see:

- The same types of alerts over and over
- Many alerts that clearly don't matter
- A small percentage that truly require action—but they're buried in the noise

This leads to **alert fatigue**: a psychological state where analysts struggle to care about each individual alert because they've seen too many that didn't matter.

2.2. The Human Cost: Burnout and Turnover

Burnout in SOCs is real:

- Night and weekend shifts
- Constant pressure to respond quickly
- Fear of missing "the one" critical alert
- Limited recognition—most of the job is preventing things that never happen

As a result:

- Talent leaves for other roles (cloud, engineering, vendor side)
- Remaining analysts carry more load
- Institutional knowledge walks out the door

Every time an experienced analyst leaves, you lose:

- Intuition for what "normal" looks like in your environment
- Familiarity with past incidents
- Rule-of-thumb shortcuts for investigation

You can hire replacements, but you can't download three years of frontline pattern recognition into their heads on day one.

2.3. Quality Degrades as Quantity Grows

Under heavy load, analysts naturally optimize for survival:

- They skim alerts rather than deeply investigate.
- They rely heavily on severity scores and default logic.
- They become more conservative or more dismissive, depending on their personality and incentives.

This increases the risk of:

- True positives being ignored because they look like "just another noisy alert."
- Investigations being documented poorly, making future learning harder.
- Shortcuts becoming unofficial standard procedure.

This is not a people problem; it is a *system design* problem. We designed SOC workflows around the assumption that humans can sustainably triage and investigate at scale. They cannot.

3. Skill Shortages and the Talent Gap

If the volume of work is going up, the logical answer is to hire more people. In security operations, that option is severely constrained.

3.1. Limited Supply, Growing Demand

The demand for:

- Tier 1 and Tier 2 analysts
- Threat hunters
- Incident responders
- Detection engineers

…has outpaced supply for years.

Organizations compete for the same pool of experienced practitioners. Salaries rise. Smaller organizations and MSSPs struggle to match offers. Even when you can hire, you often:

- Get junior candidates who need months of training
- Compete with internal teams and other projects for budget

3.2. Complexity of the Modern Stack

The skills required to be effective in a SOC have changed:

- Knowledge of on-prem infrastructure is no longer enough.
- Cloud, container, and microservices architectures bring new patterns.
- Identity-centric security requires deeper identity and access understanding.
- Threat actors are more sophisticated, using living-off-the-land techniques and blending into normal traffic.

Analysts are expected to:

- Understand multiple technology stacks
- Keep up with emerging threats and tools
- Learn new detection and response platforms regularly

This is a *moving target*. Even experienced analysts need ongoing upskilling.

3.3. The Experience Gap in Critical Moments

Many SOCs end up with an inverted pyramid:

- A wide base of junior analysts handling the bulk of alerts
- A small number of senior analysts and incident responders "on call" for escalations

This structure is fragile:

- When a major incident hits, everyone depends on a small number of people.
- If those people are unavailable, overwhelmed, or have left, response quality suffers.

You can't solve this with headcount alone. You need to:

- Codify knowledge into systems and playbooks
- Provide decision support so less experienced analysts can act effectively
- Reduce the volume of manual triage so skilled people focus on the most critical work

This is where AI, thoughtfully applied, can amplify your team rather than simply adding another tool they need to manage.

4. Fragmented Tools, Siloed Data

Most SOCs grew organically. Tools were added as needs emerged, budgets allowed, or vendors pushed their platforms. The result is often a **patchwork ecosystem**.

4.1. The "Tool Zoo" Problem

It's common to see environments with:

- Multiple log sources feeding into one or more SIEMs
- Separate EDR, NDR, email security, and cloud security platforms
- A SOAR tool (sometimes lightly used, sometimes over-customized)
- Ticketing and ITSM systems disconnected from security tooling
- Spreadsheets and ad hoc scripts filling the gaps

Each tool:

- Has its own UI, alerts, and dashboards
- Uses its own terminology and severity models
- Provides partial visibility into the environment

Analysts are forced to perform *mental correlation* across tools, which:

- Slows down investigations
- Increases the chance of missing critical relationships
- Makes training new staff harder ("Open Tool X, then Tool Y, then check Z…")

4.2. Siloed Data, Siloed Context

Critical context is rarely in one place:

- Asset importance may be in CMDB systems or in someone's head.
- Business unit ownership might live in an HR or ERP system.
- Identity attributes sit in IAM/HR directories.
- Threat intel is scattered across vendor feeds, reports, and PDFs.

The SIEM/analytics layer often has only a fraction of this context, or it has it in inconsistent, hard-to-use forms.

When data is siloed:

- Detection logic cannot incorporate all relevant context.
- Risk scoring is generic and disconnected from business impact.
- Incident reports require manual hunting for context across multiple systems.

4.3. Integration Fatigue

Every tool promises to "integrate with everything." In reality:

- Integrations are shallow (e.g., one-way alert forwarding).
- APIs change or break.
- Custom connectors have to be maintained.

Your architects and engineers spend a significant amount of time:

- Wiring things together
- Maintaining brittle scripts
- Troubleshooting why data isn't flowing correctly

This is time not spent on improving detections, response playbooks, or proactive defense.

The net effect: **the SOC is a system of systems that doesn't behave like a single, coherent organism**. It's a collection of semi-cooperating islands.

5. Why Incremental Tuning Is No Longer Enough

When faced with these challenges, the usual response is:

- Tune rules
- Adjust thresholds
- Add or remove use cases
- Improve processes

These are necessary—but no longer sufficient.

5.1. Diminishing Returns from Rule Tuning

Rule-based detections and correlation logic are still valuable, but:

- They're brittle: small changes in behavior or infrastructure can break them.
- They're reactive: rules are often written in response to past incidents or known IOCs.
- They don't scale linearly: as you add more rules, interactions and overlaps become harder to manage.

You may see temporary improvements in false positive rates, but:

- New tools and new data sources introduce new noise.
- Attackers adapt to avoid existing rules.
- Tuning efforts often must be repeated after significant architecture changes.

5.2. Process Improvements Can't Keep Up with Complexity

You can refine workflows, update RACI matrices, and enforce better SLAs. These help, but they don't fundamentally change:

- The fact that humans are still manually triaging huge alert volumes.
- The fragmentation caused by multiple tools and data stores.
- The cognitive load required to piece together investigations across systems.

You may reduce "waste" and eliminate some friction, but you won't close the gap between what's demanded of the SOC and what humans can reliably deliver under pressure.

5.3. Automation Without Intelligence Is Shallow

Many SOCs have implemented automation via SOAR:

- Automatically enrich alerts
- Automatically create tickets
- Trigger standard containment actions for high-confidence detections

This is valuable, but often:

- Automation is limited to **simple, deterministic workflows**.
- Analysts still need to manually interpret context and decide what to do next.
- Playbooks become outdated or fragmented over time.

Automation without intelligence:

- Moves work around; it doesn't fundamentally reduce cognitive load.
- Risks amplifying mistakes if not governed carefully.

To truly change the equation, we need systems that can **help us think**, not just help us click faster.

That's where AI and autonomous patterns come in—not as magical replacements for people, but as a new layer of reasoning, prioritization, and decision support.

6. What "Autonomous Defense" Actually Means

"Autonomous SOC." "Self-driving security." "AI-driven defense."

You've probably seen all of these terms in vendor decks. Before going deeper in this book, we need a clear, sober definition.

6.1. Autonomy Is a Spectrum, not a Switch

Think of autonomy as **levels**, similar to how we talk about autonomous vehicles:

- **Level 0 – Manual:**
  - Humans do everything: triage, investigation, correlation, response.
  - Tools are mostly for search, visualization, and alerting.
- **Level 1 – Assisted:**
  - Tools provide recommendations and enrichment.
  - Humans still make all key decisions and perform most actions.
- **Level 2 – Partial Automation:**
  - Certain playbooks run automatically for well-understood scenarios (e.g., basic containment).
  - Humans supervise and handle exceptions and complex cases.
- **Level 3 – Conditional Autonomy:**
  - The system can autonomously handle a subset of incidents end-to-end within defined policy boundaries.
  - Humans review summaries, override decisions in edge cases, and refine policies.
- **Level 4 – High Autonomy:**

- The system independently handles most day-to-day threats and common incidents.
- Humans focus on rare, complex, or strategic cases, oversight, and continuous improvement.

Most SOCs today operate somewhere between Level 0 and Level 2. The goal of this book is not to push you instantly to Level 4, but to help you *deliberately* move up the spectrum in a way that is safe, governed, and aligned with your business.

6.2. What Autonomous Defense Is Not

Autonomous defense does *not* mean:

- Replacing your SOC team with a black box AI.
- Turning on "full auto" and hoping for the best.
- Blindly trusting a model's outputs without verification.

It is not an excuse to:

- Ignore governance and compliance.
- Avoid building internal expertise.
- Outsource all judgment to algorithms.

6.3. What Autonomous Defense Is

Autonomous defense means:

1. **Systems that perceive and understand your environment at scale**
   - Continuously analyze large volumes of data.
   - Identify patterns, anomalies, and relationships beyond human capacity.
2. **Systems that help humans make better decisions, faster**
   - Provide contextual summaries and recommended actions.
   - Surface the most important work and hide irrelevant noise.
3. **Systems that can act within clear guardrails**
   - Execute predefined actions when confidence and impact thresholds are met.
   - Log and explain decisions for later review.
4. **A feedback-driven, learning-centric operating model**
   - Use outcomes (true positives, false positives, missed detections) to improve models and playbooks.
   - Treat the SOC as a continuously evolving system, not a static project.

In other words, autonomous defense is not just "using AI." It is redesigning how your SOC senses, decides, and acts—with AI and automation as first-class components, governed by clear rules and human oversight.

Key Takeaways from Chapter 1

- **The traditional SOC model is under structural strain.** Volume, velocity, and variety of data have outpaced what humans can realistically handle.
- **Alert fatigue and burnout are not just HR problems—they're system design problems.** Overloaded analysts lead to lower detection quality and increased risk.
- **There is no simple "hire more people" solution.** Skill shortages and a growing talent gap mean we must amplify existing teams rather than rely solely on headcount.
- **Tool sprawl and data silos fragment your view of reality.** The SOC becomes a federation of loosely connected tools instead of a coherent defensive system.
- **Incremental tuning and traditional automation are no longer enough.** They help, but they cannot fundamentally bridge the gap between demand and human capacity.
- **Autonomous defense is a spectrum of maturity.** It's about progressively augmenting and automating perception, decision-making, and action—under strong governance and human oversight.

In the next chapter, we'll strip away the hype around AI in security and focus on the **building blocks**: which types of AI matter for SOCs, how they work at a high level, and where they realistically fit into your current stack.

Chapter 2 – AI Building Blocks for Security Leaders (No Hype)

Before you can design an AI-augmented SOC, you need a clear, grounded understanding of what "AI" means in this context.

Not the marketing version.

In security operations, you don't need to become a data scientist—but you *do* need to know enough to:

1. Ask the right questions of vendors and internal teams
2. Spot unrealistic promises
3. Make sensible design and risk decisions
4. Communicate clearly with executives, boards, and regulators

This chapter breaks AI down into practical building blocks for security leaders:

1. Types of AI relevant to SOCs
2. Detection vs. decision vs. generation – three distinct roles
3. Data foundations: logs, telemetry, context, and labels
4. Where AI fits in your existing SIEM/SOAR stack
5. Limitations, hallucinations, and common failure modes
6. Principles for safe and controlled AI adoption

By the end of this chapter, you should have a simple mental model: *what AI can do for your SOC, where it lives, what it needs, and how it can fail.*

1. Types of AI Relevant to SOCs

"AI" is an umbrella term. Underneath it, there are different kinds of models and techniques, each suited to different problems.

At a high level, the SOC will encounter four broad categories:

1. Supervised learning
2. Unsupervised / anomaly detection
3. Reinforcement / decision models
4. Generative AI and large language models (LLMs)

You don't need the underlying math, but you *do* need to know what each family is good at and what to expect.

1.1. Supervised Learning

Supervised learning is about prediction from examples.

You take historical data where the desired outcome is already known—for example:

- Past alerts labelled as "malicious" vs "benign"
- Emails labelled "phishing" vs "legitimate"
- Auth events labelled "compromised" vs "normal"

The model learns patterns that distinguish one class from another and then applies those patterns to new, unseen data.

Typical use cases in security:

- Classifying alerts as high/medium/low risk
- Detecting known phishing styles or malicious URLs
- Predicting whether an endpoint event is likely malware

Strengths:

- Can be very accurate when you have *good* labelled data.
- Provides consistent decisions once trained.

Weaknesses:

- Needs a lot of quality historical data with correct labels.
- Can drift over time if the environment or attacker behavior changes.
- Can be biased by what you choose to label as "malicious" or "benign."

Supervised models are powerful for **known patterns**—they're like super-charged signatures that can generalize across variations.

1.2. Unsupervised Learning & Anomaly Detection

Unsupervised learning doesn't rely on labelled examples. Instead, it tries to find structure in data on its own.

In security, the most common application is **anomaly detection**:

- "What's unusual compared to baseline behavior?"
- "Which user's behavior looks very different from their peers?"
- "What network traffic pattern doesn't fit any known cluster?"

Examples:

- User behavior analytics (UBA/UEBA)
- Network anomaly detection (strange flows, unusual ports)
- Endpoint anomalies (process or resource usage out of norm)

Strengths:

- Useful when you *don't* have good labels.
- Can surface new, previously unseen behaviors.

Weaknesses:

- "Unusual" does not mean "malicious." It just means "different."
- Can produce many noisy anomalies that still need human interpretation.
- Baselines can be skewed if initial training data already includes malicious behavior.

Anomaly detection is valuable in complex, dynamic environments—but it must be coupled with context, prioritization, and human review. Otherwise, you just move from "alert fatigue" to "anomaly fatigue."

1.3. Reinforcement & Decision Models

Reinforcement learning and related methods are about learning **what actions to take** in a given situation to maximize some notion of reward.

In security operations, you might not always use full-blown reinforcement learning, but you will see decision models that:

- Suggest next best actions in an investigation
- Recommend containment steps based on incident type, risk, and environment
- Choose which alerts to escalate, suppress, or group

These models can:

- Learn from historical incident outcomes (what worked, what didn't)
- Optimize for metrics like time-to-contain, number of false positives, or business impact

Strengths:

- Help move from "detecting" to "acting" in a structured way.
- Can reduce decision fatigue for analysts.

Weaknesses:

- If reward definitions are poor (e.g., only minimizing alert volume), the system can learn the wrong behavior.
- Requires careful monitoring to avoid undesirable strategies (for example, always ignoring difficult alerts).

When someone says "AI-driven response," you should ask: *what kind of model is deciding which actions to take, and what objective was it trained on?*

1.4. Generative AI and Large Language Models (LLMs)

Generative AI is about **creating** new content: text, code, images, and more. Large language models (LLMs) are the most relevant type today.

LLMs are trained on massive amounts of text and learn:

- Statistical patterns of language
- How concepts relate
- How to generate plausible, coherent text given a prompt

In the SOC, LLMs can:

- Summarize long alerts, logs, and reports
- Draft incident summaries, communication emails, and documentation
- Help analysts explore data using natural language ("Show me all failed logins from unusual countries in the last 24 hours for privileged accounts.")
- Generate or refine detection logic and playbooks (with human review)

Strengths:

- Dramatically reduce the time to read, write, and explain.
- Support natural language interaction with complex systems.

Weaknesses:

- They do not "know" the truth; they generate text that *sounds* plausible.
- They can **hallucinate**: invent details, misrepresent facts, or misinterpret ambiguous input.
- They require careful control, context, and validation in security use cases.

In your mental model, treat LLMs as **very capable assistants at reading, writing, and explaining**, not as sources of ground truth.

2. Detection vs. Decision vs. Generation – Three Roles of AI

Rather than getting lost in algorithms, it's more useful to think about **what you want AI to do in the SOC**.

Most practical applications fall into one of three roles:

1. **Detection** – "Is there something suspicious here?"
2. **Decision** – "What should we do next?"
3. **Generation** – "How should this be described or documented?"

Understanding which role you are using helps you set expectations and design appropriate controls.

2.1. AI for Detection

Detection AI tries to answer: *Is this event, behavior, or pattern indicative of a threat?*

Examples:

- Classifying an email as phishing or not.
- Scoring an authentication event based on risk.
- Flagging unusual network connections.

Key questions for leaders:

- What data does the model see?
- What is it optimized for—low false negatives, low false positives, or a balance?
- How is performance measured and monitored over time?
- How easy is it to understand *why* it flagged something?

Detection AI should generally be treated as **highly influential, but not infallible**. In many cases, outputs feed into triage and prioritization, not directly into response actions.

2.2. AI for Decision

Decision AI addresses: *Given what we've detected and what we know, what should we do?*

Examples:

- Choosing whether to auto-quarantine a device or ask an analyst to review.
- Recommending which alerts to escalate to incident tickets.
- Suggesting the next step in an investigation (query this endpoint, check this user, pull this log).

Key questions:

- What actions can the system take autonomously?
- Under what conditions does it act vs. recommend?
- How do we enforce guardrails (who approves what, for which assets)?
- How are unintended consequences detected and corrected?

Decision AI is where **risk and governance** become especially critical. A misclassification is bad; an automated, wrong action can be worse.

2.3. AI for Generation

Generation AI helps answer: *How do we turn complex technical reality into understandable language, code, or configuration?*

Examples:

- Summarizing an incident in executive-friendly terms.
- Drafting detailed technical timelines for post-incident review.
- Generating first drafts of detection rules ("write a SIEM rule to detect X").
- Creating initial versions of SOPs, runbooks, and playbooks.

Key questions:

- What source data is it drawing from?
- How is that data validated?
- Who reviews and approves the generated content?
- How do we avoid hallucinations being treated as facts?

Treat generation as a **force multiplier for documentation and communication**. It accelerates humans; it does not replace the need for human oversight.

3. Data Foundations: Logs, Telemetry, Context, and Labels

All AI models, no matter how advanced, are constrained by their data. In security operations, you can think about data in four main categories:

1. Raw logs and events

2. Telemetry and metrics
3. Context and enrichment
4. Labels and outcomes

Getting these right is more important than choosing the "perfect" algorithm.

3.1. Raw Logs and Events

These are the primary feeds from:

- Network devices, firewalls, proxies
- Endpoints and EDR agents
- Cloud platforms and SaaS applications
- Identity systems, VPNs, SSO, and PAM
- Applications and APIs

For AI, key points are:

- **Coverage:** Are we seeing enough of the environment?
- **Consistency:** Are formats and timestamps usable and reliable?
- **Retention:** Do we keep enough history to learn patterns and trends?

AI models can't compensate for blind spots. If critical parts of your infrastructure aren't producing or forwarding useful logs, your AI will be "smart" about an incomplete reality.

3.2. Telemetry and Metrics

Telemetry captures *behavior over time*, not just discrete events:

- CPU and memory usage on endpoints
- Network throughput and connection patterns
- Authentication frequency and location patterns
- API call volumes and error rates

This is where many anomaly detection models operate. The more consistent and well-structured your telemetry, the more meaningful your baselines and deviations.

3.3. Context and Enrichment

Context transforms raw signals into meaningful information.

Examples:

- Asset context: criticality, owner, business function, location
- User context: role, department, seniority, typical working hours
- Threat context: known malicious IPs/domains, malware families, TTPs

- Business context: which applications support critical processes

AI models benefit enormously from context:

- A login from an unusual country looks very different for a senior executive vs. a test account.
- A vulnerability on a crown-jewel database server is more important than the same issue on a lab VM.

Investing in **good CMDB, IAM hygiene, and threat intel integration** pays dividends for both traditional analytics and AI.

3.4. Labels and Outcomes

Labels are how you tell a model: "This is what happened."

Examples:

- Was this alert a true positive or false positive?
- Was this email truly phishing?
- Did this incident cause business impact?
- Was the response timely and effective?

Without labels and outcomes:

- Supervised models can't be trained effectively.
- You can't close the loop and improve over time.
- It's hard to measure whether AI-driven changes are actually helping.

This is why **case management discipline**—consistently documenting what happened and why—becomes a strategic asset. Your past incidents are not just history; they are training data for your future SOC.

4. Where AI Fits in the Existing SIEM/SOAR Stack

Most organizations already have:

- One or more SIEM platforms
- A SOAR or orchestration tool
- An EDR/XDR solution
- A ticketing/ITSM system

The goal is not to rip everything out and "replace it with AI." Instead, you want to *layer* AI into this existing ecosystem.

You can think of AI fitting into four main layers:

1. Data & analytics layer (SIEM/XDR)
2. Automation & orchestration layer (SOAR, scripts)
3. Analyst interaction layer (consoles, AI assistants, chat interfaces)
4. Reporting & governance layer (dashboards, metrics, documentation)

4.1. In the Data & Analytics Layer

Here, AI can:

- Enhance detection: anomaly detection, behavioral models, supervised classifiers.
- Prioritize and group alerts: clustering similar events, scoring risk, deduplicating noise.
- Support natural language queries over logs and events.

Practically, this may look like:

- An AI engine integrated directly into your SIEM/XDR platform.
- A separate analytics service that ingests a subset of telemetry and returns signals/labels.

Key questions:

- How does AI interact with your existing rules and content?
- Can you see why it made certain detection decisions?
- How easily can you tune its sensitivity and behavior?

4.2. In the Automation & Orchestration Layer

In the SOAR or orchestration layer, AI can:

- Decide which playbook to run for a given incident.
- Suggest or select parameters for actions (which host to isolate, which account to disable).
- Generate or adjust playbooks over time, based on outcomes.

Here, AI is often blended with **policy**:

- "If risk score > X and asset criticality < Y, then auto-contain."
- "If AI confidence is below threshold, escalate to human instead of acting."

This is where you start approaching *conditional autonomy*: the system can take actions in certain scenarios, within predefined guardrails.

4.3. In the Analyst Interaction Layer

For analysts and threat hunters, AI can surface as:

- A chat-based AI assistant interface connected to your SIEM/SOAR/XDR.
- An inline assistant in the console that suggests next steps or queries.
- Contextual summaries attached to alerts and incidents.

This layer is where LLMs shine:

- Converting raw logs into human-friendly narratives.
- Turning analyst questions into correct queries behind the scenes.
- Drafting timeline reconstructions and impact explanations.

If designed well, this layer **reduces cognitive load** and **speeds up investigations** without hiding raw data from those who want to dig deeper.

4.4. In the Reporting & Governance Layer

AI can help you:

- Generate weekly/monthly SOC reports (for executives, clients, or regulators).
- Summarize KPI trends and notable incidents.
- Highlight recurring patterns and systemic issues.

In this layer, AI is not making security decisions—it's making it easier to **communicate** and **govern** what's happening.

5. Limitations, Hallucinations, and Common Failure Modes

No technology is perfect. AI introduces new failure modes that security leaders must understand and plan for.

5.1. Data Quality and Bias

If your data is:

- Incomplete
- Skewed toward certain environments or time periods
- Mislabelled or inconsistent

Then your models will reflect those problems.

Examples of bias:

- Models trained mostly on office hours ignoring attacks that happen at night.
- Data from one region dominating patterns, making others look "anomalous" when they're not.
- Labels applied inconsistently by different analysts.

You can't fully eliminate bias, but you can:

- Be explicit about where data comes from.
- Regularly review model performance across different segments.
- Invest in better, more consistent labelling and documentation.

5.2. Model Drift

Environments and attacker's change:

- New applications and infrastructure are deployed.
- User behavior shifts (remote work, new business processes).
- Attackers adopt new techniques or change their tooling.

Models that once performed well can become less accurate over time. This is **model drift**.

Leaders should ensure:

- There is a process for monitoring model performance.
- Models are periodically retrained or updated.
- Changes are documented and tested, not silently pushed.

5.3. Overfitting to the Past

Supervised models learn from historical data. If that data reflects:

- A limited set of attack techniques
- Specific infrastructure and configurations
- Past detection logic and gaps

Then the model may primarily detect **what you've already seen**, not what you might see tomorrow.

This is why combining:

- Supervised models (for known patterns), with
- Anomaly detection (for unknowns), and
- Human threat hunting

...remains important.

5.4. Hallucinations in Generative AI

LLMs can:

- Confidently produce incorrect statements.

- Invent logs or events that were never observed.
- Misinterpret ambiguous queries or instructions.

In a SOC, this becomes dangerous if:

- Generated content is treated as factual evidence.
- Recommended actions are not reviewed.
- Documentation combines real and invented details.

Mitigations:

- Limit LLM access to **ground-truth data sources** and clearly tell it what it is allowed to answer from.
- Require human review for any generated text that will be used in investigations, reports, or playbooks.
- Train analysts to recognize that "confident language" does not equal "correct information."

5.5. Over-Automation and Loss of Human Intuition

If you lean too heavily on AI:

- Analysts may become overly dependent on its outputs.
- Manual skills (log reading, hypothesis formation, deep investigation) can atrophy.
- When AI fails or is unavailable, your team may struggle to operate effectively.

A mature SOC treats AI as:

- A powerful tool to **amplify** human capability, not replace it.
- Something that must be balanced with ongoing training, drills, and manual practice.

6. Principles for Safe and Controlled AI Adoption in Security

Given the opportunities and risks, how should a security leader proceed?

Here are six guiding principles you can use as a checklist.

6.1. Start with Clear, Bounded Use Cases

Don't begin with "We need AI." Begin with:

- "We need to reduce time-to-triage by 30%."
- "We need to cut false positives in this specific use case."
- "We need to automate first-draft incident reports."

Bounded use cases:

- Make it easier to measure success.
- Reduce the blast radius if something goes wrong.
- Help build trust gradually among analysts and stakeholders.

6.2. Keep a Human in the Loop for High-Impact Actions

For actions that:

- Affect production systems or user accounts
- Carry legal, regulatory, or reputational consequences

…ensure that:

- AI may recommend, but a human approves.
- There is clear visibility into what AI suggested and why.
- You define thresholds and conditions for when automation is allowed.

Over time, as confidence grows in specific scenarios, you can move selected actions from "recommend" to "auto-execute under conditions X, Y, Z."

6.3. Design for Transparency and Explainability

Analysts and leaders need to understand:

- Why an alert was scored as high risk
- Why an action was recommended
- What data and rules influenced a decision

Even if the underlying model is complex, you can:

- Provide feature importance (which signals mattered most).
- Offer natural-language explanations.
- Log decisions and inputs for later review.

Transparency is essential for:

- Analyst trust
- Internal and external audits
- Regulatory scrutiny

6.4. Build Feedback Loops by Design

Every interaction with AI in the SOC is data:

- Analysts marking alerts as false positives
- Overrides of recommended actions
- Post-incident reviews and lessons learned

Turn these into **structured feedback**:

- Capture them in cases and tools, not in hallway conversations.
- Use them to correct model behavior and improve playbooks.
- Review feedback regularly as part of your SOC governance rhythm.

Without feedback loops, AI remains static and misaligned. With them, it becomes a learning component of your defensive system.

6.5. Separate Experimentation from Production

Create safe spaces to experiment:

- A lab or test tenant with synthetic or de-identified data
- Limited-scope pilots in less critical environments
- Shadow modes where AI makes recommendations but doesn't act

This allows you to:

- Evaluate new models and features without risking production.
- Compare AI decisions with human decisions over time.
- Build confidence and refine guardrails before full rollout.

6.6. Align AI Use with Ethics, Compliance, and Privacy

Security leaders must ensure that AI usage respects:

- Data minimization principles (don't send more data than needed).
- Privacy laws and contractual obligations (PII, customer logs, cross-border flows).
- Internal policies and ethical standards.

This may mean:

- Using on-prem or private-cloud AI for sensitive data.
- Masking or tokenizing certain fields before processing.
- Documenting how AI is used and what data it sees.

Being proactive here will make conversations with auditors, regulators, and privacy teams far smoother.

Key Takeaways from Chapter 2

- **AI is not one thing.** In the SOC you'll encounter supervised models, anomaly detection, decision models, and generative AI—each suited to different tasks.
- **Think in roles, not algorithms.** Frame AI as helping with detection, decision, or generation. This clarifies expectations and controls.
- **Data is the true foundation.** Logs, telemetry, context, and labelled outcomes matter more than the specific model type you choose.
- **AI fits into your existing stack as an additional layer, not a replacement.** Embed it in analytics, orchestration, analyst interfaces, and reporting—step by step.
- **Understand and plan for failure modes.** Bias, drift, overfitting, hallucinations, and over-automation are real risks that must be managed.
- **Adopt with control and intent.** Start with bounded use cases, keep humans in the loop where impact is high, design for transparency, enforce feedback loops, separate experimentation from production, and align with ethics and compliance.

In the next chapter, we'll move from concepts to architecture. We'll map how these AI building blocks come together in **reference designs for an AI-augmented SOC,** and how you can adapt those designs to your own environment and constraints.

Chapter 3 – Reference Architectures: From SOC to Autonomous SOC

Chapters 1 and 2 explained *why* the classical SOC is under strain and *what* AI can realistically do in security operations.

Now we move to the "how":

What does an AI-augmented SOC look like in architecture diagrams and building blocks?

This chapter will:

1. Define what a solid, non-AI modern SOC looks like today (your baseline).
2. Introduce AI augmentation layers that sit alongside and on top of that baseline.
3. Walk through an example reference architecture: AI sitting on top of SIEM + SOAR.
4. Explore multi-tenant and MSSP considerations.
5. Show how CTI, deception, and external telemetry plug into this model.
6. Discuss how to choose between platforms vs. building your own components.

The goal is not to promote any particular vendor, but to give you a conceptual blueprint you can adapt to your environment.

1. The Baseline: What a "Good" Modern SOC Looks Like Today

Before adding AI, you need a reasonably healthy SOC foundation. AI amplifies whatever it touches—if the base is chaotic, AI will amplify chaos.

A "good" modern SOC doesn't need to be perfect, but it usually includes:

- A **centralized log and telemetry platform** (SIEM/XDR/data lake)
- A **response orchestration layer** (SOAR, custom automation, or tightly integrated platforms)
- Clearly defined **use cases, detections, and playbooks**
- A **case management / ticketing system** with structured workflows
- **Asset, identity, and threat intelligence** integrated to some degree
- A team with defined **roles and operating model**

1.1. Core Components of the Baseline SOC

You can think of a baseline SOC as four main layers:

1. **Data Ingestion & Storage**
   - Collects logs and telemetry from: endpoints, network, cloud, identity, apps, OT/IoT, SaaS.

- o Normalizes, parses, and stores events for search and analytics.
- o Often a SIEM, XDR, or security data lake.
2. **Detection & Analytics**
   - o Content: rules, correlation, heuristics, threat intel matches, anomaly detections (even pre-AI).
   - o Dashboards, saved searches, visualizations.
   - o Basic risk scoring or priority calculations.
3. **Response & Orchestration**
   - o SOAR platform or automation engine.
   - o Playbooks: enrichment, containment, notifications, evidence gathering.
   - o Integrations with EDR, firewalls, IAM, ticketing, email, chat, etc.
4. **Operations & Governance**
   - o Case management: incident tracking, documentation, handoffs.
   - o Reporting: KPIs, SLAs, regulator, and customer reports.
   - o Procedures, policies, and training.

If this baseline is missing entirely, your first step isn't AI—it's building or stabilizing this foundation.

1.2. Characteristics of a "Healthy Enough" SOC for AI

You don't need perfection, but realistically you need:

- **Reasonable log coverage** of key infrastructure, identity, and cloud.
- At least a **basic set of documented playbooks** for common incident types.
- A **case management system** where incident outcomes are recorded.
- Some **automations already in place**, even if they are simple.

If you have none of these, AI will spend its time trying to make sense of incomplete data, unreliable workflows, and inconsistent outcomes. Your first "AI" project should arguably be:

"Use AI to help document and standardize what we already do,"
…but the underlying collection and processes still need to exist.

2. Introducing the AI Augmentation Layers

With a baseline SOC in place, you can start layering AI to amplify detection, triage, investigation, and automation.

Conceptually, think of **four AI augmentation layers**:

1. **Enrichment & understanding layer** – making data more meaningful.
2. **Triage & prioritization layer** – deciding what matters most.
3. **Analyst AI assistant layer** – helping humans investigate and reason.

4. **Automation & autonomous action layer** – acting under guardrails.

These layers don't replace your SIEM/SOAR; they sit next to and on top of them.

2.1. Enrichment & Understanding Layer

This is where AI:

- Extracts entities from logs (users, IPs, processes, apps).
- Normalizes and correlates related events.
- Adds contextual understanding ("This is a finance system used by executives").
- Summarizes raw evidence into human-readable narratives.

Technologies:

- LLMs for summarization and entity extraction.
- Traditional ML for classification of event types.
- Rule-based mappings for business context (from CMDB, IAM, etc.).

Outcome:

- Alerts and cases are enriched with context automatically.
- Analysts spend less time "gathering" and more time deciding.

2.2. Triage & Prioritization Layer

This layer helps answer: **Of all things we could look at, what should we look at first?**

Capabilities:

- Risk scoring alerts/incidents using AI models that consider:
    - Asset criticality
    - User role and behavior
    - Threat intel matches
    - Past incident patterns
- Grouping and deduplicating similar alerts into "situations" or "episodes."
- Highlighting anomalies that are truly unusual in your environment.

Outcome:

- A **rank-ordered queue** of meaningful work for analysts.
- Far fewer duplicate or low-value alerts wasting time.

2.3. Analyst AI assistant Layer

Here AI acts as a **companion for analysts and hunters**, not as an opaque engine in the background.

Capabilities:

- Natural language interface to logs and tools ("Show me all successful admin logins from new devices in the last 48 hours").
- Investigation guidance:
    - "Given this alert, here are three recommended next steps."
- Automated enrichment queries behind the scenes:
    - Fetching context from EDR, IAM, CTI, ticketing.

Outcome:

- Newer analysts operate more like mid-level analysts.
- Experienced analysts move faster and can tackle deeper investigations.
- Knowledge is encoded into the AI assistant, not lost when people leave.

2.4. Automation & Autonomous Action Layer

This layer blends **policy, playbooks, and AI-driven decisions** to execute actions under defined guardrails.

Capabilities:

- Deciding whether to trigger a playbook automatically based on:
    - AI risk score
    - Confidence level
    - Asset importance and business context
- Conditional autonomy:
    - Auto-containment in low-risk contexts
    - Human approval for high-impact actions.

Outcome:

- Routine, well-understood incidents can be contained and closed rapidly.
- Humans focus on edge cases, complex investigations, and tuning the system.

These four layers form the conceptual scaffold for the reference architecture we'll walk through next.

3. Example Architecture: AI Sitting on Top of SIEM + SOAR

Let's put all this together in a simple, vendor-agnostic reference architecture.

Imagine the core stack:

- **SIEM / XDR / Data Lake** – central data & analytics platform
- **SOAR / Automation Engine** – orchestrates response actions
- **Case Management / ITSM** – tracks incidents and work

We now add three AI-centric components:

1. **AI Analytics Service** (detection + triage)
2. **AI Assistant Service** (analyst interaction)
3. **AI Content & Documentation Service** (generation)

3.1. Data Flow: From Events to Action

At a high level, the flow looks like this:

1. **Ingestion:**
    - Logs and telemetry flow into the SIEM/XDR.
    - Threat intel and context (assets, identities, business services) are also ingested or referenced.
2. **Baseline Detection:**
    - Rules, correlation, and existing analytics generate alerts.
    - Some anomaly detection may already be in place.
3. **AI Analytics Service:**
    - Subscribes to alerts and relevant raw events from the SIEM.
    - Enriches, scores, groups, and prioritizes them.
    - Outputs: enriched alerts/incidents with risk scores and recommended actions.
4. **SOAR / Automation:**
    - Receives enriched alerts and AI recommendations.
    - Chooses playbooks (sometimes with AI's input).
    - Executes actions under policy (auto vs. human-approved).
5. **Case Management & Reporting:**
    - Incidents and actions are recorded in the case system.
    - Outcomes (TP/FP, impact, effectiveness) are fed back for retraining and tuning.
    - AI Content Service can generate reports and summaries.
6. **Analyst AI assistant:**
    - Sits alongside this whole process.
    - Provides a chat/assistant interface to query the SIEM, SOAR, and case data.
    - Helps analysts understand and navigate incidents.

3.2. AI Analytics Service: Under the Hood

This service typically includes:

- **Feature extraction:**
    - Transform raw logs into structured features (e.g., login frequency, geo variance, device profile).
- **Detection models:**
    - Supervised models for known threat patterns.
    - Anomaly detection for unknown or unusual behavior.
- **Scoring and correlation:**
    - Combine multiple alerts and signals into a single scored "episode."
- **Policy integration:**
    - Consider business rules (e.g., "Never auto-contain production databases").

The service should expose:

- **APIs** for the SIEM/SOAR to send and receive data.
- **Configurable thresholds** for risk and confidence.
- **Audit logs** showing why it scored something a particular way.

3.3. AI Assistant Service: The Analyst's Interface

The AI assistant is usually powered by an LLM with strong integrations into your tools.

Key characteristics:

- **Grounded in your data:**
    - It doesn't just "hallucinate"; it retrieves from SIEM, SOAR, CTI, and case management.
- **Secure and permission-aware:**
    - Access respects RBAC (analysts only see what they are allowed to see).
- **Task-oriented capabilities:**
    - "Investigate this alert."
    - "Summarize this incident."
    - "Draft an email to the affected business owner."
- **Explainable suggestions:**
    - When recommending a next step, it should reference the data that led to that suggestion.

The AI assistant is the human-facing part of the architecture. If your analysts love using it and trust it, adoption of the rest of the AI ecosystem becomes much easier.

3.4. AI Content & Documentation Service

While the AI assistant can generate text on demand, in many SOCs it's useful to have a **structured generation layer** focused specifically on:

- Weekly/monthly SOC reports.
- Post-incident reviews.
- Customer-facing incident notifications (for MSSPs).
- Policy and playbook drafts.

This service:

- Consumes incident and case data.
- Uses templates and LLMs to create structured documents.
- Leaves clear markers for human review and approval.

In some environments, this is just a "mode" of the AI assistant. In others, it is a dedicated component integrated with your reporting workflows.

4. Multi-Tenant / MSSP Considerations

If you are an MSSP, telco, or any provider running a **multi-tenant SOC**, AI architecture decisions come with extra complexity.

You must solve for:

- **Data separation:** tenant A must never see tenant B's data.
- **Per-tenant context:** different critical assets, users, and policies.
- **Shared vs. isolated models:** what is learned globally vs. locally.

4.1. Data Separation and Security

At the architecture level, you need to ensure:

- **Strong logical or physical segregation of data** across tenants:
    - Separate indices, schemas, or data stores.
    - Tenant IDs on all events with strict access controls.
- **AI services operating in a multi-tenant aware manner:**
    - The AI Analytics Service must never cross tenant boundaries when enriching or responding to incidents.
    - The AI assistant must enforce per-tenant RBAC and identity.

Any generative model that is allowed to "see" multi-tenant data must respect these boundaries. This may influence whether you use:

- A **centralized AI cluster** with strong tenant partitioning, or
- **Per-tenant or per-region AI instances** for higher assurance and regulatory reasons.

4.2. Shared vs. Per-Tenant Models

There are trade-offs between:

- **Global/shared models:**
    - Trained across all tenants' (appropriately anonymized/aggregated) data.
    - Better at spotting widespread campaigns and general patterns.
- **Per-tenant models:**
    - Trained on a single client's data.
    - Better at understanding that tenant's baseline behavior and quirks.

A common pattern:

- Use **shared models** for broad detection and enrichment (e.g., phishing classifiers, malware families, TTP patterns).
- Apply **per-tenant baselines** and overrides for behavior and risk scoring.

When you do learn from multiple tenants, you must:

- Ensure **explicit consent** where needed.
- Anonymize or aggregate data to protect confidentiality.
- Clearly document what is shared and how.

4.3. Multi-Tenant Views and Experiences

In an MSSP context, AI should also help with **client-facing experiences**:

- Client portals showing AI-prioritized incidents.
- AI-generated, client-specific reports.
- AI assistant features accessible to client teams (with restricted scope).

The architecture must allow:

- Different views of the same underlying incident (MSSP-wide vs. client-specific).
- Per-client governance and policy (e.g., which actions can be automated for which client).

5. Integrating CTI, Deception, and External Telemetry

Your SOC doesn't live in isolation. It draws insight from the outside world: threat intelligence feeds, deception systems, internet-facing honeypots, dark web monitoring, and more.

A well-designed AI-augmented SOC architecture treats these as **first-class inputs**.

5.1. Threat Intelligence (CTI) Integration

CTI is often:

- Consumed as indicators (IPs, domains, file hashes).
- Consumed as reports (PDFs, blogs, advisories).

AI can improve both:

1. **Indicator-level integration:**
    - Matching indicators against your logs and telemetry.
    - Scoring and prioritizing matches based on context and recency.
2. **Report-level understanding:**
    - Using LLMs to summarize CTI reports.
    - Extracting techniques, tools, and campaigns into structured data.
    - Mapping CTI to your existing detections and gaps.

Architecturally:

- CTI feeds flow into your SIEM and AI Analytics Service.
- A specialized CTI Processing component (often LLM-enabled) parses reports and enriches models and content.

5.2. Deception and Honeypot Telemetry

Deception systems and honeypots are **high-signal sources**: almost all interactions with them are suspicious.

AI can:

- Cluster attacker activity observed in honeypots to identify campaigns and toolchains.
- Correlate deception telemetry with internal logs ("Did this same IP touch production?").
- Generate hypothesis-driven hunts based on deception observations.

Architecturally:

- Deception telemetry flows into the same data plane as your other logs.
- The AI Analytics Service treats them as high-priority signals.
- The AI assistant can use them as breadcrumbs for broader investigations.

5.3. External Surface and Exposure Data

Attackers often start from your external surface:

- Exposed ports and services.
- Cloud misconfigurations.
- Publicly discoverable assets.

Integrations with:

- Attack surface management (ASM) and external scanning tools.
- Cloud security posture management (CSPM) platforms.
- DNS and certificate transparency logs.

AI can:

- Highlight mismatches between "expected" external surface and reality.
- Prioritize exposures based on likely exploitability and internal value.
- Generate remediation plans or tickets automatically.

In the architecture:

- External telemetry becomes a key input to **risk models**.
- It influences **prioritization** and **automated response** (e.g., quick blocking of newly exposed, obviously unintended assets).

6. Selecting Platforms vs. Building Your Own Components

One of the most strategic decisions you'll make is **where to buy vs. where to build**.

You will not build everything from scratch—but you also don't want to be locked into a vendor black box that you can't shape.

6.1. Where Platforms Make Sense

For most organizations, it makes sense to buy:

- **Core SIEM/XDR platforms** – mature products with deep integration ecosystems.
- **SOAR / automation engines** – widely available with broad connector libraries.
- **LLM platforms / AI infra** – managed services or enterprise AI platforms (self-hosted or cloud) that provide the foundation.

You gain:

- Security, scalability, and maintainability.
- A faster path to actionable outcomes.
- Support and continuous product improvement.

6.2. Where Customization Is Critical

Even with strong platforms, you'll likely need bespoke work around:

- **Detection content and models** tuned to your environment and threat profile.
- **Risk scoring logic** that reflects your specific business (asset criticality, regulatory constraints).
- **Playbooks and automation workflows** aligned with your processes and approvals.
- **AI assistant "skills"**: the tasks, queries, and actions your analysts care about most.

This customization can be done:

- Inside platform-provided extensibility frameworks (rules, runbooks, apps).
- Via separate microservices that interact through APIs.
- Using low-code/no-code components where appropriate.

6.3. "AI in the Platform" vs. "AI Beside the Platform"

Vendors increasingly ship **built-in AI features**. These can be valuable, but you should decide where you want:

- **Embedded AI**:
    - AI features deeply integrated into your SIEM/XDR/SOAR.
    - Pros: tight integration, less glue code.
    - Cons: limited visibility into models, less portability.
- **Sidecar AI services**:
    - Your own AI services that consume data and return enrichment, scores, recommendations.
    - Pros: greater control, transparency, and extensibility.
    - Cons: requires more in-house or partner expertise.

In many mature environments, a **hybrid** approach is ideal:

- Use embedded AI for "standard" use cases (malware classification, UEBA, etc.).
- Use sidecar AI for **differentiating capabilities**:
    - Your unique AI assistant experience
    - Your proprietary risk scoring
    - Your specialized CTI and deception analysis

6.4. Architectural Principles for Maintainability

Whatever you choose to buy vs. build, keep these principles:

- **Modularity:**
    - Each component (data plane, AI analytics, automation, AI assistant) should be loosely coupled via APIs or message buses.
- **Observability:**

- o You must be able to monitor data flows, model performance, and automation actions.
- **Testability:**
  - o New rules, models, and automations should be validated in test/staging before production.
- **Portability:**
  - o Avoid deep vendor lock-in where possible; keep your data and logic portable enough that migration is painful but feasible.

These principles will help ensure your AI-augmented SOC remains adaptable as technology and threats evolve.

Key Takeaways from Chapter 3

- **You can't skip the baseline.** AI works best on top of a reasonably healthy SOC foundation: centralized data, defined playbooks, and structured case management.
- **Think in layers.** Enrichment, triage, AI assistant, and automation layers are the core of an AI-augmented SOC architecture. Each can be implemented incrementally.
- **AI sits on top of—and beside—your SIEM and SOAR, not instead of them.** It enriches detection, accelerates investigations, and conditions automation, rather than replacing core platforms.
- **Multi-tenant environments add complexity.** Data separation, per-tenant baselines, and shared vs. local models become central design choices.
- **CTI, deception, and external telemetry are high-value inputs.** AI can turn these from passive feeds into active drivers of pre-emptive defense.
- **Platform vs. build is a strategic decision.** Use platforms for the heavy lifting and focus your custom work where it differentiates your SOC and aligns with your risk and governance needs.

In the next chapter, we'll dive deeper into the **data strategy** that supports all of this—how to build a data foundation that makes your AI-augmented SOC not only powerful, but reliable, interpretable, and sustainable over time.

Chapter 4 – Data Strategy: Fuel for Your AI-Driven SOC

AI doesn't start with models.

It starts with data.

You can buy the best "AI-powered" tools on the market, but if what you feed them is fragmented, incomplete, noisy, or context-free, you'll get disappointing results at best—and dangerous ones at worst.

In an AI-augmented SOC, data is no longer just "something you store for compliance or incident response." It becomes:

- The raw fuel for detection and triage
- The memory that models learn from
- The foundation for risk decisions and automation
- The history that lets you report, improve, and prove

This chapter is about building that foundation deliberately. We'll cover:

1. Identifying your **"golden sources"** of security data
2. Normalization, enrichment & context – turning events into information
3. Data quality and coverage – how to know if you're ready for AI
4. Feedback loops from analysts back into your data and models
5. Retention, privacy & regulatory constraints in an AI context
6. Metrics to measure data readiness and improvement over time

By the end, you should view your SOC not just as a set of tools, but as a data system that you can shape, measure, and continuously improve.

1. Identifying Your "Golden Sources" of Security Data

Not all data is created equal. Yes, you *can* ingest everything—but you probably shouldn't start there.

Your first job as a leader is to identify your **golden sources**: the data sources that give you the highest security value per unit of effort and cost.

1.1. Golden Sources vs. Nice-to-Have Sources

Golden sources are:

- **Authoritative** – they are the primary record for a particular activity (e.g., identity, endpoint, external traffic).

- **Relevant** – they consistently contain signals useful for detection, investigation, and response.
- **Stable** – they are maintained, supported, and unlikely to disappear suddenly.

Examples of typical golden sources:

- **Identity & Access:**
    - AD/Entra ID/IdPs (logins, group changes, privilege assignments)
    - VPN, SSO, MFA logs
- **Endpoint & Workload:**
    - EDR/XDR telemetry
    - OS event logs for critical servers
- **Network & Edge:**
    - Firewall, proxy, secure web gateway logs
    - VPN concentrators, WAFs, load balancers
- **Cloud & SaaS:**
    - Cloud provider audit logs (IAM, configuration, API calls)
    - Key SaaS platforms (email, collaboration, CRM/ERP where critical data lives)
- **Control Plane:**
    - IAM/PAM tooling
    - Configuration management and deployment pipelines

Nice-to-have sources might include:

- Certain application logs that are rarely used in investigations
- Low-signal telemetry from legacy systems that add noise more than value
- Highly redundant or overlapping feeds

Golden sources should be your **first priority** for:

- Proper ingestion and parsing
- Monitoring for data quality
- Integration into AI models and risk scoring

1.2. Mapping Your Current Data Landscape

Before you can decide what's golden, you need a map.

Work with your team to answer:

- What data sources are we ingesting today?
- Which business services or environments are *not* well covered?
- For each source, do we know:
    - Owner?
    - Format?
    - Volume?

- o   Retention?
- o   Current use cases (rules, dashboards, reports)?

This doesn't need to be a 200-page CMDB exercise, but you should at least have a **living inventory** of:

- Sources
- Purpose
- Health (working / partially working / broken)

1.3. Prioritizing Sources for AI

When planning AI projects, prioritize data sources that:

- Cover **identity, endpoints, and crown-jewel systems**
- Are already somewhat **clean and structured**
- Have a history of being used in past investigations

These will give the best return on early AI investments:

- AI-based triage on EDR + identity alerts
- Behavior analytics on authentication and remote access
- Risk scoring based on network + identity + asset importance

Trying to apply AI across every log source from day one dilutes focus and makes failures harder to diagnose.

2. Normalization, Enrichment & Context

Raw logs are not "data strategy." They are just raw material.

To make AI useful, you need to transform raw events into something a model—and a human—can reason about.

That transformation has three pillars:

1. **Normalization** – aligning structure and fields
2. **Enrichment** – adding missing details
3. **Context** – linking security events to business reality

2.1. Normalization: Agreeing on What Things Mean

Different systems describe similar things in completely different ways:

- One firewall logs source IP as src_ip, another as src, another as sourceAddress.

- Identity systems may refer to the same user with different identifiers.
- Time zones and timestamp formats vary wildly.

Normalization is about imposing a **consistent schema** for:

- Common fields: src_ip, dst_ip, src_user, dst_user, hostname, action, event_type, etc.
- Event categories: auth events, network connections, process executions, file changes, admin actions, etc.

For humans, this consistency:

- Simplifies searching, correlation, and rule writing.

For AI:

- It reduces noise and ambiguity, making pattern learning feasible.

Normalization doesn't have to be perfect from day one, but you should have:

- A **reference schema** (even a simple one)
- A process for updating parsers and mappings when vendor formats change

2.2. Enrichment: Filling the Gaps

Most raw logs lack important context. Enrichment fills in that context by pulling in additional information, such as:

- **Asset enrichment:**
    - Criticality rating
    - Owner and business unit
    - Environment (prod/dev/test), location, OS
- **User enrichment:**
    - Department and manager
    - Role and groups
    - Typical working hours and locations
- **Threat enrichment:**
    - Reputation of IPs/domains
    - Known malware families or campaigns
    - Mapped MITRE ATT&CK techniques

Enrichment can be:

- Static (joining against CMDB or HR data)
- Dynamic (querying EDR, CTI, or threat intel at ingestion or on demand)

For AI models, enrichment is often the difference between:

"Login from 1.2.3.4 for user X"

and

"First-time login from unusual country to a privileged finance admin account outside of working hours from a device never seen before."

The latter is far more informative for both humans and models.

2.3. Context: Connecting to Business Reality

Context is what lets you answer:

- "So what?"
- "Why does this matter?"
- "What is the potential impact?"

Contextual dimensions include:

- **Business services:** Which applications and processes are impacted by this asset or user?
- **Regulatory requirements:** Does this system store regulated data (PCI, PHI, etc.)?
- **Customer commitments:** Does downtime here affect contractual SLAs or critical clients?

When you encode this context into your data:

- Risk scoring becomes **business-aware**, not just technically precise.
- AI can prioritize incidents that actually matter, not just those that look noisy.
- Reports become immediately relevant to executives: "High-risk activity on your top revenue-generating system."

Context often lives outside traditional security tools. Part of your data strategy is to **pull it in and keep it current**.

3. Data Quality & Coverage: Are You Actually Ready for AI?

Many organizations say, "We want AI."

A more precise question is:

"Are we ready to make good use of AI with the data we have?"

You can think of readiness in two buckets:

1. **Coverage** – Are we seeing enough of the environment clearly?
2. **Quality** – Is what we collect usable, consistent, and trustworthy?

3.1. Coverage: Where Are the Blind Spots?

Key coverage questions:

- Are crown-jewel systems fully logged and monitored (endpoints, servers, databases, identity)?
- Do we capture **all critical authentication paths** (VPN, SSO, legacy auth, service accounts)?
- Are major cloud environments and SaaS platforms integrated?
- Is OT/IoT in scope for your risk profile?

The purpose is not 100% coverage on day one, but to avoid:

- Critical systems operating in the dark
- Major identity paths missing from your visibility
- Cloud assets with minimal or no telemetry

An AI-driven system trained on incomplete data may:

- Confidently ignore what it cannot see
- Overweight signals from well-instrumented areas
- Under-detect or completely miss threats in blind spots

3.2. Quality: Is the Data Clean Enough to Trust?

Typical quality issues:

- Broken parsers – fields are misaligned or missing.
- Time skew – events appear to come from the future or past due to bad clocks.
- Duplicates – repeated events due to misconfigured forwarding.
- Gaps – ingestion interruptions or overloaded collectors.

For AI (and humans), poor quality leads to:

- Bad baselines (e.g., logging bursts that are just duplicates).
- Misleading anomaly detection.
- Incorrect correlations and timelines.

You should aim to:

- Monitor for **data health** (ingestion rate, parse success, latency).
- Have alerts on significant deviations or gaps.
- Periodically review key sources for correctness.

3.3. A Simple Readiness Checklist

Before leaning heavily on AI in each area, check:

- **For the systems in scope:**
    - Do we ingest logs from all relevant components?
    - Are logs parsed into a consistent schema?
    - Is basic enrichment available (asset/user/threat)?
    - Are time and identifiers consistent enough to correlate?
- **For AI use cases:**
    - Do we have at least 3–6 months of historical data for baselining?
    - Are known gaps and limitations documented?
    - Do we have labelled cases (TP/FP) for training/evaluation where needed?

If many of these boxes are unchecked, your early AI efforts should focus on **fixing data and process**, not just deploying new models.

4. Building Feedback Loops from Analysts to Models

In a traditional SOC, analyst's close cases and move on. Notes and labels—if they exist—are mostly for compliance and audit.

In an AI-augmented SOC, those notes and labels are **training data**.

Every time an analyst:

- Marks an alert as a false positive
- Confirms a true positive incident
- Adds relevant context ("User was on approved business trip")
- Documents which actions were effective

…they're providing exactly the signal your models need to improve.

4.1. From "Case Notes" to Structured Feedback

Free-form text is useful but hard for models to consume consistently. Try to enforce a minimum level of **structured outcomes**, such as:

- Incident classification:
    - [True Positive / False Positive / Benign True Positive (accepted risk)]
- Root cause category:
    - Misconfiguration, user error, malicious insider, external attacker, test, etc.
- Action outcome:
    - Contained successfully, containment delayed, containment failed, no action needed

These can live as simple fields in your:

- Case management system
- SOAR tickets
- Incident forms

LLMs can then:

- Help extract more nuance from free-form notes.
- Summarize patterns across many cases.
- Support "lessons learned" and detection tuning.

4.2. Incorporating Feedback into Models

Once feedback is captured, you can use it to:

- Retrain supervised models:
    - "These types of alerts with these features were mostly false positives—deprioritize them."
    - "This pattern led to high-impact incidents—boost its risk score."
- Improve anomaly detectors:
    - Mark certain recurring anomalies as benign patterns to reduce noise.
- Refine decision policies:
    - If analysts frequently override a specific automated action, revisit the policy or confidence thresholds.

Importantly, this should not be ad-hoc:

- Define **who owns** model and rule tuning (often a detection engineering or "SOC product" team).
- Establish a cadence (monthly/quarterly) to review feedback and update models/rules.
- Test changes in a staging or shadow mode before rolling out broadly.

4.3. Human-in-the-Loop as a Design Principle

Human-in-the-loop isn't just about safe action approval—it also means:

- Humans are part of the **learning loop**.
- Analysts shape what the system learns to prioritize and ignore.

Practically, this may look like:

- Quick UI elements for "promote/demote this pattern."
- AI assistant prompts that ask analysts for simple classifications that feed back into training.
- Internal "bug reports" for AI behavior that seems wrong or confusing.

The more you make it natural for analysts to provide feedback, the faster your AI-driven SOC improves.

5. Retention, Privacy & Regulatory Constraints

The more you rely on AI, the more you care about **history** (for training and baselining) and **sensitivity** (because AI might see more data in aggregate than any person ever would).

That raises questions:

- How long should we keep data?
- Where is it stored and processed?
- What about PII, secrets, and customer data?

5.1. Retention: Balancing History & Cost

For AI and analytics, longer history typically means:

- Better baselines for behavior over time (seasonality, long-term trends).
- More training data for supervised models.
- Richer context for investigations ("Has this ever happened before?").

But storage and compute are not free, and retention is often limited by contract, policy, or regulation.

Key considerations:

- **Tiered storage:**
    - Keep recent data hot (fast access) for operations.
    - Move older data to colder, cheaper storage for AI training and rare investigations.
- **Use case–driven retention:**
    - Identity and endpoint logs may justify longer retention than low-value system logs.
- **Regulatory constraints:**
    - Some regulations require **minimum** retention periods; others encourage minimizing data lifetime.

For AI, you might adopt policies like:

- "We keep 12–18 months of detailed security telemetry, then aggregate or anonymize."
- "We keep full detail for crown-jewel systems longer than for generic endpoints."

5.2. Privacy & PII in an AI-Augmented SOC

Security logs almost always contain personal and sensitive information:

- Usernames, email addresses, IP addresses, device IDs
- Sometimes document names, URLs with query parameters, or even payload content

When integrating AI:

- Be explicit about **what fields are sent where**.
- Limit external or third-party AI services to **least-privilege data** (mask or hash where possible).
- Consider on-prem or private AI deployments for sensitive data (e.g., health, finance, government).

You should work with your privacy and legal teams to clarify:

- Which log data is considered personal or sensitive.
- Which jurisdictions it can be stored or processed in.
- Whether additional consent or contractual terms are required.

5.3. Transparency and Explainability for Regulators & Customers

As AI becomes more central to detection and response, external stakeholders will ask:

- "What decisions are made by AI vs. human analysts?"
- "How do you ensure fairness, accuracy, and oversight?"
- "How is my data (or my customers' data) used to train or tune AI?"

Your data strategy should include:

- **Documentation** of how AI is used, what data it sees, and how decisions are controlled.
- **Audit trails**: logs of AI-related decisions and actions, including inputs and outputs.
- **Clear statements** in customer and regulatory communications about data usage for AI.

Treat this not as a burden, but as a **trust-building exercise**. The more clearly you can articulate your data and AI practices, the more credible your SOC becomes.

6. Metrics for Data Readiness and Improvement

You can't improve what you don't measure—and that includes your data strategy.

Here are practical metrics you can track to assess and improve data readiness for AI.

6.1. Coverage Metrics

- **Source coverage:**
    - % of identified golden sources actively sending logs
    - % of critical assets (by business value) with full logging enabled
- **Identity coverage:**
    - % of authentication paths (VPN, SSO, legacy) logged
    - % of privileged accounts with complete auditable history

These metrics tell you: "How much of our environment can AI even see?"

6.2. Quality Metrics

- **Parse success rate:**
    - % of events successfully parsed into normalized schema per source
- **Ingestion latency:**
    - Average time from event occurrence to availability in SIEM/data lake
- **Data gap incidents:**
    - Number and duration of meaningful data outages per month
- **Time synchronization health:**
    - % of critical systems within acceptable NTP drift

These metrics tell you: "Can we rely on this data for accurate detection and timelines?"

6.3. Enrichment & Context Metrics

- **Enrichment coverage:**
    - % of events enriched with asset context
    - % of user events enriched with role/department
- **Threat intel hit rate:**
    - Ratio of enriched events with relevant CTI matches

These metrics show: "How much do we actually know beyond the raw event?"

6.4. Feedback & Learning Metrics

- **Incident labelling completeness:**
    - % of closed incidents with structured outcomes (TP/FP, root cause, impact)
- **Model tuning cadence:**
    - Number of model/rule tuning iterations per quarter
- **False positive reduction:**
    - Change in false positive rate for AI-influenced alerts over time
- **Analyst override rate:**
    - How often analysts override AI recommendations (should trend down as models improve)

These metrics signal: "Are we learning from experience, or just reacting?"

6.5. Governance & Compliance Metrics

- **Documented AI use cases:**
    - % of AI use cases with documented data flows and guardrails
- **Audit completeness:**
    - % of AI decisions/actions with associated audit logs
- **Data retention adherence:**
    - % of sources in compliance with defined retention & anonymization policies

These metrics demonstrate: "Are we in control of how data and AI are used?"

Key Takeaways from Chapter 4

- **AI is only as good as the data you give it.** A deliberate data strategy is foundational to any AI-augmented SOC.
- **Golden sources come first.** Focus on authoritative, high-value data sources—especially identity, endpoints, network, and crown-jewel systems.
- **Normalization, enrichment, and context transform logs into intelligence.** Without them, models and analysts both struggles.
- **Coverage and quality matter as much as quantity.** Blind spots, broken parsers, and gaps can cripple AI or lead it to false conclusions.
- **Analyst feedback is training data.** Structured outcomes and human-in-the-loop design turn your SOC into a learning system.
- **Retention, privacy, and governance are integral to the data strategy.** AI doesn't remove regulatory obligations; it intensifies them.
- **Measure your data readiness.** Coverage, quality, enrichment, learning, and governance metrics give you a roadmap for continuous improvement.

In the next chapter, we'll zoom in on a particularly high-value area: **using AI to improve alert triage and noise reduction**—one of the fastest ways to show tangible benefit to your SOC team and stakeholders.

Chapter 5 – AI for Alert Triage & Noise Reduction

If you ask most SOC teams what they want from AI, they usually don't ask for "autonomy" or "advanced analytics."

They say something much simpler:

"Please help us deal with this flood of alerts."

Alert triage is the daily grind of the SOC. It's where analysts spend a huge portion of their time, and it's where fatigue, mistakes, and missed incidents often begin.

The good news: **this is one of the areas where AI can deliver real, measurable value quickly—** if you design it correctly.

In this chapter, we'll cover:

1. Prioritization models (risk-based, asset-based, behavior-based)
2. AI-driven deduplication and correlation of alerts
3. Example workflows: from raw alerts to prioritized queues
4. Using LLMs to summarize complex alerts into plain language
5. Reducing MTTA and MTTD – what "good" looks like
6. Pitfalls: over-reliance, missed edge cases, and alert "blind spots"

By the end, you should have a clear picture of how to use AI to transform a noisy, overwhelming alert stream into a **ranked, focused queue of meaningful work**.

1. Prioritization Models: From Flat Lists to Risk-Aware Queues

Traditional alert queues often look like this:

- A flat list of alerts
- Sorted by time or vendor-provided severity
- With little or no awareness of business impact or user/asset context

This forces analysts to:

- Manually scan and filter
- Develop their own mental priors ("Ignore this rule, it's always noisy")
- Constantly context-switch between uncorrelated events

AI-driven triage replaces that with **prioritization models** that consider multiple dimensions at once.

1.1. Dimensions of Risk-Aware Prioritization

A robust prioritization model looks beyond "alert severity" and considers factors like:

- **Asset risk:**
    - Is this asset a crown jewel (e.g., payment systems, executive laptops, domain controllers)?
    - Is it internet-facing or internal only?
    - Does it hold regulated or highly sensitive data?
- **User risk:**
    - Is this a privileged admin, service account, or high-value executive?
    - Is the behavior consistent with their normal patterns?
    - Have they been involved in previous incidents?
- **Threat context:**
    - Does the alert map to known high-impact TTPs?
    - Are related indicators tied to active campaigns?
    - Has this pattern previously led to true positives?
- **Environmental context:**
    - Is there an ongoing incident or campaign with similar characteristics?
    - Is this environment already under heavy load or unusual conditions?

AI models can be trained or configured to **combine these factors into a composite risk score** for each alert or group of alerts.

1.2. Risk-Based vs. Asset-Based vs. Behavior-Based Models

You'll often hear three types of models discussed in triage:

1. **Risk-based models**
2. **Asset-based models**
3. **Behavior-based models**

In practice, they overlap, but it helps to frame them separately.

Risk-Based Models

Risk-based models focus on **impact and likelihood**:

- They ingest attributes like severity, confidence, asset importance, and threat intel.
- They output a score like "Overall risk: 0–100" or "Low/Medium/High/Critical."

These models are particularly useful for:

- Prioritizing which alerts should be looked at first.
- Driving automation policies (e.g., "Auto-contain anything above 90 on non-production hosts").

Asset-Based Models

Asset-based models emphasize **what is being targeted**:

- Assets are classified and scored (criticality, function, exposure).
- Alerts involving high-value assets are automatically boosted.

Example:

- The same type of abnormal login on:
    - A low-risk lab server → minor concern
    - The main payroll system → immediately elevated

This approach aligns triage with **business impact** rather than just technical severity.

Behavior-Based Models

Behavior-based models ask:

"Is this activity abnormal for this user, host, or environment?"

They analyze:

- Login patterns (time, location, device, frequency)
- Resource usage patterns
- Network connections and data flows
- Command/process behaviors

They're particularly good at:

- Flagging novel or evolving attacker behavior
- Finding subtle insider threats or account takeover attempts

Behavior-based findings can then be **fed into risk and asset-based models** to determine overall priority.

1.3. Combining Models into a Score

A practical implementation often looks like this:

- **Base Score (Detection):**
    - From the underlying detection logic or vendor (e.g., "Severity: High").
- **Contextual Boosters/Penalizers:**
    - +X if asset is critical
    - +Y if user is privileged
    - +Z if behavior is highly unusual
    - -W if similar alerts have historically been false positives

- **Final Composite Score:**
    - Normalized to a range (e.g., 0–100) for consistent triage.

AI can help learn the best weights and relationships between these factors based on historical outcomes.

You don't have to get this perfect from day one. Even a **first-generation composite score** that blends simple rules with AI-derived behaviors will usually outperform a flat, severity-only queue.

2. AI-Driven Deduplication & Correlation of Alerts

Alert floods are often not thousands of distinct problems—they're thousands of **symptoms of the same underlying issue**.

AI can help you collapse this chaos.

2.1. The Duplication Problem

Common duplication patterns:

- Multiple tools detecting the same event (EDR + SIEM rule + NDR).
- The same rule firing repeatedly for a persistent condition.
- Slightly different variations of alerts representing a single "episode."

Manually, analysts:

- Learn to recognize duplicates.
- Use correlation searches or dashboards.
- Close many alerts with the same comment ("Duplicate of incident #12345").

This is tedious and error prone.

2.2. Correlation and "Episode" Grouping

AI can use clustering and pattern recognition to group alerts into **episodes**:

- Time-based grouping: events within a certain window that share common attributes.
- Entity-based grouping: multiple alerts around the same user, host, or application.
- Sequence-based grouping: chains of events that match known patterns (e.g., phishing → MFA fatigue → VPN login).

An "episode" might represent:

- A single login anomaly that triggered multiple rules and detections.

- A lateral movement sequence affecting several hosts.
- A widespread phishing campaign across many users.

Instead of treating each alert as a standalone object, the SOC sees:

"Incident: Suspicious lateral movement involving 5 hosts and 3 user accounts over 2 hours."

This is far more useful—and far less overwhelming.

2.3. AI Techniques for Deduplication & Correlation

Under the hood, you'll typically see:

- **Clustering algorithms** that group similar alerts based on attributes and timing.
- **Graph-based models** that represent entities (users, hosts, IPs) and relationships (logins, connections, processes).
- **Template learning** that identifies common patterns (e.g., repeated benign bursts) and treats them as a single recurring event.

As a leader, you don't need to choose algorithms. You need to:

- Ensure the data includes enough consistent identifiers (user IDs, hostnames, IPs, correlation IDs).
- Encourage tools and teams to represent related events in ways that can be linked (for example, using shared case IDs).

The outcome you want is simple:

- Fewer, richer, more comprehensive incidents
- Less "noise scatter" across dashboards and queues

3. Example Workflows: From Raw Alerts to Prioritized Queues

Let's put the pieces together in practical workflows. We'll walk through a before-and-after view of triage using AI.

3.1. Before AI: Traditional Triage

A typical flow:

1. **Alert Creation**
   - Tools send alerts to SIEM/SOAR.
2. **Flat Queue**
   - Alerts appear in a time-ordered list with severity.

3. **Manual Filtering**
   - Analysts filter by severity, type, or source.
4. **Ad-Hoc Context Gathering**
   - For each alert, analysts manually look up:
     - Asset info
     - User info
     - Past incidents
     - Threat intel
5. **Decision & Action**
   - Close as false positive, escalate, or respond.
6. **Limited Feedback Loop**
   - Notes and labels may or may not be structured.

Problems:

- Duplicate work across similar alerts.
- High cognitive load and context-switching.
- Slow time-to-triage for meaningful incidents.

3.2. After AI: Tiered, AI-Augmented Triage

Now, let's look at a redesigned flow.

Step 1 – Initial Detection (Same as Before)

- SIEM, EDR, and other tools produce alerts from their rules and detectors.

Step 2 – AI Enrichment & Scoring

- AI Analytics Service takes each alert and:
  - Enriches it with asset/user/threat context.
  - Runs behavior models and anomaly checks.
  - Scores risk based on composite factors.
  - Tags alerts as belonging to episodes where applicable.

Output:

- Alert ID
- Enriched fields
- Risk Score (0–100)
- Episode ID (if grouped)
- Suggested "next steps" (for AI assistant and SOAR)

Step 3 – Episode Construction & Deduplication

- Alerts with the same Episode ID are grouped into a single incident view.
- Low-risk, clearly duplicate alerts may be:

- Automatically suppressed, or
- Presented only as part of the parent incident.

Analysts now see:

- A **list of episodes/incidents**, each with:
    - Overall risk score
    - Impacted assets/users
    - Brief natural-language summary
    - Number of underlying alerts

Step 4 – Prioritized Queue Presentation

- The console shows analysts a **sorted queue** of episodes, not raw alerts.
- Episodes above certain risk thresholds may be highlighted or auto-escalated.

Example view:

1. Critical – Episode #2031 – Possible domain admin compromise on DC-01
2. High – Episode #2032 – Suspicious cloud console login from new geo
3. Medium – Episode #2033 – Unusual data exfil pattern from finance app
4. Low – Episode #2034 – Known benign scanner activity from internal network

Step 5 – Analyst AI assistant Assistance

When an analyst opens Episode #2031, the AI assistant:

- Shows a timeline:
    - Suspicious login → privilege escalation → lateral movement → abnormal process activity
- Summarizes:
    - "This sequence suggests a potential domain admin credential misuse from an unusual host."
- Suggests next steps:
    - Isolate host
    - Force password reset
    - Pull EDR timeline
    - Notify on-call IR

The analyst can:

- Accept or modify suggested actions.
- Ask follow-up questions ("Show me prior logins from this user in the last 14 days").

Step 6 – Feedback Capture

When the incident is closed:

- Analyst selects: True positive / False positive / Benign true positive
- Provides a simple root-cause category.
- AI can help extract structured notes from longer text if needed.

This feedback flows back into the AI models and risk scoring logic.

4. Using LLMs to Summarize Complex Alerts into Plain Language

Technical alerts often look like this (simplified):

EventID=4625, AccountName=jsmith, WorkstationName=HR-LAPTOP-01, LogonType=3, FailureReason=Unknown user name or bad password, IpAddress=203.0.113.55

Alone, this isn't helpful to an executive—or even a busy analyst.

LLMs can take enriched event data and produce **clear, concise summaries** that accelerate understanding and communication.

4.1. From Fields to Narrative

Given structured alert data, an LLM can generate something like:

"User jsmith experienced 15 failed network logon attempts from IP 203.0.113.55 over 3 minutes to workstation HR-LAPTOP-01 from a country not previously associated with this user. The behavior is unusual compared to jsmith's past 90 days of activity."

This immediately answers:

- What happened?
- To whom?
- From where?
- Why is it unusual?

4.2. Use Cases for Summarization

LLM-based summarization is useful in multiple places:

- **Triage view:**
    - Each episode gets a short summary and, optionally, a "TL;DR" for quick scanning.
- **Incident details:**
    - Long lists of logs converted into human-readable timelines.
- **Executive reports:**
    - High-level descriptions of impact and response for non-technical audiences.
- **Customer-facing MSSP reports:**

o Clear explanations that justify actions and recommendations.

Summaries don't replace raw evidence; they **sit on top of it** for faster understanding.

4.3. Guardrails for Summarization

To avoid hallucinations and inaccuracies:

- Ground LLMs in structured, verified data (retrieved from SIEM, EDR, etc.).
- Include references in the summary (e.g., "Based on 15 failed logins in EventIDs X–Y").
- Require human review for:
  o Official incident documentation
  o Regulatory reports
  o Customer-facing communication

Treat LLMs as an **accelerator for writing and comprehension**, not a final authority.

5. Reducing MTTA and MTTD – What "Good" Looks Like

The entire point of AI-driven triage is not "better dashboards." It's **improving outcomes**:

- Lower mean time to acknowledge (MTTA)
- Lower mean time to detect (MTTD)
- Improved true-positive coverage with the same or fewer resources

5.1. Measuring Before and After

Before rolling out AI triage, capture baseline metrics:

- Average MTTA for high-severity alerts
- Average MTTD from event onset to incident creation
- Volume of alerts per day vs. incidents created
- True positive / false positive ratios by alert category
- Analyst satisfaction (surveys, interviews)

After deploying AI-based triage, measure:

- Changes in MTTA and MTTD for prioritized incidents
- Reduction in total alert volume presented to analysts
- Change in false positive load for Tier 1
- Number of incidents auto-escalated correctly (with minimal rework)

Even a **20–30% improvement** in MTTA/MTTD for critical incidents is significant.

5.2. What "Good" Might Look Like in Practice

Examples of realistic goals:

- **Alert volume presented to analysts:**
  - 40–60% reduction in raw alerts by grouping, deduplication, and suppression of obvious noise.
- **MTTA for critical incidents:**
  - Reduced from 20–30 minutes to 5–10 minutes.
- **Analyst capacity:**
  - Same team processes 1.5–2x more *meaningful* incidents without burnout.
- **False positives in prioritized queue:**
  - Reduced significantly for critical and high-priority items, even if some low-priority noise remains in the background.

"Good" doesn't mean perfect detection with zero false positives. It means:

- Your team spends most of its time on **real, impactful work**.
- High-risk incidents are **seen and acted upon quickly**.
- AI is measurably reducing manual effort and cognitive load.

6. Pitfalls: Over-Reliance, Missed Edge Cases, and Blind Spots

AI-based triage is powerful—but it also introduces new pitfalls.

You need to anticipate and design around them.

6.1. Over-Reliance on Scores

If analysts are told "trust the AI score," they may:

- Ignore low-scored alerts that are actually important edge cases.
- Overreact to high scores without critical thinking.

Mitigations:

- Train analysts to treat scores as **decision support**, not absolute truth.
- Provide transparency into **why** a score was assigned (key factors, contributing signals).
- Periodically review low-scored alerts to check for systemic blind spots.

6.2. Blind Spots from Missing Data

If certain regions, systems, or user populations are poorly instrumented:

- AI may systematically under-prioritize incidents in those areas.
- You'll get a **false sense of security** in parts of the environment you can't see well.

Mitigations:

- Document known visibility gaps and incorporate them into risk discussions.
- Use coverage metrics (from Chapter 4) to highlight blind spots.
- Avoid messaging that implies "AI sees everything" when it doesn't.

6.3. Misconfigured or Misaligned Models

If models are tuned to the wrong objective, you may see:

- Over-aggressive suppression of alerts to minimize "noise," but at the cost of missed attacks.
- Models optimizing for low false positives while tolerating too many false negatives.

Mitigations:

- Explicitly define your objective trade-offs (e.g., "For identity-related alerts, we prefer higher sensitivity").
- Monitor performance across different incident types and business units.
- Use **human review** and simulation to validate model changes before full rollout.

6.4. Model Drift as the Environment Changes

As your environment evolves:

- New apps, cloud regions, and user behaviors may make old baselines invalid.
- Behavior-based models may start flagging everything as "unusual" or fail to spot new patterns.

Mitigations:

- Monitor key performance metrics over time (false positives, missed detections, analyst overrides).
- Retrain or recalibrate models on a regular cadence.
- Treat AI as part of your **continuous SOC engineering** process, not a one-off project.

6.5. Analyst Disengagement

If triage is heavily automated:

- Some analysts may feel their role is reduced to "button clicking."
- Skills in raw log analysis and investigation may atrophy over time.

Mitigations:

- Use AI triage to **free analysts for more advanced work**, not to reduce them to passive reviewers.
- Invest in training for threat hunting, purple teaming, and advanced investigations.
- Include analysts in model and workflow design—they're not just users but co-creators.

Key Takeaways from Chapter 5

- **Alert triage is a prime candidate for AI impact.** It's where noise, fatigue, and missed incidents converge—and where AI can deliver quick, visible wins.
- **Effective prioritization goes beyond severity.** Combining asset criticality, user risk, threat context, and behavior produce richer, more meaningful risk scores.
- **Deduplication and correlation turn chaos into episodes.** Grouping related alerts into single incidents dramatically reduces noise and cognitive load.
- **LLMs transform technical noise into human understanding.** Summaries and narratives accelerate triage, investigation, and communication—but must be grounded and reviewed.
- **Measure outcomes, not features.** Success is about reducing MTTA/MTTD and false positive load, not just deploying "AI-powered" widgets.
- **Beware new risks.** Over-reliance, blind spots, misaligned objectives, drift, and analyst disengagement must be managed consciously.

In the next chapter, we shift from triage to **AI as an analyst AI assistant**—how natural-language interfaces, guided investigations, and smart enrichment can help every analyst in your SOC operate like a more experienced one.

Chapter 6 – AI assistant for Analysts & Threat Hunters

In the last chapter, we focused on AI helping you **decide what to look at**—triage and noise reduction.

In this chapter, we focus on **what happens after you've decided to look at something**:

How can AI act as an *AI assistant* for your analysts and threat hunters—guiding investigations, pulling context, and helping them think more clearly and move faster?

The idea of a "SOC AI assistant" is simple:

- It doesn't replace your analysts.
- It sits beside them—inside their console, in chat, or in the case system.
- It helps them ask better questions and get better answers, faster.

We'll cover:

1. Natural language querying of security data ("Google for your SOC")
2. Enrichment assistants: automatically pulling context (whois, VT, EDR, CTI)
3. Hypothesis generation for threat hunting (what to look for next)
4. Assisted investigation timelines and root-cause summaries
5. Training the AI assistant on your SOC's specific environment and playbooks
6. Keeping a human in the loop: review, approval, and escalation

By the end, you should have a clear mental model of what a good AI assistant looks like, what it needs under the hood, and how to roll it out safely.

1. Natural Language Querying: "Google for Your SOC"

For years, using a SIEM has meant:

- Remembering the correct query language (SQL/KQL/DSL).
- Knowing which fields exist and how they're named.
- Understanding which indices or tables to query.

That's a high bar—especially for junior analysts.

An AI assistant changes this by letting analysts ask questions in **plain language**:

"Show me all successful logins to privileged accounts from new IP addresses in the last 24 hours."

…and having the system:

- Translate that into a valid query
- Execute it against the right data sources
- Present the results in a useful format

1.1. Why Natural Language Matters

Natural language querying does three things:

1. **Flattens the learning curve**
   - New analysts no longer need to memorize query syntax before they can be useful.
   - Specialists can focus on *what* they're looking for, not on how to express it in code.
2. **Speeds up exploration**
   - Analysts can iterate quickly:
     - "OK, now show me only those logins from outside our usual countries."
     - "Filter to admin accounts only."
3. **Encodes expert knowledge in prompts**
   - Senior investigators define "investigation patterns" as reusable natural language queries, not just saved searches.
   - Over time, the AI assistant learns these patterns and can suggest them automatically.

1.2. How It Works Under the Hood (At a High Level)

You don't need the implementation details, but you should understand the flow:

1. Analyst asks a question in natural language.
2. AI assistant parses intent ("logins", "privileged accounts", "new IP addresses", "last 24 hours").
3. AI assistant maps these concepts to:
   - Data sources (auth logs, identity store, asset inventory)
   - Field names (user, src_ip, role, timestamp, etc.)
4. AI assistant generates a SIEM/XDR query and executes it.
5. Results are returned and optionally summarized or visualized.

The key dependencies:

- A **schema registry** or metadata layer (the AI assistant needs to know your fields and tables).
- Access to your query APIs.
- A way to **log and show the generated query** so analysts can review and refine it.

1.3. Design Principles for Natural Language Querying

As a leader, you should push for these principles:

- **Transparency:**
  - Always show the generated query and allow editing.
  - Analysts should be able to copy, tweak, and save it as a normal query.
- **Scoped access:**
  - Respect RBAC—analysts can only query data they're allowed to see.
- **Guardrails:**
  - Prevent overly broad or dangerous queries that could overload systems (e.g., "search everything for the last 5 years").
  - AI assistant can respond with: "This query is too broad; here's a suggested smaller scope."
- **Learning from usage:**
  - Capture frequently used natural language queries.
  - Promote them as suggested "shortcuts" or built-in investigation templates.

The goal is not to hide the SIEM behind a chatbot; it's to let analysts **discover, learn, and iterate** with far less friction.

2. Enrichment Assistants: Pulling Context Automatically

A huge part of investigations is **context gathering**:

- Looking up IP reputation
- Checking whether a file hash appears in VT or your EDR
- Confirming what assets, a host belongs to
- Determining a user's role and recent activity

Today, analysts often do this manually:

- Open a new browser tab
- Paste IPs into a threat intel portal
- Query EDR for process history
- Check CMDB or internal tools

An AI assistant can act as an **enrichment assistant** that does this automatically and consistently.

2.1. What Good Enrichment Feels Like to Analysts

In an AI assistant experience, an analyst might:

- Open an alert or episode
- Immediately see:
  - IP reputation ("Seen in 3 known malware campaigns, high risk")
  - User context ("Finance manager, based in Toronto, typically logs in 9–5 EST")

- Host context ("Critical file server, production environment, in-scope for PCI")
- File context ("Hash previously seen on 2 other endpoints; flagged as suspicious 3 times in the last week")

The analyst does **not** have to:

- Click ten links
- Log into three different tools
- Manually cross-reference identifiers

The AI assistant either pre-enriches alerts or retrieves enrichment on demand with a simple prompt:

"Enrich this alert with user, asset, and threat intel context."

2.2. Typical Enrichment Sources

Key sources the AI assistant should integrate with:

- **Threat Intelligence:**
    - IP/domain/file hash reputation
    - Malware families, campaigns, TTP mappings
- **EDR/XDR:**
    - Process tree, parent/child commands
    - Recent alerts and activities on the same host
    - Isolation status
- **Identity & Access:**
    - User groups and roles
    - Privilege level and admin rights
    - MFA usage and risk scores
- **Asset & CMDB:**
    - Asset criticality and business owner
    - Environment (prod/dev/test)
    - Location and function
- **Ticketing / Case Systems:**
    - Past incidents involving the same user/host
    - Recurring issues or accepted risks

The AI assistant doesn't replace these tools—it **orchestrates** them on the analyst's behalf.

2.3. Automation Patterns for Enrichment

There are two main patterns:

1. **Proactive enrichment**

- When a high-risk incident is created, the AI assistant automatically pulls standard context.
- Analysts always open a "fully enriched" case.
2. **On-demand enrichment**
    - Analysts ask the AI assistant to fetch specific information:
        - "Show me the last 30 days of logins for this user."
        - "Pull the EDR timeline for this host in the last 2 hours."

Both are useful. As a leader, you decide:

- Which enrichment should **always** be present (high-value, low-cost).
- Which enrichment should be on-demand (expensive queries, rate-limited APIs).

The more consistent your enrichment, the better your **AI models** perform and the faster your analysts move.

3. Hypothesis Generation for Threat Hunting

Threat hunting is fundamentally about **asking good questions**:

- "If an attacker had stolen these credentials, what would they do next?"
- "If this system were compromised, where would we see traces?"
- "What does lateral movement look like in this environment?"

Senior hunters develop these hypotheses through experience. Junior staff often struggle with:

- Where to begin
- Which queries to run
- How to interpret partial or uncertain findings

Here, an AI assistant can be a **brainstorming partner** and **pattern library**.

3.1. From Alert to Hunt: Asking "What Else Should I Check?"

Given an incident (for example, "suspicious admin login from new location"), a AI assistant can propose follow-up hunts such as:

- "Search for other logins from this IP to any other accounts in the last 7 days."
- "Look for failed logins from the same IP before the success event."
- "Check for privilege escalation events on this account in the last 24 hours."
- "Scan for similar anomalous logins to other admin accounts from unfamiliar geos."

The analyst can:

- Accept these suggestions as automated queries.

- Modify them ("Limit to domain admins only").
- Save them as reusable hunt packs.

3.2. Hunt Libraries and Pattern Sharing

A mature AI assistant doesn't just invent suggestions—it **learns and codifies**:

- Known hunting patterns from frameworks (e.g., ATT&CK)
- Internal hunt playbooks your team already uses
- Investigations that led to true positives in the past

Over time, your AI assistant becomes a **library of hunts**, surfaced at the right moment:

- When a certain type of alert appears
- When a specific technique is suspected
- When analysts ask: "What's the next logical question here?"

This helps:

- Junior analysts hunt like more experienced ones.
- Senior hunters document and reuse their knowledge without endless wiki pages.

3.3. Proactive Hunting Campaigns

Beyond reactive hunting, the AI assistant can help design and execute **proactive campaigns**:

- You define a theme:
    - "Find evidence of token theft in the last 30 days."
    - "Search for stealthy persistence mechanisms on critical servers."
- The AI assistant:
    - Suggests relevant hypotheses and queries.
    - Orchestrates searches across multiple data sources.
    - Helps track findings, false leads, and confirmed indicators.

As a leader, you can use this to:

- Run **regular themed hunts** driven by current threat intel.
- Ensure hunting activities are **structured and repeatable**, not ad-hoc heroics.

4. Assisted Investigation Timelines & Root-Cause Summaries

Investigations produce **a lot of data**:

- Dozens or hundreds of events

- Multiple hosts and users
- EDR telemetry, firewall logs, identity changes, email traces

Trying to reconstruct what happened and when is often the most time-consuming part.

An AI assistant can help build **timelines and root-cause summaries** automatically.

4.1. From Raw Events to a Coherent Timeline

Given a set of related events (or an "episode" as described in Chapter 5), the AI assistant can:

1. **Sort and correlate events by time and entity**
   - Group events by user, host, or process.
   - Identify key transitions (initial access, privilege escalation, lateral movement, exfiltration, etc.).
2. **Highlight significant steps**
   - Mark events that likely represent attacker milestones.
   - Join related events into a higher-level description ("User X logged in from IP Y, then executed process Z and accessed database A").
3. **Generate a human-readable timeline**
   - Plain language text, something like:

09:12 – User jsmith logs in from IP 203.0.113.55 (unusual geo for this user).

09:14 – jsmith successfully authenticates to VPN from the same IP.

09:16 – jsmith accesses server FIN-DB-01 for the first time in 90 days.

09:18 – jsmith executes unusual PowerShell commands on FIN-DB-01.

The analyst can then:

- Verify key points
- Add or correct details
- Use this as the backbone of incident communication and post-incident review.

4.2. Root-Cause Analysis Assistance

Understanding **how** an incident started is crucial for prevention. A AI assistant can:

- Analyze the timeline and highlight **likely initial access vectors**.
- Suggest probable scenarios ("Credentials phished," "MFA fatigue attack," "Exposed service exploited," etc.).
- Point to **missing data** that would help (e.g., "No email logs for the time period when this user's credentials were likely compromised").

It can also help draft a **root-cause summary**, such as:

"Evidence suggests that the attacker obtained valid credentials for the user jsmith, likely through a phishing campaign targeting corporate email. The credentials were used from an IP address in a country where jsmith has no prior login history. MFA was not enforced for this user at the time of the incident, enabling the attacker to gain remote access and subsequently access the FIN-DB-01 server."

Again, this is a **first draft**. Analysts and incident responders refine it—but the time savings are substantial.

4.3. Multi-Audience Reporting

Different stakeholders need different levels of detail:

- **Tier 3 / IR and forensics:**
    - Event-level detail, raw logs, exact commands, hashes, etc.
- **Security leadership (CISO, SOC manager):**
    - Attack paths, timeline, impact, control failures, remediations.
- **Business leaders and regulators:**
    - High-level narrative, impact statement, and risk mitigation summary.

The AI assistant can generate **multiple versions** of the same story at appropriate levels:

- "Technical summary"
- "Leadership summary"
- "Customer-facing summary"

This ensures consistency and saves hours of manual rewriting.

5. Training the AI assistant on Your SOC's Environment & Playbooks

Out of the box, even a good AI assistant is generic. To become truly useful, it needs to **learn your environment**:

- Your network, applications, and business services
- Your existing detection content and playbooks
- Your naming conventions and internal jargon

5.1. Data & Knowledge to Feed the AI assistant

Key inputs you should plan to provide:

- **Playbooks and SOPs**
    - Incident response procedures

- o Standard triage checklists
- o Communications templates
- **Detection content**
  - o SIEM rules, correlation logic, and use case documentation
  - o Mappings to MITRE ATT&CK, internal risk categories
- **Architecture and topology**
  - o High-level diagrams of critical systems and data flows
  - o Network segmentation and security zones
- **Glossaries and taxonomies**
  - o Names of internal systems and apps
  - o Definitions of internal severity codes, incident types, and ticket categories
- **Past incidents and post-incident reviews**
  - o What happened, how it was discovered, what worked, what didn't

The more structured and well-documented this information is, the more accurately the AI assistant can:

- Suggest relevant playbooks
- Use the right terminology in summaries and reports
- Make context-aware recommendations

5.2. SOC-Specific "Skills" for the AI assistant

Think of AI assistant capabilities as **skills** you can add:

- "Investigate phishing email"
- "Triage malware alert on endpoint"
- "Respond to suspicious VPN login"
- "Prepare monthly SOC summary report"

Each skill can be defined as:

- A set of **steps or prompts** the AI assistant follows
- Specific **data sources** to consult
- A structure for **outputs** (checklists, queries, summaries, recommended actions)

Example skill: *Investigate suspicious login*

- Inputs: user ID, timestamp, IP address
- Steps:
    1. Pull last 30 days of logins for this user.
    2. Check IP reputation and geo anomalies.
    3. Check for unusual activity following the login (new assets accessed, privilege changes).
    4. Summarize findings and suggest actions.

These skills can be implemented as:

- Pre-defined prompt templates and workflows inside the AI assistant
- Orchestration logic that interacts with SIEM/SOAR/EDR APIs

As a leader, you can:

- Prioritize which skills to build first (phishing, VPN anomalies, EDR alerts, etc.).
- Encourage analysts to propose and refine skills as they use the AI assistant.

5.3. Continuous Tuning & Localization

Over time, tune the AI assistant to:

- Use **your tone** in communications (formal vs. informal, regional spelling, etc.).
- Respect **your thresholds** (what is "critical" vs "high" in your world).
- Reflect **your specific controls and tools** ("We use product X for email security, not generic references").

This is a continuous process:

- Review AI assistant outputs regularly (reports, suggestions, timelines).
- Capture where it misunderstands or omits important local context.
- Update its knowledge base, prompts, and skills accordingly.

You're essentially training a **new team member**—one that never sleeps and can be cloned infinitely, but that still needs onboarding and coaching.

6. Keeping a Human in the Loop: Review, Approval, and Escalation

An AI assistant is not an autopilot.

If you treat it as one—especially early—you risk mistakes, miscommunications, and loss of trust.

Human-in-the-loop design is critical.

6.1. Where Human Oversight Is Essential

There are three areas where human oversight should be non-negotiable:

1. **High-impact actions**
   - Isolating production servers
   - Disabling critical user accounts
   - Blocking major network segments
2. **Official communications**
   - Customer notifications
   - Regulator reports

- Legal or HR-relevant documentation
3. **Root-cause and lessons learned**
    - Final determination of what happened and why
    - Decisions about control changes and strategic mitigations

The AI assistant can draft, recommend, and surface options. Humans approve and own the decision.

6.2. Approval Flows and Guardrails

In practical terms:

- AI assistant suggestions should be **clearly labelled** as such:
    - "Recommended next actions"
    - "Draft incident summary"
- For actions with side effects, the UI should include explicit confirmation:
    - "AI assistant suggests isolating host FIN-DB-01. Approve? [Yes / Edit / No]"
- For automation policies, you set clear conditions:
    - "Auto-contain endpoints only when:
        - Risk score > 90
        - Environment = non-production
        - Asset criticality < 'High'."

The AI assistant and SOAR can enforce these guardrails consistently—no shortcuts, no "just this once" exceptions.

6.3. Escalation and "I'm Not Sure" Cases

The AI assistant should be allowed to admit:

"I don't have enough information to make a confident suggestion."

In those cases, it can:

- Identify missing data ("Email logs from this timeframe are unavailable").
- Suggest manual steps ("Escalate to Tier 3 and consider forensic imaging").
- Provide a **structured handoff summary** for the next human.

This prevents a dangerous behavior: **forced confidence**, where the system always provides an answer even when it shouldn't.

6.4. Building and Maintaining Trust

Analysts will only use and rely on the AI assistant if they trust it.

You build that trust by:

- **Transparency:**
  - Show which data the AI assistant used and where it might be uncertain.
- **Consistency:**
  - Ensure it gives similar answers to similar questions.
- **Responsiveness to feedback:**
  - When analysts correct or override the AI assistant, those corrections should be reflected over time.
- **No punishment for questioning the AI:**
  - Encourage analysts to challenge and verify the AI assistant, not blindly follow it.

Culturally, you want a team that sees AI as:

"A powerful colleague I argue with and refine, not a boss I must obey."

Key Takeaways from Chapter 6

- **The AI assistant is about augmenting, not replacing, analysts.** It sits beside them, helping query data, gather context, generate hypotheses, and tell the story of what happened.
- **Natural language interfaces reduce friction.** Analysts can explore logs and telemetry as easily as they ask questions, while still seeing and refining the underlying queries.
- **Enrichment should be orchestrated, not manual.** A good AI assistant automatically brings user, asset, threat, and historical context into each investigation.
- **Hunting becomes more accessible and structured.** AI assistant-driven hypotheses and hunt libraries help junior staff think like seasoned hunters and make proactive campaigns repeatable.
- **Timelines and root-cause summaries are prime AI territory.** Let the AI assistant build first drafts; humans validate, correct, and adapt them for different audiences.
- **Training the AI assistant on your environment is essential.** Feed it your playbooks, architecture, past incidents, and terminology so its suggestions are aligned with your reality.
- **Human-in-the-loop is non-negotiable.** High-impact actions and official communications require human approval; the AI assistant must remain a tool, not an oracle.

In the next chapter, we'll expand from individual analysts to **AI-generated playbooks, runbooks, and reports**—how to let AI capture tribal knowledge, standardize response, and generate documentation at scale without losing control or quality.

Chapter 7 – AI-Generated Playbooks, Runbooks & Reports

In most SOCs, the real "operating system" is not the SIEM or SOAR.

It's what lives in people's heads.

- The Tier 2 analyst who "just knows" what to do with a certain kind of EDR alert
- The incident responder who remembers the three systems you *must* check after a domain admin compromise
- The senior engineer who knows which firewall policies to touch and which to avoid

This **tribal knowledge** is incredibly valuable—and incredibly fragile. It walks out the door when people leave. It degrades when teams grow. It fragments when you scale across sites and time zones.

AI gives you a way to:

- Capture that knowledge
- Turn it into **standardized playbooks and runbooks**
- Keep it **up to date** with less manual effort
- Generate **consistent reports and documentation** as a byproduct of doing the work

In this chapter, we'll cover:

1. Turning tribal knowledge into standardized playbooks
2. Using AI to draft and refine SOAR workflows
3. Automated incident reports for executives and customers
4. Generating post-incident reviews and lessons learned
5. Template library: common incident types and what AI can generate
6. Governance over AI-authored artifacts

The goal is to move from "heroes" to **systems**, without losing the expertise that made those heroes effective in the first place.

1. Turning Tribal Knowledge into Standardized Playbooks

A playbook is simply:

"Given this kind of event or incident, here is what we typically do, in what order, and who is involved."

Runbooks go deeper into **step-by-step technical actions**.

The problem is rarely that teams don't have playbooks; it's that:

- They're incomplete or out of date
- They exist as scattered documents, wikis, or memories
- They're too long and hard to follow under pressure

AI can help you **capture, structure, and maintain** these artifacts.

1.1. Interviewing Your SOC Through AI

Instead of manually writing every playbook from scratch, you can:

1. **Collect raw material**
    - Past incident tickets and case notes
    - Chat logs from major incidents
    - Existing SOPs and wiki pages
    - Informal notes from senior analysts ("Here's how I usually handle X")
2. **Have AI draft initial playbooks** by asking:
    - "Summarize the steps taken across these 10 phishing incidents into a standard playbook."
    - "From these case notes on ransomware incidents, extract common steps and sequence them."
3. **Review with practitioners**
    - Analysts and responders review the AI-drafted playbook.
    - They correct mistakes, add missing steps, clarify preconditions and exceptions.

The key advantage:

- You use AI as a **compression engine** to turn messy, distributed experience into a **structured starting point**.
- Humans refine, not create from a blank page.

1.2. Structuring a Playbook for AI and Humans

Good playbooks are useful both for:

- Humans reading them; and
- AI/automation consuming them.

A practical structure:

1. **Scope & Scenario**
    - "This playbook applies to suspected compromised user accounts detected via unusual login patterns."
2. **Prerequisites & Inputs**
    - Tools required (EDR, IAM, email security, etc.)
    - Required permissions
    - Key data (user ID, time window, alert IDs)

3. **Objectives**
   - Contain potential compromise
   - Verify legitimacy of activity
   - Minimize business disruption
4. **High-Level Flow**
   - Step 1: Validate the alert
   - Step 2: Assess risk and business impact
   - Step 3: Contain if necessary
   - Step 4: Investigate scope (lateral movement, data access)
   - Step 5: Eradicate and recover
   - Step 6: Document and close
5. **Detailed Steps**
   - Each step with:
     - Purpose
     - Actions
     - Responsible role (Tier 1, Tier 2, IR, etc.)
     - Automation opportunities (what AI/SOAR can do)
6. **Decision Points & Branches**
   - "If user confirms they were traveling and MFA logs look valid → follow branch A."
   - "If user denies activity or cannot be contacted → follow branch B."
7. **Communications & Notifications**
   - Who needs to know and when (IT, HR, legal, business owners).
8. **Data to Capture**
   - Evidence to store
   - Fields to populate in case/ticket

AI can be instructed to **always output playbooks in this structure**, making them easy to read, implement in SOAR, and update later.

1.3. Keeping Playbooks Alive

Static playbooks die. Living playbooks improve.

With AI in the loop, you can:

- Periodically feed **recent relevant incidents** into a prompt:
  - "Update this playbook based on these last 20 incidents, highlighting any new steps or changes."
- Use post-incident reviews to refine them:
  - "Incorporate the 'lessons learned' section into the playbook for this incident type."
- Ask AI to compare versions:
  - "Show me the differences between the phishing playbook v1.3 and v1.4, and summarize key changes."

The result:
Playbooks that evolve with your environment and threat landscape, without requiring a full rewrite every time.

2. Using AI to Draft and Refine SOAR Workflows

Playbooks describe **what** should happen. SOAR workflows implement **how** it happens in tools and automation.

Designing these workflows by hand can be:

- Time-consuming
- Error-prone
- Highly specialized (dependent on one or two automation engineers)

AI can accelerate the **design and refinement** of these workflows.

2.1. From Playbook Text to SOAR Workflow Draft

Given a structured playbook, you can ask AI to:

- Identify steps that can be **fully automated**
- Identify steps that should be **human-approved actions**
- Propose a SOAR workflow structure

For example, AI could output:

- Step 1: Enrich alert with user, host, and threat intel (auto).
- Step 2: If risk score > 80 and asset criticality < "high", propose auto-quarantine (needs approval).
- Step 3: If user is non-privileged and suspicious IP appears on blocklist, auto-block IP on firewall (auto under policy).
- Step 4: Create or update incident ticket with enrichment and recommended actions.

It can also generate **pseudocode or YAML/JSON** for tools that support declarative workflows.

Your engineers then:

- Review and refine the proposed flow
- Implement it in the SOAR UI or via code
- Add error handling, logging, and edge cases

2.2. AI as a Workflow Reviewer

Even if you design workflows manually, AI can act as a **reviewer**:

- "Analyze this SOAR workflow and highlight potential failure points or missing steps."
- "Does this playbook send notifications to relevant stakeholders? If not, suggest where to add them."
- "Identify where we might cause unnecessary disruption and recommend mitigations."

This is especially useful when:

- Inheriting legacy workflows
- Onboarding new automation engineers
- Scaling to many playbooks where manual review is hard

2.3. Guardrails for Automated Workflows

When creating or modifying workflows, AI should operate within **guardrails** you define:

- **Allowed actions**
    - e.g., AI may propose: isolate endpoint, reset password, quarantine email.
    - But **must not** propose: deleting data, changing firewall in core network segments, modifying backup policies.
- **Approval thresholds**
    - "Any workflow involving critical assets or privileged users must include a human approval step, regardless of risk score."
- **Audit and logging requirements**
    - "All automated actions must be logged with the reason, inputs, and outputs, in a format AI can later summarize."

You're not asking AI to "turn on full automation." You're using it to **accelerate design** while staying within tightly controlled boundaries.

3. Automated Incident Reports for Executives and Customers

Reports are where the SOC tells its story:

- What happened
- How it was handled
- What the impact was
- What will be done to prevent recurrence

They're also one of the most time-consuming and often neglected tasks.

AI is exceptionally good at turning structured case data into **clear, consistent reports** for different audiences.

3.1. Input: What the AI Needs

To generate reliable reports, your systems must capture:

- Incident metadata
    - Type, severity, impacted systems, users, timeframes
- Key events
    - High-level timeline entries from SIEM/EDR/SOAR
- Actions taken
    - Containment, eradication, recovery steps
- Outcome
    - Root cause, confirmed or suspected attacker actions, impact assessment

Most of this can be:

- Captured automatically by your tools
- Augmented with short, structured inputs from analysts during closure

3.2. Output: Multi-Audience Reports

Using this data, AI can generate different report flavors:

1. **Executive Summary**
    - 1–2 pages
    - Plain language
    - Focus on impact, business risk, and key actions
2. **Technical Incident Report**
    - Detailed timeline
    - Indicators of compromise
    - Attack chain mapped to MITRE ATT&CK
    - Evidence and logs references
3. **Customer-Facing MSSP Report (if applicable)**
    - Framed in terms of the service provided
    - What was detected, how quickly, what was done, what the customer should do
4. **Regulatory/Compliance-Oriented Report**
    - Specific fields required by regulation or contracts
    - Data breach notification details where applicable

The same underlying incident record can produce **multiple consistent outputs** with minimal additional effort.

3.3. Best Practices for AI-Generated Reports

To make AI-generated reports useful and safe:

- **Always require review and sign-off**
  - AI provides a draft; a human owner finalizes it.
- **Highlight uncertainty**
  - AI should be encouraged to say "uncertain" or "no evidence available" rather than fill gaps with guesses.
- **Use templates**
  - Create standardized report structures and instruct AI to fill those, not invent new formats every time.
- **Store the final, human-approved version**
  - Keep a clear distinction between draft and final, especially in regulated environments.

The outcome:
Reports go from "we dread writing them" to "they're a natural output of our workflow."

4. Generating Post-Incident Reviews and Lessons Learned

Post-incident reviews (PIRs) are where:

- You analyze what worked and what didn't
- You extract **lessons learned**
- You decide on **remediation and improvement actions**

They're crucial—but often rushed or skipped.

AI can help ensure PIRs happen and are of decent quality.

4.1. Drafting the Post-Incident Review

Given an incident record and timeline, AI can draft a PIR that includes:

1. **Incident Overview**
   - What happened
   - When it started and how it was detected
   - Which systems and data were affected
2. **Detection & Response Performance**
   - How quickly it was detected (MTTD)
   - How quickly it was contained and resolved (MTTR)
   - Any delays or obstacles
3. **Root Cause & Contributing Factors**
   - Technical root causes

- o Process gaps (e.g., missing controls, misconfigurations)
- o Human factors (e.g., lack of training, unclear responsibilities)
4. **What Worked Well**
    - o Controls that functioned as intended
    - o Effective actions and decisions
5. **What Needs Improvement**
    - o Detection gaps
    - o Process and communication issues
    - o Tooling and automation opportunities
6. **Action Items**
    - o Specific tasks, owners, and due dates

The PIR is then reviewed in a meeting, where stakeholders:

- Confirm or adjust analysis
- Add nuance and context
- Agree on remediation and tracking

4.2. Feeding Lessons Back into Playbooks and Models

The most important part of PIRs is not the document; it's what changes.

AI can help you **close the loop** by:

- Extracting improvement items and updating relevant playbooks:
    - o "Add an explicit step to verify MFA configuration for high-risk users after similar incidents."
- Highlighting recurring themes:
    - o "In the last 10 PIRs, 6 mentioned delays due to missing asset ownership information."
- Suggesting model and rule updates:
    - o "Consider increasing risk weighting for VPN logins without MFA from new locations."

In other words, PIRs become not just **post-mortems**, but **fuel for continuous improvement** of:

- Detection
- Playbooks and workflows
- Training and awareness

5. Template Library: Common Incident Types

Certain incident categories recur frequently across most SOCs. These are prime candidates for **AI-assisted standardization**.

Here are examples where AI-generated playbooks, runbooks, and reports are particularly effective.

5.1. Phishing & Business Email Compromise (BEC)

Playbooks / Runbooks AI can help generate:

- Triage suspected phishing email
- Contain compromised mailbox
- Investigate BEC attempts (changes to forwarding rules, finance fraud attempts)

Reports AI can generate:

- Executive summary of phishing campaigns affecting multiple users
- Customer-facing reports for MSSP anti-phishing services

5.2. Endpoint Malware & Ransomware

Playbooks / Runbooks:

- Triage suspicious EDR alert
- Confirm and contain ransomware on endpoints
- Coordinate recovery and restoration from backups

Reports:

- Technical ransomware incident reports with file hashes, TTP mappings
- Root-cause analysis on initial access (phishing, RDP exposure, etc.)

5.3. Suspicious Authentication & Account Compromise

Playbooks / Runbooks:

- Investigate unusual login from new location/device
- Respond to suspected account takeover
- Reset and monitor high-value/privileged accounts

Reports:

- Summaries of identity-related incidents with risk to data and systems
- Patterns of attempted account compromise across the organization

5.4. Data Exfiltration & Insider Threat

Playbooks / Runbooks:

- Investigate large data transfer from unusual host or user
- Triage DLP alerts with business context
- Respond to confirmed insider misuse

Reports:

- Detailed exfil timeline for legal and compliance
- Executive-level impact assessments

5.5. Cloud Security Incidents

Playbooks / Runbooks:

- Respond to public S3 bucket / storage exposure
- Investigate anomalous cloud console logins
- Handle key or token leakage incidents

Reports:

- Cloud-specific incident summaries for cloud governance teams
- Findings that feed back into CSPM and IaC pipelines

For each of these categories, AI can:

- Draft initial **playbook structures** based on your environment and tools
- Map steps to specific products (e.g., your EDR, your email gateway)
- Generate **standard report templates** tailored to each incident type

As you deploy AI across these common patterns, your SOC starts to feel:

- More **consistent** (incidents are handled similarly across shifts and locations)
- More **efficient** (less time spent reinventing the wheel)
- More **auditable** (documentation and reports are aligned and easy to produce)

6. Governance Over AI-Authored Artifacts

With AI generating playbooks, workflows, and reports, you must ask:

"Who owns this content, and how do we trust it?"

Without governance, you risk:

- Outdated or incorrect procedures creeping in
- Inconsistent formats confusing your teams
- AI-introduced errors going unnoticed into external reports

6.1. Content Ownership and Approval

Treat AI-generated artifacts like any other critical documentation:

- Assign **owners** for each playbook (e.g., phishing playbook owner = email security lead).
- Require **approval workflows** for:
    - New playbooks
    - Major revisions
    - External-facing report templates

AI can draft; **owners approve**.

6.2. Versioning and Change History

Maintain clear version control:

- Each playbook has a version number and change log.
- AI-assisted updates are logged:
    - What changed
    - Why it changed (link to incidents, PIRs, or new intel)
    - Who approved it

This helps with:

- Audit and compliance
- Forensics ("Which playbook version was in use when this incident occurred?")
- Rolling back problematic changes if needed

6.3. Validation and Testing

Before turning AI-generated playbooks into live workflows:

- **Tabletop exercises:**
    - Walk teams through simulated incidents using the new playbooks.
- **Sandbox testing:**
    - Test SOAR workflows in non-production environments.
- **Peer review:**
    - Automation, detection engineering, and IR teams review high-impact flows together.

AI can even help design and document these tests:

- "Generate a scenario to test this ransomware playbook, including sample events and expected actions."

6.4. Policy for AI Usage in Documentation

Consider codifying:

- Where AI *may* be used (drafting, summarizing, updating)
- Where AI output *must always* be reviewed and edited
- Where AI may **not** be used (e.g., specific legal or HR-sensitive documents)

This can live in your broader **AI governance** or **SOC policy**:

- "AI may be used to generate draft incident reports, but final text must be reviewed and approved by the incident owner and one additional reviewer."
- "AI-generated changes to playbooks may not be deployed without documented approval."

This clarity reassures:

- Internal stakeholders ("We're not letting a bot run the SOC")
- External stakeholders and regulators ("We have defined controls over AI use").

Key Takeaways from Chapter 7

- **Your SOC's real IP is its know-how.** AI gives you a way to capture tribal knowledge and turn it into standardized playbooks and runbooks that scale.
- **AI is a drafting engine, not the final editor.** Use it to generate first versions of playbooks, workflows, and reports; keep humans firmly in the approval loop.
- **Playbooks and SOAR workflows should evolve.** AI can continuously update them based on recent incidents and lessons learned, making your SOC a learning system.
- **Automated reporting is low-hanging fruit.** With structured incident data, AI can generate multi-audience reports that save hours and improve consistency.
- **Post-incident reviews feed improvement.** AI can help draft PIRs and feed lessons back into controls, models, and playbooks.
- **Governance is non-optional.** Ownership, versioning, testing, and clear policies are essential to keep AI-authored artifacts trustworthy and audit-ready.

In the next chapter, we'll shift from incident handling to **pre-emptive defense**—how AI can help you leverage CTI, deception, and honeypots to move from reactive response to proactive, intelligence-driven security operations.

Chapter 8 – Pre-emptive Security with AI: CTI, Deception & Honeypots

Up to now, we've mostly focused on *reactive* operations:

- An alert fires.
- The SOC triages, investigates, and responds.
- You improve the process and move on.

That's necessary—but not sufficient.

Attackers rarely appear out of nowhere. They probe, experiment, reuse infrastructure, test payloads, and run smaller-scale campaigns before they launch the "big one." If your SOC only reacts once an incident is already inside your environment, you're playing defense on **their** terms.

This chapter is about shifting your SOC toward **pre-emptive security**:

Using AI, CTI, deception, and honeypots to spot threats *earlier*, understand adversaries *better*, and feed those insights back into your detection and response machinery.

We'll cover:

1. From reactive to pre-emptive security – the mindset shift
2. Leveraging AI for external CTI processing and clustering
3. Honeypots and deception: what to collect, how to analyze it
4. Using AI to detect emerging attacker TTP patterns
5. Feeding pre-emptive insights back into detection and response
6. Example: building a continuous threat hunting and deception loop

1. From Reactive to Pre-emptive Security – Mindset Shift

Pre-emptive security isn't a product you buy. It's a way of thinking about your SOC's purpose.

A purely reactive SOC asks:

- "How fast can we respond when something bad happens?"

A pre-emptive SOC also asks:

- "How can we **see it coming**, shape attacker behavior, and reduce risk *before* they hit our core systems?"

1.1. Reactive, Proactive, Pre-emptive – Not the Same Thing

It's useful to distinguish three modes:

1. **Reactive**
    - Responding to alerts and incidents after they're triggered.
    - Focus: minimizing damage and recovery time.
2. **Proactive**
    - Threat hunting on internal data.
    - Testing controls (red teaming, purple teaming).
    - Cleaning up misconfigurations and known weaknesses.
3. **Pre-emptive**
    - Using **external intelligence** (CTI, dark web, OSINT) to understand attacker campaigns early.
    - Using **deception and honeypots** to lure, observe, and study adversaries.
    - Anticipating specific TTPs and preparing controls and detections ahead of time.

Proactive is mostly inward-looking ("What's happening in our environment?").
Pre-emptive adds outward-looking ("What are adversaries preparing and testing *against* us or organizations like us?").

1.2. Why AI Matters Specifically for Pre-emptive Work

Pre-emptive security generates **a different kind of data**:

- Large volumes of unstructured threat intel reports, blog posts, malware analyses
- Noisy, low-signal telemetry from honeypots and decoys
- OSINT from forums, paste sites, and dark web channels
- Repetitive indicators that may or may not matter to *your* environment

AI is particularly strong at:

- Reading, summarizing, and clustering unstructured text (CTI).
- Spotting patterns in noisy telemetry (deception/honeypots).
- Mapping new observations to known TTP frameworks (e.g., ATT&CK-style reasoning).
- Turning weak, early signals into **actionable hypotheses** for the SOC.

Without AI, pre-emptive work is often limited to a few specialists skimming intel feeds and manually reviewing honeypot hits. With AI, you can make it a **systematic, continuous function**.

1.3. Pre-emptive Security as a Feedback Function

Think of pre-emptive security as a **feed-in** function to your SOC:

- It does not replace detection, triage, response, or hunting.
- It feeds them with:
    - New detection ideas
    - Updated prioritization logic
    - Refined playbooks and controls
    - Concrete hypotheses for hunts

If reactive SOC answers "What just happened?",
pre-emptive SOC helps answer "What's likely to happen next if we do nothing?"—and then ensures you don't do nothing.

2. Leveraging AI for External CTI Processing and Clustering

Most organizations subscribe to multiple threat intelligence sources:

- Vendor feeds
- ISAC/industry sharing groups
- Government or regulator advisories
- Blog posts, whitepapers, and research
- Internal intel from MSSP partners or telcos

The problem is rarely "not enough intel." The problem is:

- Too much, in too many formats
- Not tailored to your environment
- Hard to convert from PDFs and blogs into detections and actions

AI—especially LLMs and clustering models—can function as your **CTI processing engine**.

2.1. From PDFs and Feeds to Structured Threat Records

A simple but powerful pattern:

1. Ingest raw CTI artifacts:
    - PDFs, HTML pages, blog text, STIX feeds, emails.
2. Ask AI to extract **structured fields**, for example:
    - Threat actor / campaign name
    - Targeted industries and geographies
    - TTPs (mapped to ATT&CK where possible)
    - Indicators of compromise (IOCs): IPs, domains, hashes, URLs
    - Initial access vectors (phishing, RDP, supply chain, etc.)
    - Tools and malware families used
3. Store these in a structured CTI repository or knowledge graph that your SOC tools can query.

Now, instead of "I read a report about XYZ ransomware," you have:

- A machine-readable representation of XYZ
- Linked to tactics, techniques, and indicators

This structured CTI can then be:

- Matched against your telemetry
- Used to generate detection content
- Mapped to existing or missing playbooks

2.2. Clustering and Prioritizing Relevant Threats

Not all CTI is equally relevant. AI can help answer:

"Which of these threats matter most to *us*?"

AI models can:

- Cluster threats by **target industry and tech stack**
- Highlight threats observed against organizations similar to yours
- Rank CTI items by potential impact, based on:
    - Your geography
    - Your cloud platforms and vendors
    - Your regulatory environment
    - Your existing incident history

For example, AI might tag some CTI content as:

- "Highly relevant – active in your sector and uses your primary cloud provider"
- "Moderately relevant – same region, but mostly targets OT environments you don't have"
- "Low relevance – niche vertical or tech stack you don't use"

This reduces "intel fatigue" and focuses your pre-emptive work where it counts.

2.3. CTI Summaries for Executives and Engineers

Different audiences need different views of the same intel:

- **Executives:**
    - "There is a growing campaign targeting telcos in your region with financially motivated ransomware. They exploit unpatched VPN gateways and weak MFA enforcement. Potential business impact: service disruption and data exposure."
- **Detection engineers:**

- o "New campaign uses TTPs: T1133 (External Remote Services), T1059 (Command and Scripting Interpreter), T1041 (Exfiltration over C2 channel). Key indicators include these IP ranges and beaconing patterns. Existing detection coverage partially overlaps with T1133 but not T1041."

AI can automatically generate:

- One-page summaries for leadership
- Technical extracts for detection and hunting teams
- Annotations that link CTI to existing rules, models, and playbooks

So, CTI stops being "pdfs in a folder" and becomes **living input** to your SOC engineering.

3. Honeypots and Deception: What to Collect, How to Analyze It

CTI tells you what others have seen. Deception and honeypots tell you **what attackers are doing to you** (or your decoy environment) *right now*.

3.1. What Deception & Honeypots Are (and Are Not)

- **Honeypots** are systems or services deployed primarily to be attacked:
    - o Fake web applications
    - o Emulated OT devices
    - o Exposed RDP services
    - o Decoy databases with fake data
- **Deception** extends this idea into production-like environments:
    - o Decoy credentials in your directory or password vault
    - o Fake shares or documents that no legitimate user needs
    - o Breadcrumbs on endpoints pointing to non-existent "backup servers" or "finance shares"

Key points:

- They're designed to look legitimate and attractive to attackers.
- Any interaction with them is either malicious or highly suspicious.
- They produce a **high signal-to-noise ratio** compared to traditional logs.

They are *not*:

- A replacement for core controls
- A silver bullet that catches every attacker
- Something you turn on and forget

They're **sensors and traps**—and AI can help you interpret what they catch.

3.2. What to Collect from Deception Systems

From honeypots and deception assets, you want to capture:

- **Network-level data:**
    - Source IPs, ports, protocols
    - Connection patterns and frequency
    - Geolocation and ASN data
- **Session and payload data:**
    - Commands executed (SSH, RDP, web shells)
    - HTTP requests and parameters
    - Uploaded files and binaries
- **Behavioral traces:**
    - Sequence of actions taken by the attacker
    - Lateral movement attempts from the decoy
    - Attempts to harvest credentials or escalate privileges
- **Timing and campaign context:**
    - When attacks happen (time of day, bursts)
    - Whether multiple honeypots see similar behavior
    - Correlation with external CTI about active campaigns

This data can be sent to:

- Your SIEM/XDR for storage and correlation
- A specialized deception analytics platform
- An AI analytics service for pattern discovery

3.3. AI's Role in Deception Analytics

AI models can help you:

- **Cluster similar attack sessions**
    - Identify recurring toolchains, scripts, and attack flows
    - Distinguish between commodity scanners and targeted activity
- **Extract and label TTPs**
    - Map observed commands and behaviors to known techniques
    - Spot novel variations or combinations
- **Prioritize what to investigate further**
    - Not every honeypot hit is worth a human deep dive
    - AI can highlight sessions that look similar to high-impact campaigns or show unusual sophistication
- **Generate IOC and behavior signatures**
    - From captured payloads and commands
    - Ready to feed into EDR, NDR, or SIEM detections

In short: AI turns deception telemetry into **structured, actionable intelligence** rather than a pile of interesting-but-unused logs.

4. Using AI to Detect Emerging Attacker TTP Patterns

Pre-emptive security isn't just about individual indicators. It's about recognizing **patterns of behavior**—TTPs—that attackers are experimenting with and may soon use more broadly.

4.1. From IOCs to TTPs

Indicators (IPs, hashes, domains) are:

- Short-lived
- Easy for attackers to rotate
- Necessary but shallow

TTPs (tactics, techniques, and procedures) are:

- More stable
- Express "how" an attacker operates, not just "from where"
- More useful for building lasting defenses

AI can help bridge the gap by:

- Observing sequences of actions across CTI, honeypots, and your own incidents
- Mapping them to existing ATT&CK techniques or suggesting new patterns
- Highlighting **emerging combinations** that might not appear in any single report

4.2. Pattern Discovery Across Multiple Data Sources

Imagine your AI system sees:

- A CTI report describing an attack chain against an organization similar to yours
- Honeypot logs showing attackers experimenting with a similar lateral movement pattern
- Internal near-miss incidents where suspicious, but inconclusive, activity matches parts of that pattern

AI can:

1. Cluster these signals together as a **candidate emerging pattern**
2. Describe it in plain language:
   - "Adversaries are testing credential theft via exported browser cookies, followed by cloud console access, then data exfiltration through legitimate storage APIs."
3. Rank its potential relevance to you based on your stack and past incidents.

This is the kind of **attacker R&D** view that humans alone rarely have time to synthesize.

4.3. Early-Warning Use Cases

Concrete examples where AI-driven TTP detection matters:

- **New persistence technique inside your specific EDR or OS ecosystem**
    - AI spots unusual registry changes or scheduled tasks in honeypots and internal logs that match emerging research.
- **Novel abuse of SaaS or collaboration tools**
    - AI clusters patterns where attackers use chat/file-sharing platforms for C2 or exfil.
- **Cloud-native exfiltration tricks**
    - AI sees multiple reports and honeypot traces of attackers abusing cross-account roles or misconfigured storage policies.

In each case, the power is not just "we saw a weird IP once." It's:

- "We're seeing a **pattern** that aligns with emerging research and early campaigns; we should act *before* it hits us at scale."

5. Feeding Pre-emptive Insights Back into Detection and Response

Pre-emptive security only creates value if it **changes how the SOC operates**.

Otherwise, you just have more interesting dashboards.

5.1. Detection Engineering: Turning Intel into Content

For each significant pre-emptive insight, you want to ask:

"What should we detect differently as a result of this?"

AI can help by:

- Generating **draft detection rules** (SIEM, EDR, NDR) based on:
    - Observed behaviors and TTPs
    - CTI descriptions
    - Honeypot payloads
- Suggesting **where to deploy** these detections:
    - Specific log sources
    - Particular segments or asset groups
- Estimating **potential noise levels**:
    - "This detection will likely have high false positives in environment X; consider restricting to admin accounts or critical hosts."

Human detection engineers review and refine these drafts, but AI handles the grunt work of translation from narrative intel to technical content.

5.2. Risk Scoring & Prioritization Adjustments

Pre-emptive insights also inform your **prioritization models**:

- If CTI and honeypots suggest attackers are targeting a particular asset type (e.g., VPN gateways), you can:
    - Increase risk weights for alerts involving those assets
    - Adjust risk models for related identities (VPN admins, network engineers)
- If a new TTP is being widely adopted, you can:
    - Temporarily boost the priority of related detections or anomalies
    - Add explicit checks in triage playbooks ("Is this related to the new XYZ technique?")

AI can generate recommendations, such as:

- "Based on recent CTI and honeypot activity, consider increasing the risk contribution of anomalous logins to cloud consoles from new devices by 20–30% for the next 60 days."

These recommendations go to the SOC engineering team for review and implementation.

5.3. Playbook & Workflow Updates

Pre-emptive insights should also tweak **how you respond** when detection triggers:

- If a new lateral movement technique is trending, your "suspicious login" playbook might add:
    - Extra checks on specific process trees or network connections.
- If a particular malware family uses distinctive file system behavior, your malware response playbook might add:
    - Additional steps to check specific registry keys, scheduled tasks, or cloud API calls.

AI can:

- Compare current playbooks with new intel and suggest inserts or modifications.
- Highlight **gaps** ("Your current playbook for ransomware doesn't address this new data exfiltration technique observed in recent campaigns.").

5.4. Training & Awareness

Finally, pre-emptive intel should influence **people**, not just tools:

- AI can generate:
  - Internal briefings for analysts: "This week's emerging TTPs and what they mean for your investigations."
  - Threat brief summaries for business stakeholders in high-risk units (e.g., finance, engineering).
  - Training scenarios for tabletop exercises and red/purple team engagements.

This ensures that **humans and machines learn together** from pre-emptive signals.

6. Example: Building a Continuous Threat Hunting & Deception Loop

To make this concrete, let's walk through an example of how AI, CTI, deception, and hunting come together in a **continuous loop**.

6.1. Step 1 – Ingest & Analyze External CTI

- New CTI comes in about a campaign targeting your sector, exploiting VPN misconfigurations and weak MFA to gain initial access, followed by lateral movement using legitimate admin tools.
- AI:
  - Extracts TTPs, IOCs, tools, and targeted technologies.
  - Flags the campaign as "highly relevant" based on your tech stack.
  - Generates detection and hunting hypotheses (e.g., "Look for unusual VPN logins followed by remote admin tool usage from new hosts").

6.2. Step 2 – Deploy or Adjust Deception Assets

- You configure or tune honeypots and deception to match this threat:
  - Expose a decoy VPN endpoint (properly isolated) that mimics your real configuration.
  - Plant fake admin credentials or "backup server" references in controlled parts of the environment.
- AI helps by:
  - Suggesting which services and banners should be emulated to look attractive.
  - Generating realistic but fake hostnames, usernames, and file names.

6.3. Step 3 – Observe Attacker Behavior in Deception

- Over the next days/weeks:
  - Honeypots start seeing login attempts and scripted scanning against the decoy VPN.
  - Some sessions manage to get past superficial checks and attempt lateral movement to decoy "internal systems."
- AI:
  - Clusters the sessions by technique, tooling, and behavior.

- Maps them to the CTI campaign, confirming overlap or revealing variations.
- Extracts potential new indicators or subtle behaviors not mentioned in CTI (e.g., specific command sequences, obscure tool flags).

6.4. Step 4 – Hunt Internally Using Deception-Driven Hypotheses

- Based on the combined CTI + deception insight, AI generates a set of targeted hunts:
  - "Find VPN logins from IPs that show similar pre-auth scanning behavior as seen on the honeypot."
  - "Search for internal use of these specific remote admin tools with similar parameters."
  - "Look for unusual access to certain network segments shortly after unusual VPN logins."
- Analysts (with AI assistant help) run these hunts across your real environment.
- They find:
  - Several unsuccessful but suspicious login attempts.
  - No confirmed compromise yet—but the pattern is clearly starting to appear.

6.5. Step 5 – Update Detection, Playbooks, and Controls

From these findings, you:

- **Detection & Controls:**
  - Deploy new or updated detections for the VPN behavior and lateral movement patterns.
  - Harden VPN and MFA policies (e.g., enforce stronger MFA on high-value accounts).
- **Playbooks:**
  - Update "suspicious VPN login" and "privileged access anomalies" playbooks to include checks for newly observed behaviors.
- **Prioritization:**
  - Temporarily raise risk scores for similar VPN anomalies to ensure rapid triage.

AI assists by:

- Drafting detection rules and playbook changes.
- Generating updated risk scoring logic.
- Producing a summary brief for leadership:
  - "We're seeing early reconnaissance from an active campaign. We've hardened controls, deployed new detections, and are actively hunting for related activity."

6.6. Step 6 – Close the Loop with Lessons Learned

After a period of monitoring:

- You review:
    - Which detections triggered
    - Whether any near misses were found
    - How effective the deception assets were at capturing attacker behavior
- AI helps you:
    - Summarize findings into a **pre-emptive PIR** (yes, you can do post-incident style reviews even when no full incident occurred).
    - Suggest sustained changes (e.g., permanent control updates, new baselines for normal VPN behavior).
    - Add this entire pattern to your **internal threat library**, so future similar campaigns are recognized faster.

The result is a **continuous loop**:

1. External CTI informs deception design and hunting.
2. Deception and hunting observations refine detection, controls, and playbooks.
3. The SOC is better prepared when (not if) the campaign or similar ones hit in force.

This is pre-emptive security in practice—not magic, but **disciplined, feedback-driven work**, greatly accelerated and scaled by AI.

Key Takeaways from Chapter 8

- **Pre-emptive security extends your SOC's mission.** It's not only about responding fast, but also about seeing campaigns forming, shaping attacker behavior, and preparing defenses early.
- **AI is critical for CTI at scale.** It turns unstructured reports and feeds into structured, prioritized intelligence tailored to your environment.
- **Deception and honeypots provide high-signal telemetry.** AI can cluster, label, and prioritize attacker activity in decoys to reveal real-world tactics and experiments.
- **TTP patterns matter more than individual indicators.** AI can detect emerging behavior patterns across CTI, deception, and internal logs, giving you an early-warning system.
- **Pre-emptive insights must feed back into the SOC.** Detection content, risk scoring, playbooks, controls, and training should all be updated based on what you learn.
- **The goal is a continuous loop.** CTI → deception → hunting → detection & control updates → lessons learned → back into CTI context. AI makes this loop faster, richer, and more sustainable.

In the next chapter, we'll shift from technology to **people and operating model**—how roles, skills, and team structures need to evolve in an AI-augmented, increasingly autonomous SOC, and what this means for hiring, training, and leadership.

Chapter 9 – People, Skills & Operating Model in an Autonomous SOC

So far, we've spent most of this book on architecture, data, and technology.

But the hard truth is this:

You can build the most advanced AI-augmented SOC in the world, and it will still fail if your **people** and **operating model** stay stuck in the old paradigm.

An autonomous or AI-augmented SOC is not just "the same team, but with more tools." It changes:

- What work looks like day to day
- Which skills are most valuable
- How teams are structured and measured
- How leaders think about capacity, ownership, and success

This chapter is about that shift.

We'll cover:

1. New roles: AI engineer, automation architect, SOC product owner
2. Upskilling existing analysts to work with AI tools
3. Shifting from ticket processors to security "product" teams
4. Designing AI-assisted workflows and RACI models
5. Measuring analyst productivity and satisfaction post-AI adoption
6. Change management: bringing the team along for the journey

Think of this chapter as the "org and people blueprint" that sits alongside your technical reference architecture.

1. New Roles in an AI-Augmented SOC

Traditional SOC org charts are built around tiers:

- Tier 1 (alert triage)
- Tier 2 (investigation and incident handling)
- Tier 3 (threat hunting, IR, content engineering)

As you introduce AI and automation, work shifts:

- Less time on low-level triage
- More time on tuning, engineering, and system design
- New responsibilities around models, workflows, and AI assistant behavior

That creates **new roles** and reshapes old ones.

1.1. AI Engineer / ML Engineer for Security

This role sits at the intersection of data science and security operations.

Key responsibilities:

- Work with SOC leads to identify AI use cases and define requirements
- Design, train, tune, and evaluate models (detection, triage, risk scoring)
- Monitor model performance and drift
- Integrate AI services with existing platforms (SIEM, SOAR, data lake)
- Collaborate with detection engineers and analysts on feedback loops

Skills:

- Strong grounding in ML concepts and tools
- Familiarity with security telemetry and SOC workflows
- Ability to explain model behavior to non-ML stakeholders

In smaller organizations, this might be a shared role (central AI team serving multiple business units). In larger ones, it can be dedicated to the SOC.

1.2. Automation Architect / SOAR Engineer

Automation was already a thing before AI, but its importance escalates dramatically in an autonomous SOC.

Key responsibilities:

- Design and maintain SOAR workflows and playbooks
- Decide what should be automated, semi-automated (with approval), or manual
- Ensure integrations with EDR, firewalls, IAM, ticketing, email, chat, etc.
- Implement AI-generated workflow ideas safely and robustly
- Build monitoring and logging for all automated actions

Skills:

- Deep understanding of SOC processes and tools
- Experience with scripting, APIs, and orchestration platforms
- "Safety-first" mindset around guardrails and rollback mechanisms

This role is critical to ensure that **AI-driven decisions actually lead to reliable, controlled actions**.

1.3. SOC Product Owner

This is a role many SOCs don't formally have—but absolutely should in an AI-augmented world.

Think of the SOC itself as a **product**:

- It has users (internal teams, customers, regulators, business stakeholders).
- It has features (detection coverage, response capabilities, reports, dashboards).
- It has roadmaps, trade-offs, and prioritization decisions.

The SOC Product Owner:

- Owns the **vision and roadmap** for the SOC's capabilities
- Prioritizes investments in detections, automation, AI use cases, and staff training
- Works with stakeholders to understand requirements (compliance, business risk, customer expectations)
- Interfaces with AI engineers, automation architects, and platform teams
- Helps define and track **success metrics** (not just alert counts)

This role transitions your SOC from "service desk that fights fires" into **a strategic security platform**.

1.4. Detection Engineer / Content Engineer (Evolved)

This role already exists in mature SOCs, but it evolves:

- Still responsible for writing and tuning SIEM/EDR/NDR detections
- Now also works closely with AI engineers to:
    - Provide labelled data and ground truth
    - Validate AI-driven detections and risk scoring logic
    - Translate CTI and deception insights into content

They become the **bridge** between:

- Threat intelligence and practical detection
- Human expertise and machine-learned patterns

1.5. Analysts & Hunters (Evolved, Not Removed)

Tier 1/2/3 titles may remain, but the work shifts:

- Less repetitive triage
- More complex investigations, hunts, tuning, and system feedback
- More use of AI assistants, automated enrichment, and AI-generated timelines

Analysts become:

- **Supervisors and editors** of AI output
- **Explorers and hunters**, not just alert processors
- **Sources of feedback** that shape how AI and automation behave over time

We'll talk more about upskilling next.

2. Upskilling Existing Analysts to Work with AI Tools

Bringing in AI is not about discarding your current team.

Your existing analysts:

- Understand your environment and threat landscape
- Know your culture, tools, and "weirdness"
- Are your best source of training data and feedback

You want to **elevate them**, not replace them.

2.1. Core Mindset Shift for Analysts

You want analysts to move from:

"I click through individual alerts and manually gather context"

to:

"I orchestrate and supervise a system that does the basics for me so I can focus on hard problems."

That means:

- Letting go of the idea that "real work" = manual steps
- Embracing AI assistants as **force multipliers** rather than threats
- Becoming comfortable **questioning and correcting AI**

You can encourage this mindset by:

- Explicitly recognizing and rewarding analysts who improve systems (not just close tickets)
- Making it clear that **human judgment is still central**
- Involving analysts early in AI design and evaluation

2.2. Practical Training Themes

You don't need every analyst to become a data scientist. But you do want them to:

1. **Understand AI's role and limitations**
   - What types of tasks AI is good at (classification, summarization, pattern recognition)
   - Where it tends to fail (edge cases, underspecified inputs, hallucinations)
   - How to interpret scores and recommendations
2. **Use AI assistants effectively**
   - How to ask good questions and give clear prompts
   - How to inspect underlying data if they disagree with AI
   - How to flag incorrect or low-quality responses as feedback
3. **Think in systems, not tickets**
   - When they see repeated patterns, they should think:
     - "How do we fix this upstream?"
     - "How do we prevent this kind of noise in the future?"
4. **Contribute to playbooks and workflows**
   - Provide input on which steps can be safely automated
   - Help write and refine playbooks based on experience
   - Validate AI-generated procedures in tabletop and live use

2.3. Training Formats That Work

You don't need a massive training program to start. Focus on:

- **Hands-on labs**
  - Give analysts a sandbox version of the AI assistant and AI triage tools.
  - Let them experiment, break things, and report back.
- **Pairing and shadowing**
  - Have early adopters or more technically inclined analysts mentor others.
- **Micro-training sessions**
  - Short (30–60 minute) sessions on:
    - "How to use the AI assistant for hunting"
    - "How to give useful feedback to AI systems"
- **Retrospectives**
  - After notable incidents, discuss:
    - How did AI help?
    - Where did it fail?
    - What could we improve in training or tools?

Remember: the goal isn't "everyone learns machine learning." The goal is "everyone knows how to **work with AI as a teammate.**"

3. From Ticket Processors to Security "Product" Teams

Many SOCs are structured like service desks:

- Work is measured in tickets closed
- Teams are grouped by shift and tier
- Priorities are driven by volume and severity

That model is not well-suited to building and evolving an AI-augmented, increasingly autonomous SOC.

You need teams that behave more like **product teams**:

- Owning specific capabilities or domains
- Continuously improving them
- Taking end-to-end responsibility for outcomes

3.1. Capability-Aligned Teams

One way to structure is around **capabilities**, for example:

- **Identity & Access Security Team**
    - Focus: identity detections, MFA risk, account compromise, privilege misuse
    - Owns: related rules, models, playbooks, and metrics
- **Endpoint & Malware Defense Team**
    - Focus: EDR, ransomware, commodity malware, lateral movement on endpoints
- **Cloud & SaaS Security Team**
    - Focus: cloud misconfigurations, control plane abuse, SaaS misuse
- **Threat Hunting & Deception Team**
    - Focus: hunts, honeypots, TTP discovery, pre-emptive defense

Each team includes:

- Analysts / hunters
- A detection/content engineer
- Some automation expertise (shared or dedicated)
- Access to AI engineering support

They own improvements within their domain: not just handling tickets but **reducing risk and toil over time**.

3.2. Outcomes vs. Activity Metrics

Product-like teams should be measured on **outcomes**, not just activity.

Examples:

- Reduction in mean time to detect/contain for identity-related incidents
- Reduction in false positive rate for EDR alerts
- Increase in coverage for critical TTPs in their domain
- Number of useful hunts or pre-emptive detections per quarter

This is a shift from:

- "How many tickets did you close?"

to:

- "How much did you reduce risk and improve the system?"

AI and automation help teams hit these goals; the teams, in turn, help shape the AI and automation.

3.3. Cross-Functional Collaboration

In a product model, you expect more collaboration across disciplines:

- SOC product owner works with capability leads to set priorities.
- AI engineers build or tune models based on detection/hunter input.
- Automation architects implement team-specific workflows.
- CTI analysts feed insights into each capability team.

This is more **horizontal** than the classic Tier 1 → Tier 2 → Tier 3 funnel, but it aligns better with an autonomous SOC that is **always evolving**.

4. Designing AI-Assisted Workflows & RACI Models

As AI and automation take on more work, you must be explicit about:

- Who does what
- Who approves what
- Who is accountable for outcomes

A fuzzy "the AI will handle it" mentality is dangerous.

4.1. RACI in an AI-Driven Context

RACI stands for:

- **R**esponsible – who executes the work

- **A**ccountable – who owns the outcome
- **C**onsulted – who provides input
- **I**nformed – who needs to know

In AI-assisted workflows, you might see patterns like:

Example: Auto-containment of suspect endpoints

- **Responsible:**
    - SOAR + AI risk engine (they execute the quarantine action)
- **Accountable:**
    - Endpoint & Malware Defense Team lead
- **Consulted:**
    - Platform/infra team (for impact assessment)
    - Business owner for critical hosts (during design phase)
- **Informed:**
    - On-call incident commander
    - Affected application owners (via notifications)

Document this clearly so that:

- When something goes wrong, you know who owns remediation and improvement.
- When designing new automations, you know which teams must sign off.

4.2. Levels of AI Involvement

For each workflow or playbook, define **how involved** AI is:

- **Level 0 – Suggest Only**
    - AI provides recommendations and summaries.
    - Humans decide and act.
- **Level 1 – Semi-Automated**
    - AI triggers actions that **always require human approval**.
    - E.g., "AI assistant suggests isolating host X; analyst clicks 'Approve'."
- **Level 2 – Conditional Autonomy**
    - AI can execute actions automatically, under defined conditions.
    - E.g., "Auto-quarantine non-critical endpoints when risk > 90 and no conflicting signals."
- **Level 3 – High Autonomy (Rare, Highly Governed)**
    - AI can handle full incident lifecycles in specific, low-risk domains.
    - Humans review periodically and step in for exceptions.

Your RACI and policies should specify **which level applies where**.

4.3. Workflow Design Principles

When designing AI-assisted workflows:

- **Start with clear use cases and guardrails.**
- **Log everything.**
  - Inputs, decisions, actions, and outcomes—so you can audit and adjust.
- **Keep humans in the loop for impactful decisions.**
- **Make it easy to override AI.**
  - A one-click "stop this automation" or "revert this action" is invaluable.
- **Involve the people who will live with it.**
  - Analysts and engineers should help design and test workflows, not just receive them from on high.

This is not just a technical exercise; it's an organizational contract about **how much autonomy you are comfortable with** in each area.

5. Measuring Analyst Productivity & Satisfaction Post-AI

If AI is working, analysts should feel:

- Less overwhelmed
- More valued
- More engaged in complex, meaningful work

If they don't, something's off.

5.1. Productivity Metrics That Actually Matter

Avoid vanity metrics like "# of AI-assisted responses."

Focus on:

- **Alert handling metrics**
  - Reduction in alerts per analyst per shift
  - Proportion of time spent on **true positives vs. false positives**
- **Investigation efficiency**
  - Average time to gather context per incident (should drop)
  - Average time from incident creation to first meaningful containment action
- **Quality improvements**
  - Reduction in repeated "noise incidents" after AI tuning
  - Increase in documented root-cause analyses
- **System-level improvements**
  - Number of playbooks updated or created per quarter
  - Reduction in manual steps in key workflows

These numbers show whether AI and automation are **actually helping** or just adding overhead.

5.2. Measuring Analyst Experience and Satisfaction

Qualitative measures are just as important:

- **Regular surveys:**
    - "Has the AI assistant made your work easier or harder?"
    - "Do you trust AI-generated recommendations?"
    - "Where does AI get in the way?"
- **Focus groups and feedback sessions:**
    - Ask analysts to share specific examples where AI helped or hindered.
    - Use these stories to guide tuning and training.
- **Retention and recruitment:**
    - Are analysts more likely to stay because they're doing higher-value work?
    - Is your SOC seen as a modern, innovative place to work?

5.3. Avoiding Metric Misuse

Be careful not to:

- Use metrics to **pressure** analysts into trusting AI blindly ("We need to increase the % of incidents fully handled by automation").
- Over-optimize for throughput at the expense of quality and learning.
- Turn metrics into weapons in performance reviews without context.

Instead, treat metrics as:

- **Instruments for navigation**, not scorecards for punishment.
- Signals of where systems need improvement, not where people need blame.

6. Change Management: Bringing the Team Along

Introducing AI and autonomy is a **change management project**, not just a technology project.

If you don't handle the human side well, you'll see:

- Resistance ("The AI is going to replace us" or "This is just management's toy")
- Workarounds ("I'll just ignore the AI assistant and do it my way")
- Misuse ("Cool, the AI said it's fine, ship it")

You need a deliberate path.

6.1. Clear Narrative and Intent

People need to know **why** you're doing this.

Your narrative might sound like:

- "We are using AI to get rid of repetitive toil, improve our visibility, and give you more time for meaningful work."
- "Human expertise is still the core of our SOC. AI is here to amplify it, not replace it."
- "We will not use AI to unilaterally cut headcount; we will use it to increase our impact and build a stronger, more resilient operation."

You don't have to promise zero change—but be honest and explicit about your goals.

6.2. Involving Practitioners Early

Don't design everything in a small leadership bubble and then "roll it out."

Instead:

- Involve analysts, hunters, and engineers in:
    - Defining use cases
    - Testing early prototypes
    - Providing structured feedback
- Identify and empower **AI champions** within the team:
    - People who are excited, curious, and willing to experiment
    - Give them visibility and support

When people feel they **helped build the system**, they are more likely to trust it.

6.3. Phased Rollout

Avoid a big-bang "new SOC overnight" approach.

Phased rollout ideas:

- **Phase 1:**
    - AI assistant for enrichment and summarization only (no actions).
- **Phase 2:**
    - AI-assisted triage and prioritization, with human control.
- **Phase 3:**
    - Limited, tightly governed auto-actions in low-risk domains.
- **Phase 4:**
    - Expansion of autonomy where it has proven reliable and valuable.

At each phase:

- Communicate what's changing and why
- Show metrics and stories of impact
- Collect feedback and adjust

6.4. Addressing Fears & Misconceptions

Common fears:

- "AI will take my job."
- "If the AI makes a mistake, I'll be blamed."
- "I don't understand how it works, so I can't trust it."

Address them directly:

- Be transparent about **job impact** and future skill needs.
- Clarify that **blame lies with system design and leadership**, not individuals, when AI workflows misbehave.
- Provide enough **explainability and training** so that people feel they can reason about AI decisions.

A good test:
If an analyst feels comfortable saying, "The AI is wrong here, and here's why," you're on the right track.

6.5. Leadership Behaviors That Matter

Leaders set the tone. In an AI-augmented SOC, strong leaders:

- **Model curiosity, not fear**
    - They use the AI assistant themselves.
    - They ask questions about how AI reached a conclusion.
- **Reward system improvements**
    - Celebrate when someone automates away a painful manual step.
    - Recognize people who provide high-quality feedback that improves models.
- **Protect time for learning**
    - Don't run the team so hot that no one has capacity to experiment and improve workflows.
- **Own the risk of change**
    - Don't push all responsibility for AI outcomes onto frontline staff.
    - Make it clear that autonomy levels and guardrails are leadership decisions.

In other words: you're not just implementing new tooling; you're **leading your team through a new way of working**.

Key Takeaways from Chapter 9

- **Technology is only half the story.** An AI-augmented SOC demands new roles, skills, and operating models.

- **New roles emerge around AI and automation.** AI engineers, automation architects, and SOC product owners become critical alongside evolved detection engineers and analysts.
- **Analysts should be elevated, not sidelined.** Upskill them to supervise AI, design better systems, and focus on complex investigations and hunts.
- **Move from ticket queues to product thinking.** Structure teams around capabilities and outcomes, not just tiers and shifts.
- **Make roles and responsibilities explicit.** Use RACI and autonomy levels to clearly define who owns which decisions in AI-assisted workflows.
- **Measure what matters: outcomes and experience.** Track MTTA/MTTD, false positives, and system improvements, but also analyst trust and satisfaction.
- **Treat AI adoption as a change-management initiative.** Clear intent, phased rollout, involvement of practitioners, and strong leadership behavior are key.

In the next chapter, we'll turn to **risk, governance, and compliance** for AI in security operations—how to ensure that your AI-augmented, increasingly autonomous SOC remains aligned with regulatory expectations, ethical standards, and your organization's risk appetite.

Chapter 10 – Risk, Governance & Compliance for AI in the SOC

By now, we've talked a lot about what AI *can* do in the SOC.

In this chapter, we deal with what it **might do wrong**—and how you stay in control.

An AI-augmented SOC introduces new kinds of risk:

- Models that drift and quietly become less accurate
- LLMs that hallucinate plausible but wrong details
- Automations that act on bad signals
- Vendors that train on data you didn't mean to share
- Regulators asking, "Explain to me how this AI made that decision."

If you don't address these explicitly, you'll end up with:

- Impressive demos
- Nervous executives
- Suspicious auditors
- And a very real risk of mistakes with operational, legal, or reputational impact

This chapter is about building a **governance framework** around AI in the SOC so that:

- You can **move fast** where automation adds real value
- You can **prove control** when questioned
- You never lose sight of who is accountable

We'll cover:

1. The risk landscape of AI in security operations
2. Defining an AI governance model for the SOC
3. Data protection, privacy, and jurisdiction issues
4. Controls: testing, validation, and ongoing monitoring of AI
5. Third-party / vendor AI risk management
6. Handling AI-related failures and incidents
7. Documentation, evidence, and audit readiness

Think of this chapter as your "safety harness" for the rest of the book.

1. The Risk Landscape of AI in Security Operations

Before you can govern AI, you need a shared language for the *kinds* of risk it introduces.

1.1. Technical Risks

These are about **how AI systems behave**:

- **False negatives & false positives**
    - Missed attacks because models under-prioritize or suppress alerts
    - Floods of noise because AI models over-trigger
- **Model drift**
    - Detection performance degrades as your environment or adversaries change
    - Behaviors that were rare become common, and vice versa
- **Hallucinations** (LLMs)
    - Invented logs or events in summaries
    - Incorrect technical explanations stated with high confidence
- **Fragility**
    - Models behaving unpredictably given unusual or adversarial inputs

1.2. Operational Risks

These are about **running the SOC**:

- **Over-automation**
    - Automated containment that disrupts critical systems
    - Chain reactions where one bad decision triggers many actions
- **Skill atrophy**
    - Analysts losing core investigation skills as they rely too heavily on AI assistants
- **Process misalignment**
    - AI workflows that bypass established approvals or communication paths
- **Dependency on vendors**
    - Losing critical capabilities if a vendor changes, degrades, or removes AI features

1.3. Legal, Regulatory & Ethical Risks

These are about **external expectations**:

- **Privacy & data protection**
    - Sending PII, customer data, or regulated logs to external AI services without proper controls
- **Explainability & accountability**
    - Not being able to explain why a system acted (or failed to act) a certain way
    - Lack of clear accountability when AI contributes to an incident
- **Bias and fairness**
    - Models systematically treating certain users, regions, or business units as "higher risk" due to skewed training data
- **Contractual and sector-specific obligations**

o MSSP clients, regulators, or auditors expecting explicit documentation of how AI is used

You don't need a separate risk framework for every AI feature. But you *do* need to acknowledge that AI adds new failure modes beyond "the rule didn't fire."

2. Defining an AI Governance Model for the SOC

Governance is simply:

"Who is allowed to do what, under which rules, with which oversight, and who is accountable if it breaks?"

For AI in the SOC, this means:

- Clear roles and responsibilities
- Clear policies and guardrails
- Clear processes for design, approval, change, and retirement

2.1. Ownership: Who Owns AI in the SOC?

You don't want AI to live in a vacuum.

Practical ownership structure:

- **CISO / Head of Security Operations**
    o Ultimately accountable for AI use in security operations
    o Approves risk appetite and autonomy levels
- **SOC Product Owner**
    o Owns the roadmap of AI capabilities in the SOC
    o Prioritizes which AI use cases to develop and maintain
- **AI / ML Engineer(s)**
    o Own model design, performance monitoring, and technical behavior
- **Automation Architect / SOAR Engineer**
    o Own how AI decisions translate into actions and playbooks
- **Data Protection / Privacy Officer**
    o Reviews how data flows into and out of AI components
    o Ensures alignment with privacy and regulatory requirements

Each significant AI capability (e.g., triage engine, AI assistant, auto-containment) should have:

- A **named owner** (human)
- A **clear description** of what it does
- A **contact** for questions, issues, or changes

2.2. Policy: What Is AI Allowed (and Not Allowed) to Do?

Create explicit SOC-level AI usage policies that answer:

- For which use cases may AI be used?
    - E.g., triage, summarization, risk scoring, workflow suggestions, *not* final legal communications
- What kinds of actions can AI trigger autonomously?
    - E.g., auto-enrich, auto-open tickets, auto-quarantine *non-critical* endpoints, but **never** modify production network configs without approval
- What data types may be sent to external AI services?
    - E.g., logs with pseudonymized user identifiers allowed
    - Raw full-content payloads only allowed to on-prem/private AI
- When is **human review mandatory**?
    - E.g., regulatory notifications, customer breach letters, high-impact playbook changes

These policies should be practical, not vague statements like "use AI responsibly." Analysts and engineers should be able to look at them and answer:

"Am I allowed to do this with AI or not?"

2.3. AI Use Case Lifecycle

Treat each AI use case as an asset with a lifecycle:

1. **Proposal**
    - Define goal, scope, risks, and expected benefits
    - Identify data inputs and outputs
2. **Design & Approval**
    - Data protection and legal review if needed
    - Security and automation design review
    - Clear definition of autonomy level (suggest-only, semi-auto, conditional auto)
3. **Pilot / Shadow Mode**
    - AI runs in recommendation-only or parallel mode
    - Compare AI results to current process
4. **Production Rollout**
    - Enable AI capability in controlled scope (e.g., certain incident types, shifts, or tenants)
5. **Monitoring & Review**
    - Track performance, errors, overrides, and incidents
    - Periodic governance review (e.g., quarterly)
6. **Change / Sunset**
    - Adapt to new threats, tools, or regulations
    - Decommission if replaced or no longer needed

This keeps you away from "we installed this AI thing 18 months ago and we're not quite sure what it's doing now."

3. Data Protection, Privacy & Jurisdiction

AI in the SOC thrives on data. Regulators and customers are increasingly strict about **how** that data is used.

You must explicitly manage:

- What data AI sees
- Where it is processed
- How long it's kept
- How it's protected and anonymized

3.1. Data Classification and AI

Start with your **data classification scheme**:

- Public
- Internal
- Confidential
- Highly confidential / regulated (e.g., PCI, PHI, PII, customer contractual data)

Then map:

- Which classes can be used by which AI systems
- Which must be masked, tokenized, or excluded

For example:

- **LLM-based AI assistant** (possibly external / cloud-based):
    - Allowed: log metadata, anonymized user IDs, non-sensitive alerts
    - Not allowed: raw packet captures, full email content, documents with sensitive data
- **On-prem ML detection models** (inside your secure environment):
    - Allowed: rich telemetry including PII, as long as retention and access are controlled

The principle: **least privilege** for AI, just like for any other system.

3.2. Jurisdiction & Data Residency

If you operate in multiple regions or regulated sectors, you may need to ensure:

- Certain logs never leave a country or region
- Certain AI models run only in specific jurisdictions
- Cross-border transfers comply with law and contracts

Common patterns:

- Use **regional AI deployments** for sensitive environments
- Route data from specific tenants or regions to **local AI clusters**
- For global AI capabilities, feed only **aggregated or pseudonymized data**

Document:

- Where each AI system is hosted
- Which data flows where
- How residency requirements are enforced

3.3. Privacy by Design in SOC AI

To align with privacy principles:

- **Minimize data**
    - Only send fields needed for the AI task
    - Avoid full payloads if metadata suffices
- **Pseudonymize where possible**
    - Replace usernames/emails with tokens when using external AI
    - Have a secure internal mapping if you need to "de-tokenize" in analysis
- **Access control & logging**
    - AI systems should respect the same RBAC as your SOC tools
    - All AI queries and responses involving personal or sensitive data should be logged for audit

Involve your privacy office early, not when a regulator knocks.

4. Controls: Testing, Validation & Monitoring of AI

AI in the SOC is **part of your control environment**. That means:

- You don't just "trust the model"
- You treat it like any other control: design, test, monitor, improve

4.1. Pre-Deployment Testing

Before enabling an AI capability in production, you should:

- Test on **historical data**

- Compare AI decisions to past incidents and outcomes
- Measure false positives/false negatives vs. your current baseline
- Run in **shadow mode**
  - Let AI make recommendations while humans still follow the old process
  - Measure alignment and differences
- Conduct **adversarial tests**
  - Simulate attacks or misconfigurations
  - See how AI behaves with incomplete, noisy, or manipulated data

Define **acceptance criteria** ahead of time:

- "We will consider AI triage ready if it correctly prioritizes 90% of known critical incidents in test data and does not suppress any incident that led to confirmed breach in the last 12 months."

4.2. Performance Monitoring & Model Drift

Once in production, monitor:

- Detection performance
  - Are critical incidents being flagged and escalated as expected?
- False positive/negative trends
  - Is the noise going up or down?
  - Are we missing things we previously caught?
- Analyst overrides
  - How often do humans disagree with AI decisions?
  - In which direction (AI too aggressive vs. too conservative)?
- Data changes
  - Are new systems, log sources, or behaviors being introduced that the model wasn't trained on?

Use these to:

- Trigger **retraining or recalibration**
- Adjust thresholds and policies
- Decide whether autonomy level is appropriate

4.3. LLM-Specific Controls

For AI assistants and other LLM-based components:

- **Grounding and retrieval**
  - Ensure responses are based on your actual data (via retrieval-augmented generation)
  - Limit free-form "imagination" as much as possible
- **Reference linking**
  - Encourage LLMs to cite which logs/cases/rules they refer to

- o   Allow analysts to click through and verify
- **Guardrails**
    - o   Block categories of responses (e.g., never fabricate logs, never claim an incident is "fully resolved" without referencing evidence)
- **Prompt & output logging**
    - o   Keep logs of what was asked and how the model responded—this is critical for reviews and audits

The goal: LLMs should behave like **helpful summarizers and translators**, not storytellers.

5. Third-Party / Vendor AI Risk Management

You will almost certainly rely on vendors for AI capabilities:

- SIEM/XDR built-in analytics
- EDR behavioral models
- Cloud-based LLM AI assistants
- Managed detection and response (MDR) services with AI under the hood

You still own the risk.

5.1. Due Diligence Questions to Ask Vendors

For each vendor AI feature, ask:

- **Functionality**
    - o   What exactly does this AI component do (triage, detection, summarization, etc.)?
    - o   Is it suggest-only or can it trigger actions?
- **Data usage**
    - o   What data do you send to their AI?
    - o   Is it used only for your service, or also to train global models?
    - o   Can you opt out of data sharing for training?
- **Location & security**
    - o   Where is the data processed and stored?
    - o   How is it encrypted in transit and at rest?
    - o   How is access to AI infrastructure controlled and logged?
- **Explainability & visibility**
    - o   Can you see why a model produced a given alert, score, or recommendation?
    - o   Are thresholds, weights, or feature importance exposed in any way?
- **Governance & compliance**
    - o   How do they handle model updates and testing?
    - o   Can they provide documentation for auditors and regulators?

You don't need perfect transparency into their models, but you do need enough information to:

- Assess whether their controls meet your standards
- Explain, at a high level, how decisions are made

5.2. Contracts and SLAs

Update contracts and SLAs to cover AI-specific aspects:

- **Data processing terms**
    - Explicitly cover how data is used for AI, training, and retention
    - Data residency commitments if needed
- **Service commitments**
    - Impact of AI performance degradation on SLAs
    - Notice requirements for significant AI changes or model updates
- **Audit and assessment rights**
    - Ability to get documentation, attend briefings, or perform independent assessments
- **Incident obligations**
    - Requirements for notifying you about AI-related incidents (e.g., model errors leading to missed alerts or wrong actions)

Treat AI capabilities as **core parts of the service**, not just cosmetic add-ons.

5.3. Vendor Lock-In & Portability

Be aware of:

- The degree to which your SOC logic, detections, and workflows depend on proprietary AI features
- How easily you could migrate if needed

Mitigations:

- Keep as much detection logic and risk policy as possible in **portable formats** (rules, queries, playbooks you can export).
- Where you build your own AI sidecars, design them to consume **generic telemetry** rather than vendor-specific formats.
- Document the logic and reasoning that underpin your SOC—even if some of it is implemented via vendor AI.

6. Handling AI-Related Failures and Incidents

AI will make mistakes. Governance is not about preventing all mistakes; it's about **detecting, containing, and learning from them**.

6.1. Defining "AI Incidents"

You should treat certain AI failures as incidents in their own right, for example:

- AI suppression or mis-prioritization that contributes to a **missed or delayed detection** of a real attack
- AI-driven automation that causes or materially worsens an outage or security event
- LLM hallucinations that lead to incorrect containment actions or miscommunication to customers/regulators
- Unauthorized or unintended use of data by AI components (e.g., misconfigured data feeds to external models)

Define criteria for when an AI issue becomes:

- A **ticket** for tuning
- An **internal incident** for deeper analysis
- A **reportable event** to customers or regulators (if it materially impacted security)

6.2. Investigation & Root Cause for AI Issues

When something goes wrong:

1. **Contain**
    - Disable or reduce autonomy of the relevant AI capability
    - Revert or mitigate harmful automated actions
2. **Investigate**
    - What was the AI output?
    - What inputs did it see?
    - Which models, rules, or workflows were involved?
    - What human decisions were made based on its output?
3. **Classify root causes**
    - Data issue (bad or missing data, poor labels)
    - Model issue (drift, misconfiguration, bad thresholds)
    - Workflow issue (unsafe automation design)
    - Human/organizational issue (misuse, lack of training, ignored warnings)
4. **Decide remediation**
    - Model retraining or recalibration
    - Changes to automation guardrails
    - Process or training updates
    - Additional logging or monitoring

AI incidents should be part of your **standard incident management process**, not a separate, opaque track.

6.3. Learning and Transparency

Decide how much transparency you'll provide to:

- Internal stakeholders
- Customers (if you're an MSSP or provide SOC services)
- Regulators (where obligations exist)

A mature posture sounds like:

"We used an AI-based triage engine that underprioritized a class of alerts. This contributed to a delayed response to incident X. We have since updated the model, tightened thresholds, and added a human review layer for similar alerts. Here is how we will prevent recurrence."

That level of candor, backed by **documented improvements**, builds credibility.

7. Documentation, Evidence & Audit Readiness

At some point, someone will ask:

- "Show me how you use AI in your SOC."
- "Prove to me this is under control."

If you've followed the principles in this chapter, you'll be ready.

7.1. What to Document

At minimum, keep:

- **AI use case catalog**
    - Description, owner, scope, autonomy level for each capability
    - Data inputs and outputs
- **Policies & standards**
    - AI usage policy (what's allowed / not)
    - Data handling rules for AI
    - Testing, deployment, and monitoring standards
- **Design docs**
    - High-level architecture showing where AI sits in the SOC
    - RACI for key AI-assisted workflows
- **Change records**
    - Model updates (what changed, when, why, who approved)

- Workflow changes involving AI decisions or actions
- **Performance reports**
  - Metrics on false positives/negatives, alert triage improvements, model drift management
- **Incident reports**
  - Any AI-related incidents and what you did about them

You don't need hundreds of pages, but you do need **organized, accessible evidence**.

7.2. Audit-Friendly AI

When designing AI components, think: "If an auditor asked, could we show them...?"

- **Decision logs**
  - Why was this alert scored 95 and auto-contained?
  - Which factors contributed (asset criticality, anomalous behavior, CTI match)?
- **Traceable workflows**
  - For any incident, can you reconstruct:
    - Which AI suggestions were made
    - Which actions were auto vs. human-approved
    - How human decisions diverged from AI recommendations
- **Model lifecycle**
  - Are there records of training data sources (at a high level), testing, and approval?
  - Do you track when models are retrained or replaced?

If auditors or regulators see that you have:

- A clear understanding of your AI
- A controlled process for introducing and changing it
- Evidence that you monitor and improve it

…they are far more likely to view AI not as an uncontrolled risk, but as part of a **mature control environment**.

Key Takeaways from Chapter 10

- **AI adds new risk and complexity—but it's manageable with deliberate governance.** Treat AI as part of your control environment, not magic.
- **Ownership and policy are foundational.** Every AI capability should have a named owner, defined scope, autonomy level, and explicit guardrails.
- **Data protection and privacy cannot be an afterthought.** Classify data, limit what AI sees, respect jurisdiction and residency, and involve privacy teams early.

- **Test, monitor, and tune AI like any critical control.** Use shadow mode, performance metrics, and analyst overrides to keep models honest and up to date.
- **Vendors don't absolve you of responsibility.** Ask hard questions, set contractual expectations, and document how third-party AI fits into your risk posture.
- **AI-related failures are incidents, too.** Detect them, investigate root cause, remediate, and be transparent where it matters.
- **Documentation is your ally.** A simple but structured record of AI use cases, policies, and changes will make audits, regulatory reviews, and board conversations far smoother.

In the next chapter, we'll pull everything together into **a practical roadmap and maturity model**—how to move from today's classical SOC to an AI-augmented, increasingly autonomous SOC in sensible, governed steps, without betting the farm or losing control.

Chapter 11 – AI Guardrails & Safe Autonomy in the SOC

In earlier chapters, we talked about AI in the SOC in terms of **capabilities**:

- Triage and risk scoring
- AI assistants for analysts
- Automated workflows and playbooks
- Pre-emptive hunting, CTI, and deception

We also looked at **governance, risk, and compliance**—the high-level policies and responsibilities around AI.

This chapter zooms in on something more concrete:

How do we put *practical guardrails* around AI so it can act quickly without putting the SOC or the business at risk?

Guardrails are the difference between:

- A SOC that uses AI to dig out of alert overload safely, and
- A SOC that wakes up one morning and realizes an AI-driven workflow just quarantined 300 critical servers.

We'll cover:

1. What "AI guardrails" really mean in a SOC context
2. Design principles for safe autonomy
3. Guardrails across the four layers: data, model, workflow, enforcement
4. Guardrails for LLM-based AI assistants
5. Guardrails for automation and Level 2 autonomy
6. Testing and validating guardrails (before they hurt you)
7. How to know when guardrails are too tight—or too loose

Use this chapter as the "engineer's blueprint" for turning your AI policy into concrete, enforceable controls.

1. What AI Guardrails Really Are

"Guardrails" is a popular word, but in the SOC it needs a specific meaning.

AI guardrails are the technical and procedural constraints that limit what AI can see, decide, and do—so that failures are contained and recoverable.

They are not just "we have a policy." They are implemented as:

- **Data constraints** – what data AI can access, in what form
- **Decision constraints** – which decisions AI is allowed to influence or make
- **Action constraints** – what AI-driven automation can actually do, and where
- **Context constraints** – which environments, tenants, or assets are in scope

Good guardrails do three things:

1. **Limit blast radius** – if AI is wrong, the damage is small and containable.
2. **Preserve human control** – humans can see, override, and shut things down.
3. **Stay transparent** – you can explain what the guardrails are and how they work.

We'll build those guardrails layer by layer.

2. Design Principles for Safe Autonomy

Before we talk mechanics, it's useful to anchor on a few key principles.

2.1. Least Autonomy Principle

Grant AI the minimum autonomy necessary to deliver real value.

Just as we apply least privilege to users and service accounts, we should apply **least autonomy** to AI:

- Start with **Level 0** (suggest-only) and **Level 1** (human-in-the-loop).
- Move to **Level 2** (conditional autonomy) only for:
    - Well-understood patterns
    - Low-impact actions
    - Guardrails that you've tested and monitored

2.2. Defense in Depth

Guardrails work best in **layers**:

- Data layer (what's visible)
- Model layer (how decisions are made)
- Workflow layer (how decisions become actions)
- Enforcement layer (what actually changes in the environment)

A mistake at one layer shouldn't instantly become an outage—other layers should catch or limit it.

2.3. Reversibility

Anything AI can do, you should be able to **undo** (or at least mitigate quickly).

Examples:

- Isolation that can be reversed
- Policy changes that can be rolled back
- Tickets or notifications that can be corrected

Irreversible actions (deleting backups, wiping disks, dropping user accounts, altering core network topology) should **never** be fully autonomous.

2.4. Observability & Explainability

Guardrails are useless if you can't see what AI is doing.

- Log what decisions were made, on what inputs, and why (where possible).
- Make it easy for analysts to see **which actions were AI/automation-driven vs manual**.
- Favor models and rules where you can at least explain "what factors matter."

2.5. Simplicity Over Cleverness

Guardrails that are too complex are:

- Harder to implement correctly
- Harder to test
- Harder to explain to auditors and leadership

Aim for **simple rules with clear boundaries**:

- "Only isolate endpoints in this asset group."
- "Never modify firewall rules in these zones automatically."
- "Never send emails directly to customers without a human review."

3. Guardrails Across the Four Layers

Think of your AI-enabled SOC as four stacked layers:

1. **Data layer** – what the AI sees
2. **Model layer** – how it makes sense of the data
3. **Workflow layer** – how decisions move through playbooks
4. **Enforcement layer** – where real-world changes happen

Each layer needs its own set of guardrails.

3.1. Data Layer Guardrails

Data guardrails answer:

"What can the AI **see**, and in what form?"

Key controls:

1. **Scope of data sources**
   - Limit AI to **relevant telemetry** for the use case:
     - For login anomaly detection: identity + VPN + device context
     - For endpoint malware triage: EDR + asset inventory
   - Don't blindly ingest *everything* including highly sensitive data that isn't necessary.
2. **Data minimization & masking**
   - Replace personal identifiers (usernames, emails) with **tokens** where possible—especially for external AI services.
   - Strip or mask payloads (email body, file contents) unless truly required.
   - Store mappings internally, not in the AI system.
3. **Tenant and environment isolation (MSSP / multi-env)**
   - Per-tenant data separation: AI cannot mix telemetry or context between clients.
   - Environment tags: PROD vs DEV vs OT; AI may be allowed more freedom in **DEV** and **lab** than in PROD.
4. **Log integrity & validation**
   - Sanity check inputs before they feed models:
     - Timestamps not in the far future/past
     - IPs and hostnames in expected ranges
     - Event volumes within reasonable thresholds
   - If a data source starts behaving strangely (e.g., duplication or corruption), **downgrade** the AI's trust in that source—or temporarily exclude it.

Data guardrail rule of thumb:

If the AI doesn't strictly need the data to do its job, don't feed it.

3.2. Model Layer Guardrails

Model guardrails answer:

"What **decisions** is the AI allowed to make, and how confident must it be?"

Key controls:

1. **Decision scope**

- Define what the model outputs:
    - Risk scores (0–100)
    - Classifications (benign / suspicious / malicious)
    - Clusters or episodes (which alerts likely belong together)
- Explicitly **forbid** other behaviors:
    - "Never directly instruct an enforcement system."
    - "Never claim certainty where none exists—always express uncertainty as a score or range."
2. **Confidence thresholds and bands**
    - Use **bands**, not a single magic number:
        - 0–39: Mostly benign → candidate for auto-closure (with guardrails)
        - 40–69: Needs human review → Level 0/1 only
        - 70–89: High suspicion → prioritize for human investigation
        - 90–100: Very high suspicion → eligible for conditional auto-actions on low-criticality assets
    - Guardrail: **never** use model outputs in the "gray band" for autonomous actions.
3. **Model explainability hooks**
    - Where possible, models should expose:
        - Top features contributing to a score
        - Simple "because" statements ("High risk due to admin account, new country, and CTI match.")
    - Even if it's not deep math, this helps analysts **challenge AI** intelligently.
4. **Human override as a first-class signal**
    - When analysts:
        - Downgrade a "high risk" alert
        - Upgrade a "low risk" alert
    - Capture the override **and the reason**.
    - Use these overrides as training or tuning signals in future iterations.

Model guardrail rule of thumb:

Treat AI decisions as strong hints, not absolute truth—especially in the middle confidence bands.

3.3. Workflow Layer Guardrails

Workflow guardrails answer:

"How do AI decisions flow through playbooks—and where do humans stay in the loop?"

This is where the **Level 0 / 1 / 2** autonomy model becomes concrete.

1. **Explicit autonomy per playbook step**
   For each step in a playbook, decide and document:

- **Manual only** – human must decide and act
- **AI-suggested** – AI drafts or suggests; human approves
- **Auto-if-safe** – automation can run based on AI, but only under defined constraints

Example for an endpoint malware playbook:

- Parse alert → AI can assist (Level 0)
- Isolate host → Auto-if-safe for non-critical laptops only (Level 2)
- Disable domain admin account → Manual only (no AI autonomy)

2. **Approval gates and dual control**
   - For any significant change:
     - At least one human must explicitly confirm ("Approve isolation for HOST-123").
   - For very sensitive actions, use **dual control**:
     - IR lead + platform owner approval for things like firewall rule changes in core data centers.
3. **Context-based branching**
   Workflow logic can use context to enforce guardrails:
   - If asset criticality == "high" → force human approval, regardless of AI confidence
   - If tenant == "regulated client" → no auto-actions, only suggestions
   - If environment == "lab" → allow more aggressive automation for testing purposes
4. **Safety timeouts and throttles**
   - **Rate limiting**:
     - "Never isolate more than N endpoints in 10 minutes without an explicit override."
   - **Safety pauses**:
     - If the same automation fires unusually often ("30 isolations in 5 minutes"), pause it and ask for human review.

Workflow guardrail rule of thumb:

Every path from AI decision to real-world change should cross human checkpoints, context checks, or rate limits.

3.4. Enforcement Layer Guardrails

Enforcement guardrails answer:

"What systems can actually be changed automatically—and how do we keep that safe?"

Key areas:

1. **System scope**
   - Decide which systems are **eligible** for any automatic changes:
     - EDR agent actions on user laptops
     - Email security rules for spam or phishing quarantines
   - Decide which systems are **never automatically changed**:
     - Core routing and switching
     - OT / ICS controllers
     - Backup and restore infrastructure
     - Identity providers for privileged accounts
2. **Privilege separation**
   - The automation engine should:
     - Have **limited rights** in each system
     - Use separate service accounts per domain (EDR vs firewall vs IAM)
   - Avoid a single "super-service-account" that can touch everything.
3. **Rollback capability**
   - For every automated action, define a **rollback path**:
     - Un-isolate host
     - Undo block rule
     - Re-enable account
   - Where rollback is impossible (e.g., deleting data), that action **must not** be automated.
4. **Auditable enforcement logs**
   - For each action, log:
     - Who/what initiated it (AI assistant, automation workflow, human analyst)
     - When and where it ran
     - Result (success, partial, fail, error)
   - Keep these logs in your central logging / SIEM for investigation and audits.

Enforcement guardrail rule of thumb:

If an action can cause widespread outage or irreversible change, it should never be fully autonomous.

4. Guardrails for LLM-Based AI Assistants

LLM-based AI assistants are powerful but bring unique risks:

- **Hallucination** – making up plausible but false details
- **Prompt injection** – malicious inputs trying to steer the model
- **Data exfiltration** – leaking sensitive info in outputs

Guardrails here focus on **inputs, outputs, and integration**.

4.1. Input Guardrails

1. **Input sanitization**
   - If you feed logs or tickets that may contain user-supplied text (e.g., phishing emails, web requests), treat that content as **untrusted**.
   - Avoid allowing arbitrary log content to change the AI assistant's **system instructions**. Use strict separation between instructions and data.
2. **Sensitive data stripping**
   - Before sending data to an external AI assistant:
     - Strip secrets, passwords, tokens, PII where feasible
     - Replace real identifiers with placeholders (USER-123, HOST-456)
3. **Context limiting**
   - Give the AI assistant **only the context needed** for the current task:
     - Don't automatically expose all internal playbooks, configs, or tickets for every prompt.
   - Use retrieval: only fetch relevant documents based on the query.

4.2. Output Guardrails

1. **No direct enforcement commands**
   - The AI assistant should **not** directly call enforcement APIs.
   - Instead, it should propose actions in a structured form that:
     - Flows into a separate automation system
     - Applies its own policy/guardrails and approvals
2. **Confidence and uncertainty**
   - Encourage patterns like:
     - "This is likely X because Y, but you should check Z before acting."
   - Discourage:
     - Overconfident language on ambiguous evidence.
3. **Reference linking**
   - Where possible, the AI assistant should:
     - Refer to specific logs, events, or tickets that support its conclusions
     - Make it easy for analysts to **click through to verify**.
4. **Style constraints**
   - For external-facing drafts (emails to customers, regulators):
     - AI drafts must be reviewed and edited by humans.
     - The assistant should avoid committing to facts that aren't confirmed (e.g., "No data was exfiltrated" unless you're certain).

4.3. Integration Guardrails

1. **Role-aware behavior**
   - The AI assistant should know which **type of user** it is helping:
     - Tier 1 vs Tier 2 vs IR lead vs non-SOC user
   - Limit what it can suggest or access:

- A Tier 1 user shouldn't get guidance on changing core firewall configs.
2. **Logging assistant usage**
    - Log:
        - Prompts
        - Responses (or at least summaries)
        - Any actions proposed by the assistant
    - This is invaluable for:
        - Debugging
        - Training
        - Auditing
3. **Safe defaults**
    - If the AI assistant is unsure or lacks sufficient context:
        - It should **ask for clarification** or more data
        - Not fabricate details or push for high-risk actions.

LLM guardrail rule of thumb:

Treat the AI assistant like a very smart but occasionally overconfident junior analyst whose work must be checked.

5. Guardrails for Automation & Level 2 Autonomy

When AI decisions begin to **trigger actions**, guardrails need to be especially clear.

Here we focus on those Level 2 cases: **conditional autonomy** in bounded scenarios.

5.1. Scoping Autonomy by Use Case

Good candidates for Level 2 autonomy:

- Auto-isolating **non-critical** endpoints for high-confidence malware
- Auto-quarantining emails that match exact threat intel patterns
- Auto-closing alerts that:
    - Match a well-understood "benign pattern"
    - Have been repeatedly closed as FPs by humans

Guardrails per use case should define:

- **Conditions to enable autonomy**
    - Minimum risk score
    - Asset criticality thresholds
    - Environment tags (e.g., not OT, not critical production)
- **Conditions to force human review**
    - VIP users
    - Sensitive systems

- Tenants with strict agreements
- **Maximum rate / volume limits**
  - "Do not auto-isolate more than 5 devices per hour without human review."

5.2. Escalation & Fallback Paths

For each autonomous action, define:

- What happens if:
  - The action fails (e.g., isolation fails)
  - The action appears to be triggering too often
  - A human flags it as inappropriate

Examples:

- If N rollback events occur in 24 hours → automatically downgrade that playbook from Level 2 back to Level 1 and alert the platform owner.
- If an autonomous action fails repeatedly due to permissions or configuration issues → raise a ticket to the SOAR/platform team, and stop retrying automatically.

5.3. Separation of "Decide" vs "Do"

A powerful guardrail pattern:

AI decides, SOAR enforces, guardrails sit between them.

- The AI system outputs **recommendations** and structured action proposals.
- The SOAR/automation engine:
  - Applies policy checks, asset/tenant rules, rate limits
  - Decides whether to actually perform the action

This way:

- You can improve or swap out AI models without rewriting all your guardrails.
- Guardrails are implemented in a **single control plane** (SOAR / orchestration), not scattered.

6. Testing & Validating Guardrails

Guardrails are only real if you've **tested** them.

6.1. Pre-Deployment Testing

1. **Tabletop simulations**
   - Walk through scenarios:

- "EDR raises 50 high-severity alerts from a new campaign."
                - "AI misclassifies a benign maintenance script as malware."
        - Ask:
            - What would the AI assistant propose?
            - Which automations would trigger?
            - Where do guardrails stop bad outcomes?
2. **Replay historical incidents**
    - Run past real incidents through your AI + guardrail stack.
    - Check:
        - Would the system have caught these earlier?
        - Would automation have taken appropriate actions?
        - Did any guardrails block necessary actions incorrectly?
3. **Synthetic "failure" tests**
    - Deliberately inject:
        - Outlier data
        - Broken feeds
        - Extreme volumes
    - Validate that:
        - AI performance degrades gracefully
        - Guardrails step in (e.g., rate limits, fallback to human-only mode)

6.2. Ongoing Validation

1. **Metrics & dashboards**
Track:
    - Number of autonomous actions per period
    - Override rates (how often humans disagree)
    - Rollback events
    - AI-related incidents or near-misses
2. **Guardrail drift checks**
    - Periodically review:
        - Are conditions still appropriate (e.g., asset criticality changes)?
        - Have we added new systems that are not covered by guardrails yet?
        - Are any "temporary exceptions" quietly permanent now?
3. **Red-teaming and adversarial testing**
    - Where possible, include AI in red-team exercises:
        - See if prompt injection or crafted logs can manipulate AI decisions.
        - Validate that automation guardrails prevent actual harm.

Testing rule of thumb:

Never rely on "it should be fine." Make guardrails prove themselves in safe experiments before trusting them in live incidents.

7. Knowing When Guardrails Are Too Tight—or Too Loose

Guardrails can fail in two directions:

- **Too loose** → risk of outages and incident impact
- **Too tight** → AI becomes irrelevant, stuck in pilot mode, and you get no real benefit

You can use a few signals to tune them.

7.1. Signs Guardrails Are Too Loose

- AI-driven workflows trigger **unexpected actions** that surprise analysts.
- Analysts frequently **rollback or override** automation **with concern**, not just minor preferences.
- Near-misses:
  - Automation almost impacted a critical system, but a human caught it.
- Regulators or risk/compliance teams express discomfort because:
  - They can't clearly understand or explain which actions are autonomous.

If you see these:

- Tighten autonomy scope (fewer playbooks at Level 2).
- Raise thresholds for auto-actions.
- Add more explicit approvals for sensitive contexts.

7.2. Signs Guardrails Are Too Tight

- AI assistant is widely ignored because:
  - It never has enough data or authority to be useful.
- Analysts still spend most of their time in **low-value, repetitive tasks** that AI could handle.
- Automation is present but mostly used:
  - To create tickets
  - To send notifications
  - Not to reduce workload or improve response times

If you see these:

- Identify **low-impact, repetitive incidents** with clear patterns.
- Carefully open up Level 2 autonomy for those specific, low-risk cases.
- Reassure staff that autonomy is being introduced *to remove toil*, not to replace them.

Key Takeaways from Chapter 11

- **AI guardrails are not a buzzword; they are concrete constraints on what AI can see, decide, and do.**
- Design guardrails using **least autonomy, defense in depth, reversibility, observability, and simplicity**.
- Implement guardrails **layer by layer**:
    - Data – what the AI sees
    - Model – how it scores and classifies
    - Workflow – how decisions flow through playbooks
    - Enforcement – what systems actually change
- LLM-based **AI assistants need specific guardrails** for inputs (sanitization, masking), outputs (no direct commands, clear uncertainty), and integration (role-aware, fully logged).
- Level 2 **autonomy should be scoped** to narrow, low-impact, well-understood cases—with explicit preconditions, rate limits, and easy kill-switches.
- Guardrails must be **tested and validated** with simulations, historical replays, and adversarial tests.
- Watch for signals that guardrails are **too loose** (scary overrides, near-misses) or **too tight** (no real benefit, AI ignored) and tune accordingly.

This chapter gives you the **engineering toolkit** for turning your AI governance into reality—so your SOC can safely enjoy the benefits of AI-assisted and semi-autonomous operations, without handing the keys of your environment to a black box.

Chapter 12 – Measuring Value: Metrics, ROI & the Business Case for AI

When you talk to executives about AI in the SOC, sooner or later you'll get some version of:

"What do we get for this spend, and how will we know it's working?"

If you can't answer that clearly, AI becomes a **science project** or a **nice-to-have toy**. This chapter is about turning it into a **business decision**—with numbers and a story.

We'll cover:

1. What "value" means for AI in the SOC
2. Core metrics to track (operations, risk, people)
3. How to establish baselines before deploying AI
4. Linking specific AI capabilities to measurable outcomes
5. Simple ROI models and worked examples
6. How to build an internal business case for AI
7. AI-specific KPIs and dashboards
8. Common pitfalls in measuring value
9. A 90-day measurement plan you can start tomorrow

Use this chapter to justify the investment, tune your program, and give leadership confidence that AI in the SOC is more than just hype.

1. What "Value" Means for AI in the SOC

AI in the SOC delivers value in **three main dimensions**:

1. **Operational efficiency**
    - Less time on repetitive toil
    - Faster triage and investigation
    - Better use of scarce analyst time
2. **Risk reduction**
    - Faster detection and response for real attacks
    - Fewer missed or late high-severity incidents
    - Better coverage of attack techniques
3. **Human impact**
    - Lower burnout and turnover
    - Faster onboarding for new analysts
    - Higher quality and consistency of work

You need **all three** in your story:

- Efficiency speaks to **CFOs and operations leaders**.
- Risk reduction speaks to **CISOs, boards, regulators**.
- Human impact speaks to **SOC managers and HR**, and ultimately keeps the SOC functioning.

The good news: many of these are measurable with the data you already have—if you take the time to instrument them.

2. Core Metrics: What to Actually Measure

You don't need 50 KPIs. Start with a small set you can **reliably track** and that AI can realistically influence.

2.1. Operational Metrics

These are the easiest to quantify and usually where you see the **first wins**.

2.1.1. Alert Volume & Triage Load

- **Total alerts per day/week**
- **Alerts per analyst per shift**
- **Percentage of alerts auto-closed / suppressed**

AI impact:

- AI-assisted triage and clustering can **reduce the number of items a human must touch**.
- Automation can safely auto-close clearly benign or duplicate alerts.

2.1.2. Time to Triage and Investigate

- **Average time to initial triage per alert**
- **Average investigation time per incident**

AI impact:

- AI assistant reduces time to understand, enrich, and summarize.
- AI-generated queries and timelines accelerate analysis.

2.1.3. MTTA, MTTD, MTTR

- **MTTA** – Mean Time To Acknowledge
- **MTTD** – Mean Time To Detect (or to confirm detection)
- **MTTR** – Mean Time To Respond / Remediate

AI impact:

- Better triage → critical alerts bubble up faster → MTTA/MTTD drop.
- Automation for containment → MTTR drops for repeatable scenarios.

You don't have to hit "magic numbers"—you just need to **show improvement** tied to specific AI use cases.

2.2. Detection & Risk Metrics

These are harder but important for a **risk-based argument**.

2.2.1. True Positive / False Positive Balance

- Percentage of alerts that become **confirmed incidents** vs noise.
- For key use cases (phishing, malware, identity), track:
    - Detection coverage
    - FP rate
    - Number of missed or late high-severity incidents

AI impact:

- AI triage can **push real attacks higher in the queue**.
- Better coverage of TTPs via AI-assisted detection engineering.

2.2.2. Dwell Time for Confirmed Incidents

- Time between **first malicious activity** and:
    - Detection
    - Containment

AI impact:

- Better triage + pre-emptive CTI/deception + automation should reduce dwell time, especially for repeatable attack patterns.

2.2.3. Coverage of Key Threat Scenarios

You can express this as:

- **% of prioritized TTPs with at least one detection and a playbook**
- **% of high-risk assets with adequate logging and detections**

AI impact:

- AI-supported CTI processing and hunting campaigns → quicker conversion of intelligence into detections & hunts.

2.3. Human & Organizational Metrics

These are softer but powerful for SOC managers and leadership.

2.3.1. Time Allocation of Analysts

Rough breakdown of time per week:

- % on **low-value repetitive tasks** (copy/paste enrichment, report drafting)
- % on **actual investigations**
- % on **improvement work** (detections, runbooks, tuning, training)

AI impact:

- AI assistant and automation are largely about **shifting time from toil → investigation → improvement**.

2.3.2. Onboarding & Skill Growth

- **Time to get new analysts productive** (e.g., from 6 months to 3)
- Number of **knowledge base entries/playbooks** improved or created

AI impact:

- AI assistant as a "mentor" that explains alerts and guides next steps can **shorten ramp-up** and spread expertise.

2.3.3. Analyst Satisfaction & Burnout Signals

Even simple surveys help:

- "On a scale of 1–5, how overwhelmed do you feel by alert volume?"
- "How helpful do you find the AI assistant / automations?"

AI impact:

- If done right, analysts report **less grind and more interesting work**.
- If done badly, they report confusion or mistrust of tools.

3. Establishing Baselines (Before AI)

You can't prove improvement without a **"before" picture**.

3.1. Pick a 30–90 Day Baseline Window

Before switching on major AI capabilities:

- Choose a **recent, representative period** (e.g., last 60 days).
- Extract metrics from your **SIEM, SOAR, ticketing, EDR**, and any time tracking if available.

Priority metrics to baseline:

- Alerts per day / per analyst
- MTTA, MTTD, MTTR for key incident types
- Average time per triage / investigation
- Basic FP rate (even via sampling)
- A rough split of analyst time (even if estimated)

3.2. Use What You Already Have

Data sources:

- **Ticketing/case system**
    - Open/close times, status transitions, incident types.
- **SIEM/XDR**
    - Detection timestamps, alert counts, severities.
- **SOAR**
    - Workflow durations, automation success/fail stats.
- **Simple surveys/interviews**
    - "How long do you typically spend on X?"
    - "What feels like the biggest time sink?"

Don't aim for perfection. A **reasonable baseline** is better than waiting for a perfect one you never record.

4. Linking AI Capabilities to Specific Metrics

You don't measure "AI" generically. You measure **each capability or use case**.

4.1. Capability → Metric Mapping

Here's a simple mapping you can use.

AI capability: AI assistant for triage

- Metrics:
    - Average time to triage
    - Alerts handled per analyst per shift
    - MTTA / triage backlog

AI capability: AI assistant for investigations

- Metrics:
    - Average investigation time
    - Time to build timelines
    - Analyst satisfaction with tooling

AI capability: AI assistant for reporting & documentation

- Metrics:
    - Time spent writing incident reports
    - Time from incident resolution to report completion
    - Consistency/quality of KB articles (maybe via peer review)

AI capability: AI-assisted triage scoring & clustering

- Metrics:
    - FP rate (per rule/use case)
    - % of high-severity incidents caught earlier in the queue
    - Change in MTTA/MTTD for those incident types

AI capability: AI-supported automation (low-risk domains)

- Metrics:
    - MTTR for those incident types
    - Number of manual steps removed
    - Number of auto-actions vs manual actions
    - Override/rollback rate

4.2. Control vs Experiment Where Possible

You can treat some of this like an A/B test:

- For a given period, apply AI-assisted triage to **subset A** of alerts and not to subset B.
- Compare average triage time, MTTA, and FP/TP breakdown.

Or:

- Turn AI assistant on for **Tier 2** only at first and compare their case metrics against Tier 1.

The more you can isolate a change, the stronger your story becomes.

5. Simple ROI Models & Worked Examples

You don't need a PhD in finance. A few **simple, transparent calculations** go a long way.

5.1. Time-Savings ROI

Step 1 – Estimate time saved per use case

Example:

- Before AI assistant, average triage of an alert: **6 minutes**
- After AI assistant, average triage: **3 minutes**
- Savings: **3 minutes per alert**

If you triage 5,000 alerts/month:

- Time saved = 5,000 × 3 minutes = 15,000 minutes
- 15,000 minutes ÷ 60 = **250 hours per month**

Step 2 – Convert hours to FTE value

If one FTE ~ 160 working hours/month:

- 250 hours/month ≈ **1.56 FTE equivalents**

If loaded cost per analyst is $150,000/year:

- Cost per FTE per month ≈ $150,000 ÷ 12 ≈ $12,500
- 1.56 FTE equivalent ≈ 1.56 × $12,500 ≈ **$19,500/month** in reclaimable time

You won't necessarily fire people; instead, you can say:

"This AI capability frees up the equivalent of 1.5 FTEs of time per month to focus on higher-value work, rather than hiring additional headcount."

Step 3 – Compared to AI/tool cost

If the AI platform + implementation costs:

- $250,000 per year

Then yearly time value reclaimed:

- $19,500 × 12 ≈ $234,000

You're very close to **break-even just on triage time**. Once you add:

- Faster incident handling
- Fewer missed high-severity incidents
- Savings from not hiring additional staff

...the ROI becomes much easier to justify.

5.2. "Analysts Avoided" / Capacity ROI

Alternative model:

- Without AI, you project needing **+3 analysts** over 18 months to handle volume.
- With AI, you can handle growth **with +1 analyst** plus AI platform spend.

Roughly:

- Avoided cost: 2 analysts × $150,000/year = **$300,000/year**
- AI spend: $200,000/year

Net: ~$100,000/year in avoided staff cost **plus** better coverage and lower burnout.

5.3. Risk Reduction ROI (Simplified)

Risk math can get very complex. Keep it simple and scenario-based:

Example scenario:

- You handle ~5 high-severity incidents/year that could, if mishandled, cost **$1–3M** each (regulatory fines, downtime, etc.).
- With improved AI triage & automation, you cut average dwell time and chance of escalation so that you reduce **probability of worst-case outcome** by, say, 10–20%.

Even conservatively:

- 10% reduction of expected loss on $5M/year exposure = **$500,000/year** risk reduction.

Combine this with operational savings and you get a credible story:

"Between reclaimed analyst time and reduced probability of major incidents, we expect AI-enabled SOC capabilities to be worth ~$600–800k/year to the organization, against a spend of $200–300k."

The key is to **explain assumptions clearly**, not pretend you have perfect precision.

6. Building the Business Case for AI

Metrics are the raw material. A **business case** is the story you tell with them.

6.1. Structure of a Strong Business Case

- **Problem / Pain**
    - Alert overload, hiring constraints, risk of missed incidents.
    - Use 2–3 concrete numbers (e.g., 30,000 alerts/day, average MTTA 6 hours).
- **Vision / Target State**
    - AI-augmented SOC with:
        - Faster triage
        - Analysts focused on real threats
        - Selective, safe automation
- **Proposed Capabilities**
    - AI assistant for triage & investigations
    - AI-assisted triage scoring
    - Automated low-risk containment/actions
- **Expected Impact (Backed by Metrics)**
    - Time savings: X hours/month → Y FTE equivalents
    - MTTA/MTTR improvements for key incident types
    - Reduction in noisy alerts and better detection coverage
- **Investment & Timeline**
    - License + implementation cost
    - 90-day pilot, 12-month rollout
- **Risk & Governance**

- o   Guardrails, autonomy levels, AI policy
- o   Testing & monitoring plan
- **Ask**
  - o   Budget, headcount, and executive support you need.

6.2. Slide-Friendly Narrative

For execs, think in terms of **5–7 slides**, maximum:

- **Today's SOC Reality**
  - o   Metrics showing overload and key risks.
- **What AI in Our SOC Means (No Hype)**
  - o   Specific capabilities we will deploy.
- **Quantified Impact**
  - o   Table with time saved, FTE equivalent, and risk reduction estimate.
- **Investment & Payback**
  - o   1–3 year view with break-even point.
- **Safety & Governance**
  - o   Guardrails, autonomy limits, kill switches.
- **Roadmap (90 Days / 12 Months)**
  - o   Concrete milestones.
- **Decision & Next Steps**
  - o   What you need from the audience.

Your earlier chapters and appendices give you almost all the ingredients; this chapter is just about **assembling them into a narrative**.

7. AI-Specific KPIs and Dashboards

Beyond traditional SOC metrics, you need KPIs specific to your **AI components**.

7.1. AI Triage & Scoring KPIs

- Percentage of alerts scored **Low / Medium / High / Critical**
- Percentage of **high-severity incidents** that originated from **AI-elevated alerts**
- Analyst **override rate**:
  - o   How often humans adjust AI severity or disagree with AI grouping
- **False signal rate**:
  - o   Cases where AI suppressed or deprioritized an alert that became a confirmed incident

7.2. AI Assistant Usage KPIs

- Number of **prompts/queries** per analyst per week

- Time per investigation **with vs without AI assistant** (sampled)
- Analyst **satisfaction score** with the AI assistant
- **Knowledge base growth** supported by AI (e.g., AI-generated drafts that were accepted)

7.3. Automation & Autonomy KPIs

- Number of **automated actions** triggered per week (by type)
- **Success vs failure** rates of automations
- Number of **rollbacks/overrides**
- Number of **AI-related incidents or near-misses**

A simple dashboard that combines:

- SOC operational KPIs
- AI performance KPIs

…goes a long way to proving ongoing value and catching issues early.

8. Common Pitfalls in Measuring Value

Be aware of traps that undermine your credibility.

1. **Overclaiming causal impact**
   - Don't say "AI reduced incidents by 50%" when you simply tuned a few rules.
   - Instead: "During this period, after deploying AI triage and tuning content, we saw X% reduction in noisy alerts and Y% improvement in MTTA."
2. **Ignoring data quality and process changes**
   - If you also changed logging, rules, or staffing, acknowledge it.
   - Position AI as part of a **bundle of improvements**, not the only magic ingredient.
3. **Measuring only efficiency, not risk**
   - If all your charts are about time saved, you'll look like you're optimizing a factory, not reducing risk.
   - Always include at least a few risk-oriented indicators (dwell time, coverage, high-severity incidents).
4. **Measuring only risk, not efficiency**
   - Conversely, boards and CFOs will want to see that you're **using human capital wisely**.
   - Show both: fewer missed attacks **and** better use of people.
5. **Using metrics nobody believes**
   - If numbers feel unrealistic ("we saved 10 FTEs overnight"), you lose trust.
   - Be conservative and transparent in assumptions. Under promise, overdeliver.

9. A 90-Day Measurement Plan

Here is a practical **step-by-step plan** to put this chapter into action.

Weeks 1–2: Decide What to Measure

- Pick **3–5 core SOC metrics**:
    - e.g., Alerts per analyst, MTTA, investigation time, FP rate sample.
- Pick **3–5 AI-specific metrics** for your first AI capability:
    - e.g., triage time, AI usage, override rate.

Weeks 2–4: Establish Baselines

- Pull **30–90 days of historical data** for those metrics.
- Capture any **qualitative baseline** via short analyst surveys.
- Document clearly:
    - Time period
    - Data sources
    - Any known anomalies

Weeks 4–8: Launch AI in Suggest-Only Mode

- Deploy your first AI capability (assistant or triage scoring) in Level 0 / Level 1.
- Track the same metrics continuously.
- Collect anecdotal stories:
    - "This saved me 30 minutes on this incident."
    - "This alert would have been buried in the queue before."

Weeks 8–12: Compare, Tune, and Tell the Story

- Compare baseline vs post-AI metrics:
    - Where did you see improvements?
    - Where did you see nothing (or regression)?
- Tune:
    - Prompts
    - Rules
    - Guardrails
- Build a **short internal report or slide deck** summarizing:
    - Baseline vs now
    - Lessons learned
    - Recommendations for scaling or adjusting scope

At the end of 90 days, you'll be able to say:

- "Here's how AI is helping today, in numbers."
- "Here's where we still need work."

- "Here's why the next phase of investment makes sense."

Key Takeaways from Chapter 12

- You can't sell or scale AI in the SOC without **credible metrics and a business case**.
- Value comes from **operational efficiency, risk reduction, and human impact**—measure all three.
- Start with a **small set of metrics** you can reliably track, and establish a **baseline** before deploying AI.
- Link each AI capability to specific metrics (triage time, MTTA, FP rate, etc.), not "AI" in general.
- Use simple, transparent **ROI models** based on time savings, avoided hires, and risk reduction.
- Build a business case that combines **numbers + governance + roadmap**, not just cost.
- Track **AI-specific KPIs**: override rates, automation behavior, AI-related incidents.
- Avoid overclaiming; be conservative and honest about what AI changed vs other improvements.
- Implement a **90-day measurement plan** so your AI program is grounded in reality from day one.

With this chapter, you have the tools to make AI in the SOC **not just technically sound**, but **financially and strategically defensible**—the kind of investment a board or executive team can say "yes" to with confidence.

Chapter 13 – AI Tooling Buyer's Guide for the SOC

AI in the SOC is no longer a single product you "turn on." It's a **capability layer** that shows up inside:

- SIEM and XDR
- EDR and email security
- SOAR/orchestration tools
- Cloud platforms
- Standalone AI assistants and data platforms

That makes buying decisions harder, not easier.

This chapter is your **practical buyer's guide** for AI-enabled SOC tooling: how to cut through marketing, ask the right questions, and pick tools that fit your environment, your maturity, and your risk appetite.

We'll cover:

1. The main categories of AI in SOC tooling
2. Core evaluation principles (beyond hype)
3. Key evaluation dimensions & questions
4. Differences between SIEM/XDR, EDR, SOAR, and standalone AI assistants
5. MSSP / multi-tenant considerations
6. Red flags & "too good to be true" patterns
7. Example scorecard / evaluation template

Use this as a companion to your RFPs, POCs, and vendor meetings.

1. Categories of AI in the SOC Tooling Landscape

When vendors say "we have AI," they can mean very different things. It helps to sort offerings into **categories**.

1.1. Native AI Features in Existing Platforms

Most existing tools now include some AI functions:

- **SIEM / XDR**
    - Alert correlation and grouping
    - Risk scoring and anomaly detection
    - Natural-language search / "ask the SIEM"
- **EDR / Endpoint Platforms**
    - Behavioral models for malware/ransomware

- - "Suspicious activity" detections, storyline graphs
  - Automated remediation suggestions
- **Email / Web / Identity Security**
  - Phishing detection
  - "Identity risk" scoring
  - UEBA (user and entity behavior analytics)

These are **embedded** in platforms you may already own. You evaluate them as **features of a larger platform**, not standalone products.

1.2. AI Assistants / "Security Copilot"-Style Tools

These are **LLM-based AI assistants** designed to:

- Answer natural language questions ("Summarize this incident")
- Generate queries and hunts
- Summarize logs, cases, and CTI reports
- Draft reports, playbooks, and communications

They may be:

- Built into existing tools (e.g., SIEM or XDR assistant)
- Standalone but integrated with your stack via APIs

These tools are **directly visible to analysts** and heavily influence workflows.

1.3. AI-Powered Analytics / Data Platforms

Some vendors offer **data platforms** with AI-native capabilities:

- Security data lakes with ML analytics
- UEBA platforms
- Graph analytics / entity-centric modeling

They focus more on **behavior analytics and big-picture patterns** than on single alerts.

1.4. SOAR / Automation Platforms with AI

SOAR tools are adding AI for:

- Playbook generation and recommendation
- Intelligent routing and case categorization
- AI-assisted decision points inside workflows

The AI here is less about discovering threats and more about **orchestrating response** and **reducing manual steps**.

1.5. CTI, Deception & Specialist AI Tools

Niche tools using AI for:

- CTI summarization and threat clustering
- Attack path modeling and exposure management
- Deception/honeypot analysis

You evaluate these per **specific use case**, not as generic SOC engines.

2. Core Evaluation Principles (Beyond AI Hype)

Before we dive into checklists, a few **mindset principles**:

2.1. Use Cases First, Technology Second

Start with:

- The **problems you want to solve** (e.g., triage overload, slow investigations, limited hunting, reporting overhead).
- The **use cases** you care about (Chapters 5–7 and your roadmap).

Then evaluate tools on:

How clearly they support those specific use cases—not on how fancy their AI pitch deck is.

2.2. Data & Integration Are King

Most AI features will fail if:

- Your logs are incomplete or messy
- The tool can't integrate with key platforms
- Data can't be joined with user/asset context

Your evaluation should prioritize:

- How well the AI tooling ingests, normalizes, and **understands your data**, not just synthetic demos.

2.3. Guardrails & Control Matter More Than Cleverness

A clever model with weak guardrails is dangerous in security operations.

Always ask:

- How do we **limit** what this AI can see, decide, and do?
- What **autonomy levels** are supported?
- How fast can we **rollback** or **turn off** something that misbehaves?

2.4. Transparency & Observability

You want tools that can:

- Explain (at least at a high level) why something was scored/flagged
- Log AI decisions and automated actions
- Provide metrics over time (performance, override rates, etc.)

If it's a total black box, you'll struggle with:

- Analyst trust
- Tuning
- Audits and regulators

2.5. Avoid "One Giant Bet"

Don't try to buy a single **mega-platform** that promises to do everything with AI overnight.

- Start by making **incremental improvements** where value is obvious.
- Ensure tools play nicely together via **APIs and open integration**.

3. Key Evaluation Dimensions & Questions

Here's a structured way to evaluate AI tooling, with **questions you can ask vendors**. (We'll turn this into an RFP-style list in Appendix F.)

3.1. Use Cases & Capabilities

What you're looking for:

- Clear mapping from AI features → **your SOC use cases**
- Real examples, not just generic promises

Questions to ask:

1. **Which SOC workflows is your AI specifically designed to support?**
    - Triage, investigation, hunting, reporting, CTI, automation, etc.
2. **Can you show us customer examples that closely match our environment?**
    - Similar industry, size, cloud stack, regulation.
3. **What can your AI not do (or not do well)?**
    - Any limitations or scope boundaries.
4. **How does AI behave when it doesn't have enough data or context?**
    - Does it fail safely? Ask for more info? Guess?

3.2. Data & Integration

What you're looking for:

- Strong integration with your **current tools**
- Sensible data models and **normalization**
- Support for your **clouds, SaaS, and critical systems**

Questions to ask:

1. **Which data sources and platforms do you support natively?**
    - SIEM, XDR, EDR, identity, cloud, email, etc.
2. **How do you handle data normalization and schema differences?**
    - Do you use a standard schema (e.g., ECS, OCSF), or your own?
3. **How do you enrich data with user and asset context?**
    - Connectors to CMDB, HR, identity, asset inventories.
4. **How do you perform correlation across multiple sources?**
    - Latency, performance, and how "deep" the joins can go.
5. **What is the typical data volume and retention model?**
    - On-prem vs cloud, hot vs cold data.

3.3. Autonomy, Guardrails & Control

What you're looking for:

- Built-in support for **autonomy levels** (suggest-only, human-in-loop, conditional auto)
- Clear, configurable **guardrails**
- Easy **kill switches** and rollback

Questions to ask:

1. **How do you represent autonomy?**
   - Can we configure certain actions as:
     - Suggest-only
     - Requires approval
     - Allowed to run automatically under conditions
2. **Can you show us how to define guardrails?**
   - Asset criticality checks
   - Environment filters (dev vs prod vs OT)
   - Tenant isolation (for MSSP)
3. **What's the process for disabling or rolling back an AI-driven feature?**
   - Is there a single place to turn off certain types of automation?
4. **How are automated actions logged and audited?**
   - Can we see which actions were AI-driven vs manually triggered?

3.4. Model Transparency & Performance

What you're looking for:

- Basic explainability
- Performance metrics you can understand
- A plan for **model updates and tuning**

Questions to ask:

1. **What type(s) of models do you use for key features?**
   - Anomaly, supervised, rules + ML hybrid, LLM, etc.
2. **How do you measure the accuracy and performance of your models?**
   - Do you have TP/FP metrics from real deployments?
3. **Can we see feature contributions or high-level "reasons" for decisions?**
   - Even if approximate.
4. **How are models updated?**
   - Frequency of updates
   - Whether updates can be tested in shadow mode before going live
   - Can we *opt-out* of certain model updates?
5. **How do we provide feedback (labels, overrides) to improve models?**
   - Is analyst feedback first-class?

3.5. Security, Privacy & Data Usage

What you're looking for:

- Strong story on **data security and privacy**
- Clear answers on **training data, retention, residency**
- Configurable settings for **sensitive data**

Questions to ask:

1. **How is customer data stored, encrypted, and isolated?**
   - At rest, in transit, in multi-tenant environments.
2. **Do you use our data to train global or shared models?**
   - If yes, under what conditions and what controls do we have?
3. **Can we opt out of having our data used for training beyond our tenancy?**
4. **Where is data processed and stored?**
   - Regions, data residency, cross-border flows.
5. **What controls exist for redacting or tokenizing sensitive fields before they reach AI components?**
6. **Do you have documentation or certifications relevant to AI security and privacy?**
   - Not just generic ISO, but any AI-specific practices.

3.6. Multi-Tenant & MSSP Features

If you're an MSSP or have multiple business units/tenants, this is crucial.

What you're looking for:

- Strong **tenant isolation** in data, models, and UI
- Per-tenant customization of rules, thresholds, and guardrails
- Flexible reporting and access control

Questions to ask:

1. **How do you separate data and AI decisions across tenants?**
   - Is there any shared model logic that can cross-contaminate?
2. **Can we set different policies, thresholds, and automations per tenant?**
3. **How does your AI assistant behave in a multi-tenant context?**
   - Can it accidentally "see" or summarize cross-tenant data?
4. **How do you handle per-tenant reporting, SLAs, and access control?**
5. **For MSSP: How easy is it to onboard/offboard tenants at scale?**

3.7. Operations, UX & Adoption

Even the best AI is useless if analysts don't use it.

What you're looking for:

- UI that fits existing workflows
- Minimal context switching
- Good in-tool guidance

Questions to ask:

1. **Where and how do analysts interact with your AI features?**
   - Inside the main console, separate UI, browser extension, IDE-style assistant?
2. **Can AI output be embedded directly into our case management workflow?**
3. **What training and enablement do you provide?**
   - Documentation, playbooks, prompt libraries, workshops.
4. **Do you support role-specific experiences?**
   - Tier 1 vs Tier 2 vs IR vs detection engineer.
5. **Can we see usage metrics?**
   - How often the assistant is used
   - Which features are adopted or ignored

3.8. Pricing & Licensing

What you're looking for:

- Predictability
- Clear relationship between **value and cost**
- Understanding of how AI features are priced (separately or bundled)

Questions to ask:

1. **Are AI features included in existing licenses or priced separately?**
2. **If separate, how is pricing structured?**
   - Per user? Per query or token? Per data volume? Per tenant?
3. **What limits apply?**
   - Rate limits, maximum concurrency, maximum prompts, etc.
4. **Can we start with a limited scope / pilot license?**
5. **How do costs scale over 1–3 years as we expand use?**

3.9. Vendor Maturity & Roadmap

What you're looking for:

- Evidence that they're serious about AI beyond buzzwords
- A realistic roadmap—not just hype slides

Questions to ask:

1. **How long have your AI features been in production with customers?**
2. **How many customers are using them in critical workflows?**
3. **What major AI improvements did you ship in the last 12–18 months?**
4. **What's on your AI roadmap for the next 12–24 months?**
5. **How do you incorporate customer feedback into the roadmap?**

4. Buying SIEM/XDR vs AI Assistant vs SOAR vs Analytics

Many organizations will combine:

- A **primary SIEM/XDR** platform with native AI
- One or more **AI assistants**
- **SOAR** for orchestration
- Possibly a **security data lake / analytics** layer

Here's how to think about each.

4.1. SIEM/XDR with AI

Evaluate as:

- Your **core detection and triage engine**
- The place where **most alerts and context live**

Focus on:

- Quality of built-in detections + AI insights
- How well it supports **AI triage, grouping, risk scoring**
- How easy it is to integrate with other tools and AI assistants

4.2. AI Assistant (Cross-Tool)

This is the "front end" for analysts.

Focus on:

- Which **tools and data sources** it can access
- How well it handles **summarization, investigations, hunts, and reporting**
- Whether it respects **guardrails and data privacy**

If the assistant is tied to one vendor, ask:

- Can it see data beyond that vendor's stack (e.g., other SIEMs, custom logs, CTI sources)?

4.3. SOAR & Automation Platforms

These are the **execution engines** for actions.

Focus on:

- Integration breadth (EDR, identity, cloud, network, ticketing)
- How AI is used to recommend or partially automate steps
- Support for **autonomy levels** and **guardrails**

Even if your SIEM/XDR has some automation, a dedicated SOAR might still be your **central control plane** for cross-tool workflows.

4.4. Analytics / Data Platforms & UEBA

These support:

- Entity-centric risk scoring
- Behavior analytics
- Big-picture patterns

Focus on:

- How are results exposed to analysts (dashboards? AI assistant?)
- How insights feed back into SIEM rules and SOAR playbooks
- Whether they require **duplicating data** or can sit on top of existing stores

5. MSSP & Multi-Tenant Buyer Considerations

If you're an MSSP or have strong internal separation (multiple BUs, geos), AI adds extra challenges.

Key points:

- **Per-tenant autonomy and policy**
    - Some tenants may allow more aggressive automation; others won't.
- **Per-tenant explainability and reporting**
    - Clients will ask "Why was this alert handled this way?"
    - Your tools must help you answer that at tenant level.
- **Per-tenant data residency and compliance**
    - Some clients may require local processing or EU-only data.
- **Economics at scale**
    - Pricing per tenant, per volume, or per user matters a lot.
    - Look for multi-tenant features designed *for* MSSPs (not just repurposed enterprise tools).

When evaluating, ask explicitly:

"How many MSSP customers do you have using your AI features today? Can we speak to one?"

6. Red Flags & "Too Good to Be True" Patterns

A few warning signs to watch for.

6.1. Pure "Magic Box" Marketing

Red flag phrases:

- "We use proprietary AI to find all threats automatically."
- "Just flip the switch and let the AI handle everything."

Better vendors will:

- Talk about specific **use cases**, **data needs**, and **guardrails**.
- Acknowledge limitations and the need for **human oversight**.

6.2. No Clear Data Story

Red flag:

- Vendor can't explain how your **actual data sources** will be ingested, normalized, and used.

Danger:

- Beautiful demos on clean, synthetic data; chaos in real deployments.

6.3. No Metrics, No Benchmarks

Red flag:

- Hand-wavy claims like "customers see huge improvements" with no concrete numbers or ranges.

Ask for:

- Ranges for typical improvements (e.g., "Customers often see 20–40% reduction in time-to-triage for these alert types").
- At least **anonymized** before/after graphs.

6.4. No Story on Guardrails & Autonomy

Red flag:

- Vendor is excited about auto-remediation but vague on:
    - Safeguards
    - Kill switches
    - Logging

Danger:

- Difficult to defend to your change advisory board, auditors, and regulators.

6.5. Lock-In Without APIs

Red flag:

- Limited or no **open APIs**
- AI features that only work in a "walled garden"

This makes it hard to:

- Combine tools
- Use cross-platform AI assistants
- Migrate in the future

7. Example Scorecard / Evaluation Template

Here's a sample **scorecard structure** you can adapt into a spreadsheet.

Dimensions (score 1–5)

1. Use Case Fit
2. Data & Integration
3. Guardrails & Autonomy
4. Model Transparency & Performance
5. Security & Privacy Posture
6. Multi-Tenant & MSSP Readiness (if relevant)
7. UX & Adoption Potential
8. Pricing & Commercial Fit
9. Vendor Maturity & Roadmap

For each vendor/tool:

Dimension	Weight (%)	Vendor A (1–5)	Vendor B (1–5)	Notes
Use Case Fit	20%	4	3	
Data & Integration	15%	5	3	
Guardrails & Autonomy	15%	3	2	
Transparency & Performance	10%	3	4	
Security & Privacy	10%	4	4	
Multi-Tenant / MSSP (if needed)	10%	5	2	
UX & Adoption	10%	4	3	
Pricing & Commercials	5%	3	4	
Vendor Maturity & Roadmap	5%	4	3	

Calculate a weighted score and combine with **qualitative comments** from the SOC team.

Key Takeaways from Chapter 13

- You're not buying "AI"—you're buying **AI-augmented SIEM/XDR/EDR/SOAR**, plus possibly **AI assistants** and **analytics platforms**.
- Evaluate tools based on **your specific use cases and pain points**, not generic AI hype.
- Focus heavily on **data & integration**, **guardrails**, and **observability**, not just detection claims.
- Ask clear questions about **model behavior, feedback loops, security, and privacy**.
- If you're an MSSP or multi-tenant environment, ensure strong **tenant isolation** and per-tenant control.
- Watch out for **magic box** marketing, missing data stories, and tools with no clear way to control autonomy.

- Use a structured **scorecard** to compare vendors in a way that reflects your strategy and roadmap.

With this buyer's guide, you can approach AI tooling decisions like an architect and product owner—not just a shopper—and assemble an AI-enabled SOC stack that's **effective, safe, and sustainable** over the next 3–5 years.

Chapter 14 – Roadmap & Maturity Model for the Autonomous SOC

By now, you have all the building blocks:

- Reference architectures (data, SIEM, SOAR, AI sidecars)
- Data strategy and quality
- AI triage, AI assistants, and automation
- CTI, deception, and pre-emptive security
- People, operating model, and governance

The remaining question is the one executive will ask:

"Okay, but **what do we actually do first, next, and after that**?"

This chapter turns the ideas into a **practical roadmap and maturity model**, so you can:

- Assess where you are today
- Define a realistic target state
- Plan incremental steps that demonstrate value early
- Avoid the traps of "AI everywhere" chaos or "we'll wait until it's perfect" paralysis

We'll cover:

1. Why you need a roadmap (and not a big-bang "AI SOC" project)
2. A simple 5-level maturity model for AI in the SOC
3. A 90-day "foundations & quick wins" plan
4. A 12–24 month roadmap to an AI-augmented SOC
5. Long-term target state: toward selective autonomy
6. Adjusting the roadmap for different org types (enterprise, MSSP, regulated)
7. Common pitfalls and anti-patterns to avoid

Think of this chapter as the "glue" that connects all the concepts from earlier chapters into a coherent journey.

1. Why You Need a Roadmap (Not a Big Bang)

When organizations first get excited about AI in the SOC, they often oscillate between two unhelpful extremes:

- **Big-bang transformation:**
    - "In 12 months we'll have a fully autonomous SOC with AI everywhere."
    - Result: overly ambitious projects, disappointment, technical debt, and trust issues.

- **Paralysis and pilot purgatory:**
    - "We'll run endless small POCs and see what happens."
    - Result: scattered experiments, no systemic change, and no story for leadership.

A roadmap gives you a **third path**:

"We will move through **defined stages** of maturity, with **clear outcomes** at each stage, building on what we already have."

Characteristics of a good roadmap:

- **Incremental:** Each step makes your SOC better even if you never reach the "end state."
- **Value-driven:** Early steps focus on use cases that deliver visible improvements (triage, enrichment, reports).
- **Governed:** Autonomy increases only as data, processes, and trust improve.
- **Adaptive:** It survives tool changes and vendor decisions because it's based on principles, not product names.

The maturity model in the next section is the backbone of that roadmap.

2. A Simple 5-Level Maturity Model for the Autonomous SOC

We'll use a 5-level model:

- **Fragmented & Manual SOC**
- **Instrumented SOC**
- **Augmented SOC**
- **Semi-Autonomous SOC**
- **Selectively Autonomous SOC**

You don't need to hit every capability at every level. Think of this as a **map**, not a certification scheme.

2.1. Fragmented & Manual SOC

Typical characteristics:

- Logs are scattered; some go to a SIEM, others to local files or vendor consoles.
- Detection content is mostly default/vendor out-of-the-box rules.
- Triage is largely manual; analysts swivel-chair between tools.
- Playbooks are tribal knowledge or ad-hoc checklists.
- Reporting is mostly manual copy-paste.

AI status:

- At most, individual tools may claim "AI features," but there is no deliberate AI strategy in operations.

Goal at this level:

- Stabilize and **instrument** the environment (Level 1) before adding significant AI.

2.2. Instrumented SOC

Key outcomes:

- Centralized log and telemetry platform (SIEM/XDR/data lake) for key sources:
    - Identity, endpoint, network/edge, cloud, crown jewels.
- Baseline set of documented **playbooks** for common incident types (phishing, malware, suspicious login, etc.).
- Basic SOAR or scripting for **simple automations** (ticket creation, basic enrichment).
- Case management is structured (fields, categories, outcomes).

AI status:

- Limited, mostly vendor-native analytics (UEBA, anomaly detection).
- Maybe one or two localized experiments (e.g., an LLM used to draft incident summaries).

What's possible at this level:

- AI **summarization and enrichment** pilots.
- Basic AI assistant for natural language queries over logs (if data quality is decent).

Next step:

- Move to **Level 2 – Augmented SOC**, where AI becomes a deliberate layer, not scattered features.

2.3. Augmented SOC

Here, AI is **meaningfully integrated** into daily operations, but humans still drive decisions.

Key outcomes:

- **Data quality & coverage** are actively managed:
    - Normalization and enrichment in place for golden sources.

- o Basic health metrics (parse success rate, ingestion latency) monitored.
- **AI assistant** for analysts:
  - o Natural language queries into SIEM/XDR.
  - o Automated enrichment lookups (user/asset/CTI).
  - o Incident summaries and timeline drafts.
- **AI-assisted triage** (suggest-only or semi-automatic):
  - o Risk scoring that considers asset criticality, user risk, and behavior.
  - o Grouping/correlation of alerts into episodes, but **humans decide priority**.
- **Playbooks & reports**:
  - o AI drafts playbooks and incident reports; humans approve and refine.

Human role at Level 2:

- Analysts and engineers **shape the AI**, provide feedback, and use it as a co-worker.
- No critical actions are fully autonomous.

Next step:

- Introduce **carefully governed auto-actions** and pre-emptive AI in threat hunting and deception (Level 3).

2.4. Semi-Autonomous SOC

Now AI doesn't just suggest; under **strict guardrails**, it **acts** in bounded domains.

Key outcomes:

- **AI-driven triage** with conditional automation:
  - o Certain low-risk, well-understood incident types (e.g., commodity malware on non-critical endpoints) can be:
    - Auto-contained
    - Auto-resolved with human post-review
- **Pre-emptive AI use**:
  - o CTI is processed and structured by AI.
  - o Honeypot and deception telemetry is analyzed by AI for patterns and emerging TTPs.
  - o AI suggests hunts, detection content, and playbook updates.
- **AI assistant deeply integrated**:
  - o Standardized "skills" (investigate phishing, suspicious login, etc.) are built into the AI assistant.
  - o Analysts frequently rely on AI assistant for investigations.
- **Governance & monitoring**:
  - o Autonomy levels are defined (suggest-only / semi-auto / conditional auto).
  - o Metrics for AI performance, override rates, and incidents are tracked.
  - o AI-related incidents are managed within the main incident process.

Human role at Level 3:

- Humans **approve high-impact actions**, design guardrails, and own outcomes.
- Analysts focus on complex cases, hunts, and system improvement.

Next step:

- Expand autonomy where proven, especially in narrow, well-controlled domains (Level 4).

2.5. Selectively Autonomous SOC

This is not "no humans needed." It's **autonomy where it makes sense**, with humans designing and supervising the system.

Key outcomes:

- **Fully autonomous handling** (within strict scope) for specific patterns:
  - Known benign alerts and noise classes are auto-suppressed.
  - Routine, repetitive incidents are fully auto-handled end-to-end, with periodic human review (e.g., commodity phishing blocked, user notified, ticket auto-closed).
- **Adaptive risk models**:
  - AI risk scoring adjusts based on feedback, emerging CTI, and deception data.
  - Human teams manage **policies and guardrails**, not individual thresholds.
- **Learning loops fully operational**:
  - Post-incident reviews, CTI, hunting, model performance, and playbook updates all feed into a continuous cycle.
- **Mature governance and auditability**:
  - Clear documentation of AI architectures, decisions, and controls.
  - Regulators and auditors receive coherent explanations and evidence.

Human role at Level 4:

- Humans become **system designers, overseers, investigators of the unusual, and strategic decision-makers.**
- The SOC operates as a **platform**, not just a team.

Most organizations won't reach (or need) full Level 4 everywhere. The roadmap is about identifying **where** autonomy adds value and risk is acceptable.

3. The First 90 Days: Foundations & Quick Wins

No matter where you are, you can do something meaningful in 90 days without buying an entire new stack.

3.1. Baseline Assessment (Weeks 1–2)

Deliverables:

- Inventory of:
    - Data sources and coverage for identity, endpoint, network, cloud, and crown jewels.
    - Current playbooks (even if messy) and automations.
    - Existing "AI" features in tools.
- Map yourself roughly to the maturity model (0–4).

Questions to answer:

- Which parts of the SOC are most overloaded (triage, investigations, reporting)?
- Where do analysts spend the most low-value time (copy-paste, enrichment lookups, report writing)?
- Where is data quality clearly a problem (broken parsers, missing logs)?

3.2. Choose 2–3 High-Impact Use Cases (Weeks 2–3)

Don't start with "autonomous SOC." Start with **specific pain points**.

Common good choices:

1. **AI-assisted alert triage** (suggest-only at first):
    - Risk scoring for a noisy alert class (e.g., EDR alerts).
2. **AI assistant for investigations**:
    - Natural language queries + enrichment for a small group of analysts.
3. **AI-generated reports or summaries**:
    - Turn incident data into executive summaries and technical reports.

Pick use cases that:

- Are **visible** (people will notice improvement).
- Are **bounded** (you can measure success or failure).
- Don't require perfect data across everything.

3.3. Data & Process Tune-Up for Those Use Cases (Weeks 3–6)

For each chosen use case:

- Ensure the necessary **data sources are reliable** (coverage, parsing, enrichment).
- Clarify the **current manual process**:
    - How analysts triage these alerts today
    - What info they look up
    - How they decide what's important
- Capture **a sample of recent cases** (e.g., 50–100 incidents) to use as reference and test material.

3.4. Pilot AI in Shadow / Suggest Mode (Weeks 6–10)

Implement a **pilot**:

- AI assistant gives suggested queries, enrichment, and summaries.
- Triage AI assigns risk scores and groups alerts into episodes, but **does not change the actual queue order** yet.

Track:

- How often analysts agree with AI suggestions.
- Whether suggested triage ordering "would have" helped in real incidents.
- Time saved on enrichment and reporting.

3.5. Decide What to Industrialize (Weeks 10–12)

At the end of 90 days:

- Identify **what worked well enough** to scale:
    - "We'll roll out AI assistant to all Tier 2 analysts."
    - "We'll turn the triage scoring into an actual sort order, but still no automated actions."
- Identify **what needs more data or tuning**.
- Produce a simple **one-page summary**:
    - Baseline metrics vs. pilot metrics
    - Stories from analysts
    - Lessons learned
    - Recommended next steps

You now have **real evidence** and a better intuition for where AI helps. That de-risks the next 12–24 months.

4. A 12–24 Month Roadmap to an AI-Augmented SOC

Think of this as moving from Level 1 → Level 2 → early Level 3.

4.1. Phase 1 (Months 0–6): Consolidate & Augment

Objectives:

- Strengthen data and process foundations.
- Expand AI assistant & enrichment.
- Deploy AI-assisted triage in production (human-in-the-loop).

Key activities:

1. **Data & coverage uplift**
   - Ensure golden sources (identity, endpoint, network edge, cloud, crown jewels) are ingested, parsed, and enriched.
   - Implement basic data health monitoring.
2. **Standardize playbooks**
   - Use AI to draft playbooks for top 5–10 incident types.
   - Review and finalize with analysts.
3. **Roll out AI assistant**
   - Provide AI assistant access to Tier 2+ analysts.
   - Train them on prompts, verification, and feedback.
4. **AI triage in production (no auto-actions)**
   - Use risk scores and episode grouping to organize alert queues.
   - Track impact on MTTA/MTTD and analyst workload.

Deliverables at ~6 months:

- A **visible reduction** in alert noise perceived by analysts.
- AI assistant becoming a normal part of investigations.
- Documented playbooks and early AI governance policies.

4.2. Phase 2 (Months 6–12): Governed Automation & Pre-emptive Intelligence

Objectives:

- Introduce carefully controlled auto-actions.
- Start pre-emptive AI: CTI processing, basic deception analytics.

Key activities:

1. **Define autonomy policies & RACI**
   - For each playbook, define:
     - Which steps are suggest-only, which require approval, which can be auto.
   - Document RACI for AI-assisted workflows.
2. **Implement low-risk auto-actions**
   - Example domains:

- Quarantining low-value endpoints with confirmed commodity malware.
- Auto-blocking known malicious IPs/domains from curated threat feeds.
  - Always with:
    - Strong logging
    - Easy rollback
    - Human review of samples
3. **CTI & deception integration**
   - Use AI to:
     - Parse and structure CTI reports.
     - Summarize relevance to your environment.
   - Stand up basic honeypots or deception assets.
   - Feed their telemetry into AI analytics (even if manually reviewed).
4. **Feedback loops & metrics**
   - Formalize structured feedback from analysts on AI triage and AI assistant outputs.
   - Review model performance and override rates monthly or quarterly.

Deliverables at ~12 months:

- Some **real incidents handled faster** due to AI-driven triage and limited automation.
- Early wins in pre-emptive detection driven by CTI + deception insights.
- Governance mechanisms that auditors and leadership can understand.

4.3. Phase 3 (Months 12–24): Toward Semi-Autonomous SOC

Objectives:

- Scale governed auto-actions to more incident types.
- Make pre-emptive loops (CTI → detection → deception → hunts) routine.
- Mature operating model.

Key activities:

1. **Expand automation by domain**
   - Identity, endpoint, cloud, email—each with its own:
     - Auto-actions
     - Playbooks
     - Ownership and metrics
2. **Continuous detection engineering powered by AI**
   - AI generates draft detections from CTI, deception, and PIRs.
   - Detection engineers validate and deploy on a regular cadence.
3. **Pre-emptive hunting campaigns**
   - Quarterly or monthly themed hunt campaigns designed with AI and executed by hunters.

- Incorporate deception findings and CTI trends.
4. **People and org evolution**
    - Move toward capability-based teams (identity, endpoint, cloud, etc.).
    - Establish SOC product owner role if not already present.
    - Embed AI/automation expertise in or adjacent to SOC.
5. **Governance and audit maturity**
    - Finalize AI risk and usage policies.
    - Maintain a catalog of AI capabilities, their autonomy levels, and evidence of control.

Deliverables at ~24 months:

- SOC operating at **Level 2 and parts of Level 3**:
    - Analysts heavily augmented by AI.
    - Certain incident types semi-autonomously handled.
    - Pre-emptive threat intelligence feeding back into operations.
- A leadership-ready narrative:
    - What AI is doing
    - What risk it reduces
    - How it is governed

5. Long-Term Target State: Selective Autonomy (3+ Years)

Beyond 24 months, the roadmap becomes less about time and more about **ambition and risk appetite**.

You're aiming for **Level 3–4** in the areas that matter most.

5.1. What "Good" Looks Like in 3+ Years

- **Human work has shifted**:
    - Minimal manual triage of commodity alerts.
    - Human energy focused on complex incidents, hunting, system tuning, and strategic work.
- **Autonomy is selective and explainable:**
    - For well-understood patterns, the SOC acts autonomously.
    - For novel, ambiguous patterns, the system surfaces rich context for humans.
    - For high-impact decisions, human approvals remain in place.
- **AI is just "how the SOC works," not a separate topic.**
    - New detections, playbooks, and workflows assume AI for enrichment, triage, and documentation.
    - AI performance metrics sit alongside traditional SOC KPIs.
- **The SOC is a learning system:**

- o Every incident, near-miss, CTI report, and deception finding feeds back into content and models.
- o Data, models, and playbooks are continuously and visibly improving.

5.2. Where Not to Automate (On Purpose)

Even at high maturity, you may deliberately **not** automate:

- Highly sensitive actions on critical infrastructure or safety systems.
- Legal, HR, and regulatory communications.
- Strategic risk decisions (e.g., "Do we shut down this business service as a precaution?").

Autonomy should be seen as a **tool**, not a virtue on its own.
The test is always:

"Does autonomy here reduce overall risk and improve outcomes, with controls we trust?"

6. Adjusting the Roadmap for Different Organizations

Not every organization has the same starting point or constraints.

6.1. Large Enterprise, Single-Organization SOC

Constraints:

- Complex, diverse environments
- Multiple stakeholders and risk appetites

Focus areas:

- Data strategy and platform consolidation (Chapters 3–4).
- Strong governance and AI risk management (Chapter 10).
- Capability-oriented teams (identity, endpoint, cloud, etc.).

Approach:

- Lean heavily on existing platforms' AI features where they fit, but keep control in your architecture and policies.
- Invest in detection engineers and SOC product ownership early.

6.2. MSSP / Service Provider / Telco

Constraints:

- Multi-tenancy, strict client separation
- SLAs and commercial expectations

Focus areas:

- Multi-tenant architecture and AI tenancy design (Chapter 3).
- Client-specific context and reporting (Chapters 7–8).
- Pre-emptive CTI and deception pipelines that benefit **many clients**.

Approach:

- Use global/shared models for broad pattern detection, plus per-tenant baselines for noise reduction.
- Focus on capabilities that generate **visible value for clients**: better reports, faster response, proactive findings.
- Treat AI as part of your **service differentiation**—but governed and explainable.

6.3. Highly Regulated or Critical Infrastructure

Constraints:

- Tight regulation, heavy audit, and documentation demands
- Very low tolerance for automation failures

Focus areas:

- Governance, risk, and compliance for AI (Chapter 10) **from day one**.
- On-prem or private AI deployments for sensitive data.
- Conservative autonomy: more AI assistant, less fully automated action.

Approach:

- Use AI first for **summarization, enrichment, and decision support**.
- Introduce **very limited** auto-actions only after extensive testing and with strong oversight.
- Make documentation and explainability central—not an afterthought.

6.4. Small / Mid-Market SOC or "SOC-of-One"

Constraints:

- Limited headcount and budget
- Often heavily dependent on managed services and SaaS tools

Focus areas:

- Use AI to **multiply a small team**, not to build a big stack.
- AI assistants and AI features embedded in cloud-native security tools.
- Strong vendor selection and integration strategy.

Approach:

- Start with:
  - AI assistant features in your cloud/SaaS security tools.
  - AI-powered triage and reporting from vendors.
- Focus your own effort on:
  - Governance and integration
  - Selecting vendors whose AI you can understand and trust

Even small teams can operate at **Level 2–3** if they lean on the right platforms.

7. Common Pitfalls & Anti-Patterns to Avoid

As you implement this roadmap, beware of traps that repeatedly derail organizations.

7.1. "AI First, Data Later"

Trying to deploy sophisticated AI on top of:

- Missing logs
- Broken parsers
- No enrichment
- No case structure

…is a recipe for frustration.

Fix:

- Follow Chapters 3–4: **data and process health** first.
- Start AI where your data is already "good enough."

7.2. "Pilot Forever"

Running endless POCs that never graduate to production:

- Confuses the team
- Wastes goodwill
- Produces no systemic change

Fix:

- For each pilot, define:
    - Success criteria
    - Decision point date (go/no-go)
    - A clear path to production **or** to retire the idea

7.3. "Automation Without Guardrails"

Turning on auto-containment or aggressive AI without:

- Clear scopes
- Rollback mechanisms
- Monitoring

…can cause outages and damage trust.

Fix:

- Explicit autonomy levels (suggest / semi-auto / conditional auto).
- Always start with **low-impact domains** and build trust incrementally.

7.4. "Magic Box Mentality"

Treating AI (especially vendor AI) as:

- Unquestionable
- Opaque
- Not your responsibility

…is dangerous.

Fix:

- Insist on at least high-level explainability and documentation.

- Log and review AI decisions just like any other control.
- Train analysts to question AI, not worship it.

7.5. "Ignoring People and Org Design"

You can't drop AI into a SOC that:

- Measures people only on ticket counts
- Never gives time for improvement or learning
- Doesn't reward system-level changes

Fix:

- Apply Chapter 9: new roles, product thinking, capability teams, and change management.
- Celebrate **system improvements** (better detections, fewer false positives) as much as individual heroics.

Key Takeaways from Chapter 14

- **You need a journey, not a jump.** Moving to an AI-augmented or selectively autonomous SOC is a multi-stage process, not a big bang.
- **A simple maturity model helps you communicate and plan.** Levels 0–4 give a language to describe where you are and where you're going.
- **The first 90 days are about foundations and visible wins.** Clean data, a few high-impact AI use cases (triage, AI assistant, reports), and real feedback.
- **The 12–24 month horizon is about integration and governance.** AI assistants become normal, triage is AI-assisted, some low-risk auto-actions are in place, and pre-emptive CTI/deception loops begin.
- **Beyond 24 months, autonomy is selective and deliberate.** You choose where AI can act alone under guardrails and where humans must always decide.
- **Different organizations have different paths.** Enterprises, MSSPs, critical infrastructure, and small teams all apply the same principles with different emphases.
- **Avoid the common traps.** Don't do AI on bad data, live in pilot limbo, turn on automation without guardrails, or forget the people side.

In the concluding chapter, we'll step back and look at the **bigger picture**: what an AI-augmented SOC means for the future of cybersecurity, how to communicate this journey to boards and non-technical leaders, and how to stay adaptable as both threats and AI technologies continue to evolve.

Chapter 15 – Real-World Stories: Wins, Failures & Lessons Learned

Frameworks are great. Runbooks are useful. But nothing sticks like **stories**—where real teams tried to use AI in the SOC and things actually happened.

This chapter gives you **fictionalized but realistic composites** drawn from patterns across many organizations. Names and details are sanitized, but the **problems, missteps, and breakthroughs** are all very real.

We'll look at:

1. A global enterprise that used AI triage to reduce alert fatigue
2. An automation "faceplant" where containment went too far
3. An MSSP scaling from 20 to 80 customers with AI
4. A highly regulated organization using AI under strict scrutiny
5. A small "SOC of One" that used AI to punch above its weight

For each case, we'll cover:

- Context & pain
- What they did
- What worked
- What went wrong
- Metrics and outcomes
- Lessons you can reuse

Use these as **conversation starters** with your own team:
"Which story are we closest to—and what can we steal from it?"

1. Global Enterprise: Killing Alert Fatigue with AI Triage

Context

- Industry: Global manufacturing and logistics
- SOC size: ~35 analysts across 3 regions
- Stack: SIEM + EDR + email security + basic SOAR
- Problem: ~30,000 alerts/day, chronic backlog, high turnover

Symptoms:

- Tier 1 analysts triaged alerts mechanically, with little context.
- Important identity and cloud alerts were buried in queues.
- Leadership was skeptical of "yet another tool," but something had to change.

What They Did

They decided to start with **AI-assisted triage**, not full automation:

1. **Defined clear use cases**
    - Prioritize identity and cloud access alerts.
    - Deprioritize obviously benign noise (repeated low-risk patterns).
2. **Deployed an AI triage engine (Level 0/1 only)**
    - The AI assistant scored alerts on a 0–100 scale and suggested:
        - "Likely benign"
        - "Suspicious – needs human review"
        - "High risk – work first"
    - No auto-closing, no auto-containment. Just ranking and tagging.
3. **Enriched alerts automatically via SOAR**
    - For each alert, SOAR fetched:
        - User role, department, and past behavior
        - Asset criticality and location
        - Threat intel for IPs/domains/hashes
    - AI used this context to refine scores.
4. **Ran in shadow mode for 60 days**
    - AI generated scores **but did not influence queues**.
    - They compared AI "would have" rankings with real analyst decisions.
5. **After validation, integrated into queue management**
    - Tier 1 console showed "AI priority score" and default sort order was by score.
    - Analysts could still override ordering, add filters, or ignore suggestions.

What Worked

- **Backlog dropped significantly**
    - They didn't magically reduce alert *volume*, but they drastically reduced time wasted on trivial alerts.
    - Analysts spent more time at the **top of the queue** where risk was highest.
- **Better focus on real attacks**
    - Identity-based attacks (impossible travel + MFA tampering) surfaced quickly.
    - Cloud misconfigurations and suspicious API usage were handled sooner.
- **Analysts felt supported, not replaced**
    - The team framed the AI assistant as "a junior colleague that pre-sorts your inbox."
    - Analysts could see when AI got it wrong and override it.
- **Concrete metrics**
  Over the first 6 months:
    - **Average time-to-first-triage (MTTA)** for high-risk identity alerts:
        - Before: ~3 hours
        - After: ~40 minutes
    - **Alerts handled per analyst per shift** (without increasing fatigue):
        - Before: ~80–100
        - After: ~140–160

- **Approximate triage time per alert**:
  - Before: ~6 minutes
  - After: ~3–4 minutes

What Went Wrong

It wasn't all smooth:

- **Initial model bias toward certain rules**
  - The AI over-weighted one noisy EDR rule that fired constantly for a legacy app.
  - Those alerts often ended up near the top of the queue without good reason.
  - Analysts started to distrust scores for endpoint alerts.
- **Data quality issues surfaced**
  - Assets with missing criticality tags got odd scores.
  - A server mis-tagged as "lab" led to under-prioritization of several meaningful alerts.

They responded by:

- Adjusting the model's feature weights
- Fixing CMDB and asset tagging
- Creating a "Do not prioritize based solely on rule X" guideline

Lessons Learned

1. **Start with prioritization, not auto-actions.**
   - It's low-risk, high-visibility, and easy to explain.
2. **Data quality will become painfully obvious.**
   - AI amplifies both good and bad data. Use that to justify fixes.
3. **Treat overrides as gold.**
   - They logged when analysts disagreed with AI scores and used that feedback to retrain.
4. **Win analyst trust early.**
   - Showing visible improvements in triage experience built support for later automation.

2. Automation Gone Wrong: When Containment Overreached

Context

- Industry: Regional healthcare group
- SOC size: ~12 analysts + 1 IR lead
- Stack: EDR with strong containment features; SIEM; SOAR
- Problem: Frequent commodity malware infections on user endpoints

They wanted to **reduce response time** and free analysts from repeating the same steps.

What They Did

They created an **automated playbook**:

- Trigger: High-confidence malware detection from EDR on a user endpoint.
- Actions:
    1. Isolate endpoint from the network
    2. Kill malicious process
    3. Block file hash in EDR policies
    4. Create ticket and notify helpdesk

They set this to **Level 2 autonomy** (conditional auto) with guardrails:

- Only endpoints tagged as "non-critical workstation"
- Only if detection confidence > certain threshold
- Only during business hours

It worked well in testing and for the first few weeks.

What Went Wrong

Then a **perfect storm** hit:

1. The EDR vendor pushed **a detection logic update** that mis-classified a widely used internal application DLL as malicious.
2. The SOC had **not fully tested** the updated logic in their environment.
3. Overnight, several dozen endpoints triggered the "known malware" detection.

Result:

- The SOAR playbook started to auto-isolate these endpoints.
- A large group of clinical staff arrived for morning shifts to find their endpoints disconnected.
- No immediate patient safety impact, but significant **operational disruption** in non-critical workflows.

How They Detected the Issue

- A spike in **isolation actions** appeared in SOAR logs.
- Analysts noticed many tickets with the same incident type but **no actual malicious behavior** on review.
- IT staff escalated user complaints quickly.

Response & Recovery

They:

1. **Hit the kill switch**
    - Disabled the malware auto-isolation playbook.
    - Placed similar alerts back into manual review mode.
2. **Rolled back containment**
    - Un-isolated affected endpoints via SOAR.
    - Coordinated with IT to validate the business application.
3. **Investigated root cause**
    - Identified the vendor logic change.
    - Added a pre-deployment test step for future detection updates.
4. **Updated guardrails**
    - Added rate limiting:
        - "Never auto-isolate more than N endpoints per 30 minutes."
    - Added an extra precondition:
        - Require at least one corroborating signal (e.g., suspicious process behavior, network IOCs) before auto-isolation.

Metrics & Impact

- About **40 endpoints** were auto-isolated incorrectly.
- Roughly **2–3 hours** of operational disruption for affected departments.
- No patient harm, but strong feedback from operational leaders and IT.

The SOC was able to recover in half a day, but trust took longer to rebuild.

Lessons Learned

1. **Guardrails need rate limits, not just conditions.**
    - Even correct logic can cause chaos if triggered at scale.
2. **Test automations after vendor rule changes.**
    - Especially when those changes involve high-confidence detections.
3. **Always have a visible kill switch and rollback path.**
    - Leadership calms down faster when you show you can stop and undo.
4. **Communicate boundaries clearly.**
    - After this, they documented:
        - "We will not auto-isolate anything in this subnet or with this tag."
        - "When detection engines change, automations go into monitored mode for X days."

Ironically, this "failure" made their automation program stronger and more mature—once the pain faded.

3. MSSP: Scaling from 20 to 80 Customers with AI

Context

- Organization: Managed Security Service Provider
- SOC size: ~25 analysts, 5 detection/automation engineers
- Customers: SMEs across multiple sectors
- Problem: They were stuck around **20 fully managed customers**; onboarding more meant hiring heavily. Margins were tight.

They wanted to use AI to **scale without burning out analysts** or diluting service quality.

What They Did

They focused on three pillars:

1. **Standardized multi-tenant runbooks**
   - Created **baseline playbooks** for common incident types:
     - Phishing, endpoint malware, identity anomalies, web attacks.
   - Added **per-tenant variations** (e.g., specific escalation contacts, critical asset lists).
2. **AI-assisted triage across tenants**
   - Integrated an AI triage engine and AI assistant with their multi-tenant SIEM and SOAR.
   - AI helped with:
     - Cross-tenant alert classification
     - Suggesting priority per tenant based on criticality and SLAs
     - Summarizing incidents into **client-ready narratives**
3. **AI-assisted reporting**
   - Quarterly reports and monthly summaries were a major time sink.
   - They wired an AI assistant into their ticketing and SIEM data to:
     - Draft client-specific incident summaries
     - Provide "Top 5 incidents this month" bullet lists
     - Generate graphs and narrative intros that analysts edited

What Worked

- **Onboarding workload dropped**
  - A new customer could be onboarded with a **standard package** of rules and runbooks.
  - AI helped suggest initial tuning options based on similar tenants.
- **Analyst efficiency increased**
  - Instead of deep-diving into each tenant console, analysts used:
    - Multi-tenant views with AI-driven prioritization
    - AI assistant summaries to quickly understand context
  - The SOC could comfortably grow to **80+ customers** over 18 months.

- **Reporting quality improved while time dropped**
    - Time spent per monthly report per tenant dropped from:
        - ~3–4 hours → ~1–1.5 hours
    - Yet clients felt they were getting **more insight**, not less:
        - Clearer narratives
        - More consistent structure
        - Faster turnaround

What Went Wrong

- **Early multi-tenant data confusion**
    - At first, the AI assistant sometimes mixed context between tenants in its narratives:
        - Mentioned assets or users from Tenant A in Tenant B's draft report.
    - This didn't leak raw logs outside the SOC, but it created trust issues internally.
- **Per-tenant policies were not adequately encoded**
    - Some tenants were more sensitive to auto-containment than others.
    - Initially, automations were too "global"; they had to add **per-tenant guardrails**.

They fixed it by:

- Making tenant context a **mandatory parameter** for AI queries and prompts.
- Forcing strict tenant-specific filtering in the retrieval layer before sending anything to the AI assistant.
- Creating **per-tenant autonomy profiles** (e.g., "Conservative", "Standard", "Aggressive") that the SOAR enforced.

Metrics & Outcomes

Over ~18 months:

- Customers: from ~20 → ~80 managed tenants.
- Analysts: modest increase from 25 → 32 (vs >50 projected without AI).
- Time spent on reporting: reduced by ~50–60%.
- AI adoption:
    - AI assistant used in ~70% of investigations.
    - AI-supported triage on >80% of alerts.

Lessons Learned

1. **Standardization + AI is the MSSP superpower.**
    - Start with repeatable playbooks, then let AI accelerate and adapt per tenant.
2. **Tenant boundaries must be enforced technically, not just "in our heads."**
    - Hard isolation in data retrieval and prompts is non-negotiable.
3. **Reporting is low-risk, high-value AI territory.**
    - Clients care deeply about clear reporting; AI can save huge time here with minimal risk.

4. **Per-tenant autonomy profiles avoid one-size-fits-all.**
    - Some clients want aggressive containment, others want maximum human review.

4. Highly Regulated Org: AI Under the Microscope

Context

- Industry: Financial services, heavily regulated
- SOC size: ~50 across regions, with dedicated risk/compliance partners
- Problem: Growing complexity of cloud and SaaS; static headcount

They had **zero tolerance** for "black box" systems. Everything needed to be explainable and auditable.

What They Did

They approached AI in the SOC as a **governance-first project**:

1. **Created an AI-in-SOC policy and RACI**
    - Documented allowed use cases:
        - Triage support, investigation summaries, CTI processing, reporting
    - Defined **disallowed** areas:
        - Autonomous high-impact actions
        - Direct modification of trading systems or core banking infrastructure
2. **Deployed AI assistants in suggestion-only mode (Level 0)**
    - AI assistant integrated with SIEM, case management, and CTI.
    - Analysts used it to:
        - Summarize incidents and logs
        - Draft incident reports
        - Suggest queries and hunts
3. **Instrumented everything**
    - Logged: prompts, responses, and any incident updates linked to AI assistance.
    - Created dashboards for:
        - AI usage
        - Time saved per case (estimated via case timing data)
4. **Engaged risk, legal, and audit early**
    - Demoed workflows and logs.
    - Showed how AI decisions were **advisory-only** and never directly changed controls.
    - Developed **AI incident** criteria (e.g., harmful hallucination or misleading recommendation used in a real case).

What Worked

- **Investigations and reporting sped up**

- o Average time to produce a **draft** incident report dropped significantly.
- o Analysts used AI to quickly explain complex multi-system logs in plain language.
- **Regulators were surprisingly receptive**
  - o When audits asked, "How are you using AI?", they could show:
    - Concrete policy
    - Example logs of AI usage
    - Clear human oversight at every step
  - o AI was framed as part of their **risk management improvement**, not a new risk.
- **Internal stakeholders saw practical value**
  - o Risk/compliance teams found AI-generated summaries useful for their own reviews.

What Went Wrong

- **Initial mistrust from analysts**
  - o Some feared being "graded" or replaced by the AI.
  - o Others assumed AI was more capable than it really was and followed early bad suggestions too closely.
- **Early hallucinations in CTI summaries**
  - o The AI sometimes over-interpreted CTI reports and implied stronger evidence of targeting than actually existed.

They responded by:

- Adding a **short training**:
  - o "AI assistant is a tool, not your boss. Here's how to challenge it."
- Adding a rule:
  - o For any CTI-based statement, the AI had to **reference specific report excerpts**.

Metrics & Outcomes

- Draft incident report time:
  - o Before: 90–120 minutes per significant incident
  - o After: 40–60 minutes (with AI drafts, human editing)
- CTI processing:
  - o Time from new CTI report → internal digest and recommended hunts dropped from **days** to **hours**.
- No AI-related adverse findings from internal audit or regulators over first 18 months.

Lessons Learned

1. **In regulated environments, suggestion-only AI is a strong first step.**
   - o It still delivers value without triggering autonomy concerns.
2. **Logging and explainability are not optional.**
   - o They are the price of entry if you want regulator trust.
3. **Train humans on how to use AI, not just how to configure it.**
   - o Cultural acceptance and critical thinking are key.

4. **CTI summarization is high-leverage but needs careful phrasing.**
   - "Based on this report, the actor has previously targeted…" is safer than "The actor is definitely targeting us now."

5. The "SOC of One": Punching Above Its Weight with AI

Context

- Industry: SaaS startup (~300 employees)
- Security team: 1 security engineer doing "SOC stuff" plus other responsibilities
- Stack: Cloud-native (cloud provider logs, SaaS security, EDR on laptops, simple SIEM)

Problem:
The "SOC of one" couldn't:

- Triages all alerts daily
- Run meaningful threat hunts
- Keep up with CTI and changing attack patterns

What They Did

They built a **lightweight AI-augmented SOC** without massive tooling:

1. **Consolidated logs in a simple SIEM**
   - Focused on:
     - Identity (IdP, VPN)
     - Cloud control plane logs
     - EDR on laptops
2. **Used an AI assistant for investigations & hunts**
   - Wired the SIEM to export recent relevant logs for a given incident.
   - Used the AI assistant to:
     - Summarize suspicious sessions
     - Suggest queries ("Find similar activity in last 7 days")
     - Draft Jira tickets and incident notes
3. **Automated a few low-risk playbooks via cloud-native tools**
   - Examples:
     - Force MFA for certain high-risk sign-ins
     - Auto-alert engineering on suspicious IAM changes
4. **Turned CTI into hunts with AI help**
   - Pasted CTI bulletins into the AI assistant.
   - Asked: "Turn this into 5 specific hunts for our stack."

What Worked

- **Single person could manage a reasonable detection footprint**

- o They couldn't cover everything—but they could cover **the most important things consistently**.
- o AI helped them "jump to the interesting part" instead of drowning in logs.
- **Hunts became realistic**
  - o Instead of copying queries from blogs, they had AI adapt them to their environment and log formats.
- **Documentation improved**
  - o Each significant incident ended up with notes and summaries that looked like they came from a larger team.

What Went Wrong

- **Over-reliance in the beginning**
  - o The security engineer sometimes accepted AI explanations without verifying them in raw logs.
  - o They almost misclassified a rare-but-benign admin job as malicious due to an over-enthusiastic AI summary.
- **No clear boundary between "engineering" and "SOC" tasks**
  - o AI freed up time, but that time was quickly eaten by other engineering work.
  - o Without explicit time allocation, the "SOC work" still risked being squeezed.

They corrected by:

- Building a habit:
  - o Always cross-check AI conclusions with at least one raw log query.
- Blocking dedicated **SOC hours** each day, protected by management.

Metrics & Outcomes

- The "SOC of one" could:
  - o Review high-risk alerts daily.
  - o Run at least one meaningful hunt per week.
  - o Produce clear incident documentation for leadership and customers when needed.
- They were able to **pass security reviews with larger clients**, who were impressed by the clarity of their incident process even if the team was small.

Lessons Learned

1. **AI won't replace headcount—but it can give a tiny team a fighting chance.**
   - o Especially for cloud-native startups.
2. **You still need discipline and time allocation.**
   - o AI can't fix prioritization of your own time.
3. **Verification is non-negotiable.**
   - o The more you rely on AI to interpret logs, the more you must sanity-check.
4. **Good documentation is a hidden superpower.**
   - o AI-assisted documentation improved customer and leadership confidence.

6. Bringing It Back to Your SOC

Across all five stories, common themes emerge:

- **Start small and safe.**
    - Prioritization, summarization, and reporting are excellent first AI use cases.
- **Guardrails are not optional.**
    - Rate limits, per-asset/per-tenant policies, and kill switches are what separate a clever lab demo from a safe production deployment.
- **Data quality and context drive AI value.**
    - Fix your asset tags, user context, and log normalization—it pays off twice with AI.
- **Human skills and culture matter as much as tools.**
    - Training analysts to **question** AI, provide feedback, and use it creatively is key.
- **Failures are normal—as long as they're survivable and learned from.**
    - Every mature program has at least one "Automation Gone Wrong" story. What matters is how you respond and improve.

In the next chapters, you'll see how these real-world patterns map into **concrete patterns & anti-patterns**, **role-based guides**, and **forward-looking roadmaps** that help you design your own AI-in-SOC journey with open eyes and solid footing.

Chapter 16 – Role-Based Guides: What This Journey Means for You

The AI-augmented SOC is not just a technology project.
It's a **people and roles** project.

The same changes that make the SOC faster and more effective will also:

- Change how **CISOs** talk about risk and investment
- Change how **SOC managers** run shifts and measure performance
- Change what **analysts** do hour to hour
- Change how **detection, automation, CTI, and platform teams** work together

This chapter translates the journey into **concrete guidance by role**:

1. For CISOs / Heads of Security
2. For SOC Managers / Leads
3. For Detection / Content Engineers
4. For Automation / SOAR / Platform Engineers
5. For SOC Analysts – Tier 1
6. For SOC Analysts – Tier 2 / Incident Responders
7. For Threat Hunters
8. For CTI Analysts
9. For IT / Cloud / Application Owners (Your Partners)
10. For Risk, Compliance & Audit

Each section covers:

- How AI changes your world
- What you're responsible for in an AI-augmented SOC
- What to do in the **next 90 days**
- Pitfalls to watch for

You can skip directly to the sections that match your role—or read everything to understand how your teammates see this journey.

---

1. For CISOs / Heads of Security

How AI Changes Your World

AI in the SOC:

- **Changes the economics** of detection and response (more coverage per person).

- **Changes the risk profile** (new failure modes: bad automation, model drift, data leakage).
- **Changes expectations** from boards and executives ("If AI exists, why are we still overwhelmed?").

Your job is to turn AI from a hype-fueled risk into a **governed, measurable capability** that supports your broader security strategy.

Your Responsibilities

1. **Define the "why" and desired outcomes**
    - Less alert fatigue?
    - Better response to high-severity incidents?
    - Scaling SOC coverage without linear headcount?
2. **Set risk appetite and autonomy boundaries**
    - Where are Level 0–1 (suggest-only / human-in-loop) acceptable?
    - Where, if anywhere, is Level 2 (conditional autonomy) acceptable?
    - Where is autonomy **never** acceptable (critical infra, OT, trading, safety)?
3. **Secure budget and cross-functional support**
    - Tools + people + process change, not just licenses.
    - Work with CIO, CTO, CRO, COO, etc.
4. **Integrate AI-in-SOC into governance**
    - Policies, standards, risk registers, incident classification.
    - Ensure AI failures and AI-related incidents are in scope.
5. **Communicate clearly to the board and executives**
    - Show progress using metrics from Chapter 11.
    - Be honest: "AI helps here, but not magically everywhere."

Your 90-Day Actions

- Ask your SOC lead for a **simple baseline**:
    - Alerts per day, MTTA/MTTR, key pain points.
- Approve 1–3 **low-risk AI use cases**:
    - E.g., AI assistant for incident summaries; AI triage suggestions.
- Commission an **AI-in-SOC policy draft** (use Appendix B).
- Decide and document **red lines**:
    - "No automation that can impact X systems without dual control."

Pitfalls to Avoid

- Treating AI as a side experiment with no clear owner.
- Demanding autonomy before the basics (data, process) are in place.
- Overpromising to the board ("AI will solve everything next quarter").
- Ignoring cultural fears in the SOC about replacement and monitoring.

2. For SOC Managers / Leads

How AI Changes Your World

AI changes:

- How you manage **queues and workloads**
- How you **measure performance**
- How you design **shifts, roles, and training**

You are the person who turns AI from "a feature in tools" into **daily, repeatable practice**.

Your Responsibilities

1. **Translate strategy into operations**
    - Which playbooks get AI assistance first?
    - Where does AI sit in your daily workflows?
    - How do we measure whether it is actually helping?
2. **Own AI adoption and feedback loops**
    - Ensure analysts know **how and when** to use the AI assistant.
    - Collect feedback: what works, what doesn't, false positives/negatives.
    - Feed that back to detection/automation/AI owners.
3. **Adjust roles and KPIs**
    - Move from "how many alerts did you close?" to:
        - How well did you handle priority incidents?
        - How much time did you invest in improvement work?
    - Reward analysts for **using AI wisely**, not just clicking faster.
4. **Protect team morale**
    - Frame AI as a way to **reduce toil**, not grade or replace people.
    - Encourage analysts to **question AI outputs**.

Your 90-Day Actions

- Identify **3–5 workflows** where AI can help immediately:
    - Alert summaries, initial triage, incident documentation, report drafts.
- Work with detection/automation teams to integrate AI into **case management views**.
- Run a **brief training session**:
    - What the AI assistant can do
    - Example prompts
    - How to override and flag bad outputs
- Start tracking:
    - Time per triage (before/after AI)
    - Analyst usage of AI (rough counts)
    - Qualitative feedback

Pitfalls to Avoid

- Treating AI usage as optional "if you feel like it" forever.
- Or, opposite extreme: forcing AI usage without addressing shortcomings.
- Not giving analysts time to **experiment and learn** the assistant.
- Ignoring metrics—if you don't measure, you can't defend or tune.

3. For Detection / Content Engineers

How AI Changes Your World

AI doesn't replace detection engineering; it **multiplies** it.

- AI helps you **draft rules**, not decide what to detect.
- AI can cluster and score alerts, but **you define logic and thresholds**.
- Your work becomes the **bridge between CTI, incidents, and AI models**.

Your Responsibilities

1. **Design detection content with AI in mind**
   - Clear rule descriptions, tags, and metadata for AI to interpret.
   - Consistent naming conventions and severity levels.
   - Enrich rules with references (CTI, MITRE ATT&CK).
2. **Use AI as a partner**
   - Generate initial rule drafts from CTI or incident stories.
   - Ask AI to propose test cases, attack simulations, regression tests.
   - Use AI to suggest **related detections** for a given TTP.
3. **Feed AI with ground truth**
   - Label alerts: TP / FP / "Legacy rule; ignore" where feasible.
   - Document why rules were tuned or disabled.
   - Provide clean examples of "good vs bad" for training/validation.
4. **Review AI-generated detections and logic**
   - Never deploy AI-suggested rules blindly.
   - Evaluate performance metrics (TP/FP, coverage of known incidents).

Your 90-Day Actions

- Take **1–2 high-volume rules** and:
  - Use AI to analyze false positives and propose improvements.
  - Run a test campaign with improved logic.
- Choose a recent incident and:
  - Use AI to draft detection content covering multiple stages of the kill chain.
  - Review, refine, and push to test.
- Work with SOC manager to:
  - Set up a simple process to capture **labelled outcomes** from analysts.

Pitfalls to Avoid

- Over-trusting AI to "know what to detect" out of thin air.
- Generating too many complex rules that are impossible to understand or maintain.
- Failing to close the loop: letting AI suggest logic, but never measuring how it performs.
- Treating detection engineering as "just rule writing" instead of **system design**.

4. For Automation / SOAR / Platform Engineers

How AI Changes Your World

You become the **safety engineer** for the SOC's AI.

- AI proposes and scores; your automations **enforce and act**.
- You encode **guardrails, rate limits, and kill switches**.
- You own the logs and observability that prove to leadership that AI is safe.

Your Responsibilities

1. **Implement autonomy levels and guardrails**
    - Explicitly mark each playbook step:
        - Manual only
        - AI-suggested, human-approved
        - Auto-if-safe, with preconditions
    - Use:
        - Asset tags
        - Tenant IDs
        - Environment flags (dev/prod/OT)
        - Rate limits
2. **Centralize control**
    - Make SOAR the **control plane** where AI suggestions become actions.
    - Avoid scattered scripts that bypass guardrails.
3. **Instrument automations for observability**
    - Log **inputs, decisions, and actions**.
    - Track:
        - Number of auto-actions
        - Overrides and rollbacks
        - Failures and near-misses
4. **Test and simulate**
    - Build test harnesses for playbooks.
    - Replay historical incidents with new automation + AI logic.

Your 90-Day Actions

- Inventory existing automations and classify:
    - Safe for potential Level 2 (conditional auto)
    - Human-in-loop only

- Too dangerous for autonomy
- For 1–2 **low-risk incident types** (e.g., commodity malware on non-critical endpoints):
  - Design or refine playbooks with **clear preconditions** and **rate limits**.
- Implement a **kill-switch mechanism**:
  - E.g., a central flag or config that can disable specific playbooks instantly.
- Start a small dashboard showing:
  - Auto-actions over time
  - Overrides/rollbacks
  - Failures

Pitfalls to Avoid

- "Everything-autonomous" mindset; trying to automate high-risk steps too soon.
- Lack of visibility—no idea what automations are currently doing or how often.
- Letting AI directly call enforcement APIs without your guardrails in between.
- Underestimating **multi-tenant complexity** if you're an MSSP.

5. For SOC Analysts – Tier 1

How AI Changes Your World

Your job becomes less about:

- Copy-pasting data between consoles
- Writing repetitive ticket notes

And more about:

- **Validating AI summaries and scores**
- Deciding what to escalate and how
- Providing feedback that makes rules and AI smarter

The AI assistant is a **power tool**—you still decide what gets cut.

Your Responsibilities

1. **Use the AI assistant actively (not passively)**
   - Ask for:
     - Alert summaries
     - Context ("What has this user/host done in last 24–72h?")
     - Suggested next steps or queries
2. **Critically evaluate AI output**
   - Check AI's summary against raw alerts and logs.
   - If something feels off, dig deeper.
3. **Make clear decisions and document them**

- o FP / TP / escalate / close with reason.
- o Your decisions become **training data** and tuning signals.
4. **Flag AI problems**
   - o When AI recommends something wrong or misses important context, note it.
   - o Use defined channels to send feedback to your lead or engineers.

Your 90-Day Actions

- Learn a **handful of core prompts** (from Appendix A) and practice daily:
   - o "Summarize this alert in 3–5 bullet points for a Tier 1 analyst."
   - o "Show me recent activity for this user/host/IP in the last 24 hours."
   - o "Suggest 3 questions I should answer before deciding on escalation."
- Start writing **slightly richer notes**:
   - o Don't just write "False positive."
   - o Write "False positive because X; rule seems to trigger on Y."
- Keep a **personal list of where AI helps you most**:
   - o Have a 10–15 minute retro at the end of a week:
     - ▪ "Where did the AI assistant save me time?"
     - ▪ "Where did it confuse me?"

Pitfalls to Avoid

- Copy-pasting AI conclusions without verification.
- Not using the assistant at all and falling back into old habits.
- Being afraid to say, "The AI is wrong here."
- Thinking "If I use AI, leadership will think I'm lazier or less skilled." (It's the opposite when used well.)

6. For SOC Analysts – Tier 2 / Incident Responders

How AI Changes Your World

Your focus shifts further toward:

- **Complex investigations and coordination**
- **Hypothesis-driven analysis**, not just alert handling
- Acting as **editor-in-chief** for AI-assisted outputs.

Your Responsibilities

1. **Direct the AI assistant with high-quality questions**
   - o Multi-step investigations:
     - ▪ "Build a timeline of events related to this user and host between T1 and T2."
     - ▪ "Group these alerts into plausible incidents and describe each one."

2. **Lead containment decisions**
    - Use AI for context and options, **you** decide containment paths.
    - Ensure Level 2 automation is appropriate for the scenario.
3. **Mentor Tier 1s in using AI effectively**
    - Share prompts, "do/don't" examples.
    - Show how to validate AI outputs.
4. **Feed improvements back into detections and playbooks**
    - From each major incident, identify:
        - What AI did well
        - Where it misled you
        - What new detection or automation ideas come out of the case

Your 90-Day Actions

- Use AI to **draft timelines and incident reports** for your next few major cases.
- After each incident, spend 10–15 minutes answering:
    - "What could the AI assistant have done better?"
    - "What new rule/playbook idea came from this?"
- Pair with detection/automation engineers:
    - Share 2–3 incidents where AI insights could be codified into rules or workflows.

Pitfalls to Avoid

- Treating AI assistants as infallible "brains" instead of junior helpers.
- Failing to capture insights in the KB / wiki because "AI can just regenerate it later."
- Ignoring AI-related oddities that might indicate **model drift** or poor integration.

7. For Threat Hunters

How AI Changes Your World

AI becomes your **accelerator and research assistant**.

- Converts CTI and past incidents into hunt ideas faster.
- Helps generate and refine complex queries.
- Summarizes large volumes of log output and weird patterns.

Your Responsibilities

1. **Turn AI into a hypothesis engine**
    - "Given this TTP, propose 3–5 hunts across our SIEM/EDR/identity logs."
    - "Compare behaviors across similar hosts/users and highlight anomalies."
2. **Validate and refine AI suggestions**
    - Discard nonsense or low-value hunts.
    - Focus on hunts that are both plausible and impactful.

3. **Feed hunts back into detections and models**
      - Turn successful hunts into:
        - Permanent detections
        - Hunt templates
        - Training data for anomaly models
   4. **Document repeatable patterns**
      - Use AI to help write hunt runbooks and notes.
      - Ensure others can reproduce hunts, not just you.

Your 90-Day Actions

- Take 1–2 CTI bulletins and:
  - Use AI to propose hunts customized to your environment.
  - Run them, then refine both the hunts and the prompts.
- Start a "Hunt Library":
  - For each new hunt:
    - Hypothesis
    - Data sources
    - Queries
    - Example outputs
    - Possible detections
- Work with AI/detection teams:
  - Identify which hunts are good candidates for **ongoing detection**.

Pitfalls to Avoid

- Chasing AI-generated "cool" hunts that don't align with your threat model.
- Over-hunting on poor-quality or sparse data that AI made look interesting.
- Not closing the loop from hunts → detections → training signals.

8. For CTI Analysts

How AI Changes Your World

AI can chew through:

- Long CTI reports
- Feeds and blog posts
- OSINT

...and help you:

- Summarize quickly
- Map threats to your environment
- Generate detection and hunt ideas

Your Responsibilities

1. **Curate and contextualize, don't just summarize**
   - AI can summarize, but you decide:
     - Is this relevant to us?
     - Which business units / geos / tech stacks are at risk?
2. **Turn intelligence into actions**
   - With AI assistance, generate:
     - Detection suggestions
     - Hunt templates
     - Hardening recommendations
3. **Ensure accuracy of AI summaries**
   - Cross-check AI output with original reports.
   - Avoid overstating targeting or certainty.
4. **Collaborate with detection, hunting, and SOC teams**
   - Deliver CTI in **SOC-friendly formats**:
     - Short, structured, actionable.

Your 90-Day Actions

- For each major CTI report:
  - Use AI to draft:
    - Executive summary
    - Technical summary
    - "Actions we should take in our environment"
- Start a "CTI → Action" tracking list:
  - CTI source
  - Related detections/hunts created
  - Status

Pitfalls to Avoid

- Letting AI exaggerate threat relevance ("They are targeting us!" when unproven).
- Flooding SOC with AI-generated CTI junk.
- Skipping the **relevance filter** that only a human with context can apply.

9. For IT / Cloud / Application Owners (Your Partners)

How AI Changes Your World

AI in the SOC will:

- Trigger **more and faster requests** for configuration changes, fixes, and hardening.
- Possibly auto-contain or auto-block in domains you care about.

You become a key **stakeholder** in decisions about autonomy and guardrails.

Your Responsibilities

1. **Clarify criticality and business impact**
   - Maintain accurate tags for:
     - Critical apps
     - Sensitive data stores
     - Production vs test
   - These tags directly affect AI-driven prioritization and automation.
2. **Agree on where autonomy is acceptable**
   - Work with SOC to define:
     - Which endpoints or services can be auto-isolated
     - Which changes always require human approval
3. **Participate in playbook and guardrail design**
   - Validate that automation steps match reality:
     - Maintenance windows
     - Known exceptions
     - Legacy quirks

Your 90-Day Actions

- Review asset tagging/CMDB for **glaring gaps** affecting automation decisions.
- Join at least one **playbook design session** for a scenario touching your systems (e.g., app server malware, database exfil alert).
- Agree with SOC on:
  - "What's too risky to automate."
  - "What's safe to automate for speed."

Pitfalls to Avoid

- Letting SOC guess about app criticality and acceptable downtime.
- Ignoring SOC requests for tagging and configuration support.
- Being surprised when an automation affects your environment because you weren't involved in guardrail discussions.

---

10. For Risk, Compliance & Audit

How AI Changes Your World

AI in the SOC touches your concerns directly:

- **Model risk, data privacy, operational risk**
- New **documentation and audit trails**
- New types of incidents ("AI-related incident")

Your role is to ensure AI **reduces risk overall**, while being explainable and compliant.

Your Responsibilities

1. **Integrate AI into risk frameworks**
   - Add **AI-in-SOC** topics into:
     - Risk registers
     - Control libraries
     - Internal audit plans
2. **Review AI-in-SOC policies and guardrails**
   - Ensure documented:
     - Autonomy levels
     - Use cases
     - Data usage and residency
     - Roles & responsibilities
3. **Check logging and explainability**
   - Confirm:
     - AI recommendations and automated actions are logged.
     - There is a way to reconstruct "why" an action was taken.
4. **Participate in AI incident reviews**
   - When AI misbehaves or contributes to an incident, be part of:
     - Root cause analysis
     - Control improvements

Your 90-Day Actions

- Review the **AI-in-SOC policy** draft (Appendix B style) and provide feedback.
- Ask SOC to demonstrate:
  - Where AI is used today
  - How decisions and actions are logged
  - Where humans remain in control
- Add a section to your **audit or risk plan**:
  - "Controls for AI-enabled security operations."

Pitfalls to Avoid

- Treating AI purely as a risk to be minimized rather than a control to be harnessed.
- Asking for "zero AI risk" (impossible) instead of **managed, documented risk**.
- Caricaturing AI as magic or as inherently non-compliant.

Key Takeaways from Chapter 16

An AI-augmented SOC is a **team sport**:

- **CISOs** set direction, risk appetite, and secure investment.
- **SOC managers** operationalize AI and manage adoption.

- **Detection and automation engineers** translate strategy into content, workflows, and guardrails.
- **Analysts, hunters, and CTI** turn AI from a generic tool into **applied insight**.
- **IT, cloud, app owners, risk and audit** ensure AI operates safely in the real business context.

If you read only your own section, here's the one universal message:

AI is your assistant, not your replacement. Your judgement is still the control that ultimately matters.

In the next chapter, we'll zoom out again to look at **patterns and anti-patterns** across organizations—concrete do's and don'ts that you can check against your own AI-in-SOC journey, regardless of your role.

Chapter 17 – Patterns & Anti-Patterns for AI in the SOC

By this point, we've seen architectures, guardrails, stories, and role guides. This chapter is the **cheat sheet**: what tends to *work* in real SOCs—and what tends to *hurt*.

Think of it as:

- A pattern library you can **copy on purpose**, and
- A list of traps you can **spot early and avoid**.

We'll cover:

1. Why patterns & anti-patterns matter
2. Core patterns for AI in the SOC
3. Common anti-patterns (and how to fix them)
4. A quick pattern vs anti-pattern comparison table
5. A self-check you can run on your own program

1. Why Patterns & Anti-Patterns Matter

When you add AI to the SOC, you're not starting from zero. You're layering AI onto:

- Existing processes
- Existing tools
- Existing culture and skill levels

Patterns and anti-patterns help you answer:

- "Are we moving in a direction that tends to work elsewhere?"
- "Does what we're doing *feel* right—but has actually burned other teams before?"

You'll never copy a pattern 1:1, but you can use these as **north stars and warning signs**.

2. Core Patterns for AI in the SOC

These are the patterns that show up again and again in successful AI-enabled SOCs.

2.1. Pattern 1 – "Suggest First, Then Automate"

What it is

You introduce AI in **Level 0 (suggest-only)** and **Level 1 (human-in-loop)** modes first:

- AI assistant for summarizing alerts, incidents, and CTI
- AI scoring and prioritizing alerts, but **not closing or containing**
- AI drafting reports and timelines that humans edit

Only after this is stable do you move a small number of flows to **Level 2 (conditional autonomy)**.

Why it works

- Builds trust with analysts and leadership
- Exposes data quality problems without causing outages
- Gives you time to refine prompts, models, and workflows

Signals you're doing it

- Most AI usage lives in:
    - Triage suggestions
    - Investigation assistance
    - Documentation & reporting
- You can point to at least 1–2 **concrete improvements** (time saved, better MTTA) before any auto-actions.

2.2. Pattern 2 – "Decisions in AI, Actions in SOAR"

What it is

You keep a clear separation:

- AI systems **decide and recommend**:
    - Risk scores
    - Classifications (benign/suspicious/malicious)
    - Proposed actions
- SOAR / orchestration **enforces**:
    - Executes actions with guardrails
    - Applies policy, asset tags, tenant logic, and rate limits
    - Logs everything centrally

Why it works

- Guardrails and policies live in **one control plane** (SOAR), not scattered.
- You can improve or swap AI models without rewriting all enforcement logic.
- Easier to explain to auditors:
    - "AI suggests, SOAR enforces under policy."

Signals you're doing it

- AI outputs go into structured fields (e.g., suggested_action, risk_score).
- SOAR workflows check:
  - Asset criticality
  - Tenant
  - Time of day
  - Rate limits
- AI never directly calls firewall / IAM / EDR APIs.

2.3. Pattern 3 – "Guardrails by Design, Not by Accident"

What it is

You design guardrails as **first-class objects**, not afterthoughts:

- Autonomy levels defined per playbook and action
- Preconditions (score thresholds, asset/tenant filters) are explicit
- Rate limits and kill switches are documented and tested
- Rollback steps are built into playbooks

Why it works

- Limits blast radius when something goes wrong
- Makes leadership and regulators more comfortable with automation
- Makes it easier to iterate without fear

Signals you're doing it

- You can:
  - Show a **list of automations**, their autonomy level, and their owners
  - Demonstrate a **kill switch** in a test environment
  - Explain for any playbook:
    - "This part is AI-suggest-only."
    - "This part can auto-run, but only for these endpoints/tenants."

2.4. Pattern 4 – "Standardize First, Then Scale with AI"

What it is

Before you lean heavily into AI, you:

- Standardize **playbooks** for your top incident types
- Standardize **ticket fields** and incident categories
- Standardize **detection naming** and metadata

Then:

- AI assists with those standard workflows
- You expand from a small, consistent base

Why it works

- AI thrives on consistent patterns and fields
- Makes metrics and ROI clearer (same process, now faster/better)
- For MSSPs, makes per-tenant variance manageable

Signals you're doing it

- You have:
    - A documented set of high-volume playbooks
    - Standard incident types and fields
    - A detection catalog with owners
- AI prompts reference **common structures**, not one-off quirks.

2.5. Pattern 5 – "Data-First AI"

What it is

You prioritize:

- Reliable ingestion of key data (identity, EDR, network/edge, cloud)
- Normalization and enrichment (user/asset context, CTI, tags)
- Observability for data quality (missing sources, parsing errors)

Only then do you expect AI to:

- Triage effectively
- Spot anomalies
- Support good hunting

Why it works

- AI amplifies data quality: good in → great value out; bad in → chaos.
- Data investments benefit **both AI and traditional detections**.

Signals you're doing it

- You monitor:
    - % endpoints reporting
    - % critical assets onboarded

- Log ingestion errors / gaps
- Adding a new log source includes:
    - Parsing
    - Mapping
    - Context enrichment

2.6. Pattern 6 – "Human Feedback Loops"

What it is

You treat analysts' interactions as **training signals**, not noise:

- They can easily mark:
    - "AI was wrong here (and why)"
    - "This suggestion was helpful"
- Their labels (TP/FP, reason, context) feed back into:
    - Detection tuning
    - Model retraining
    - Playbook improvements

Why it works

- AI and detections evolve based on **real-world use**, not theory.
- Analysts feel involved instead of overruled.

Signals you're doing it

- You can show:
    - A place in the UI where analysts give feedback
    - Periodic reviews of that feedback by detection/AI owners
- You have at least a basic process:
    - "Every month we look at overrides and adjust where needed."

2.7. Pattern 7 – "Safe Early Wins"

What it is

You start AI usage in **low-risk, high-annoyance** areas:

- Incident summaries
- Report drafts
- CTI digesting
- KB article drafts
- Case timelines

Why it works

- Delivers immediate visible value
- Has low operational risk
- Builds confidence and usage habits

Signals you're doing it

- Analysts:
    - Regularly use AI to draft reports and summaries
    - Still review and adjust them
- CTI teams:
    - Use AI to turn long reports into SOC-ready actions

2.8. Pattern 8 – "Multi-Tenant and Context-Aware by Design"

(Especially for MSSPs or large enterprises with multiple BUs.)

What it is

You design AI and automation to **respect boundaries**:

- Tenant-aware queries and prompts
- Per-tenant policies and autonomy levels
- Context-aware decisions (e.g., environment, region, line of business)

Why it works

- Prevents cross-tenant data leakage or confusion
- Lets you tailor risk tolerance and autonomy individually
- Makes reporting and SLAs manageable

Signals you're doing it

- Tenant ID / BU / environment are **explicit parameters** in AI calls and automations.
- You can point to:
    - A "conservative" profile for some tenants
    - A "standard" or "aggressive" profile for others

2.9. Pattern 9 – "Metrics-Driven AI Adoption"

What it is

You:

- Establish baselines (Chapter 11)
- Track a small set of KPIs before and after AI
- Use numbers to decide:
    - Expand this use case
    - Rework or kill that one

Why it works

- Helps you justify spend and changes
- Avoids running AI "because it's cool"
- Focuses effort on what moves the needle

Signals you're doing it

- You know:
    - How triage time changed after AI assistance
    - How often AI suggestions are overridden
    - Whether automation actually impacts MTTR

3. Common Anti-Patterns (and How to Fix Them)

Now the fun (and slightly painful) part: the **things that look appealing but typically burn teams.**

3.1. Anti-Pattern 1 – "AI First, Data Later"

What it looks like

- You turn on AI features while:
    - Key logs are missing
    - Asset/user context is incomplete
    - Data is noisy and unnormalized

You hope AI will "figure it out" anyway.

Why it's harmful

- AI surfaces nonsense and misses important context
- Analysts lose trust in the tool quickly
- You make bad decisions based on incomplete pictures

How to fix it

- Pause or scope AI usage to **narrow domains** where data is solid.
- Run a **data readiness review**:
    - Identity, EDR, cloud, critical assets.
- Invest in normalization and enrichment before expanding AI.

3.2. Anti-Pattern 2 – "Big Bang Automation"

What it looks like

- You massively expand auto-remediation based on:
    - "High-confidence" detections
    - Vendor encouragement
- Many playbooks jump from manual → fully autonomous at once.

Why it's harmful

- High risk of business disruption (Case 2 in Chapter 14).
- No time to validate in shadow mode or semi-auto.
- One bad rule or vendor update can isolate or block half your environment.

How to fix it

- Roll back to:
    - **Suggest-only** for most actions (Level 0–1).
    - Level 2 autonomy only for:
        - Narrow, well-understood, low-impact cases.
- Add:
    - Preconditions
    - Rate limits
    - Kill switches
    - Clear rollback steps

3.3. Anti-Pattern 3 – "Magic Box Vendor"

What it looks like

- Vendor promises:
    - "We detect all threats automatically with our proprietary AI."
    - "Just send us your logs; no tuning or context needed."

No clear explanation of:

- Data requirements
- Error modes

- How analysts interact with it

Why it's harmful

- Misaligned expectations with leadership
- Difficult to tune or debug
- Hard to defend to auditors or in post-incident reviews

How to fix it

- Demand:
  - Concrete use-case demos on **your data**, not generic slides
  - Explainability at least at a high level
  - Integration points and feedback loops
- If you get vague or evasive answers, treat as a **major risk**.

3.4. Anti-Pattern 4 – "Pilot Forever"

What it looks like

- AI features live in a **permanent POC**:
  - A few enthusiasts use them in a corner.
  - No formal adoption, metrics, or roadmap.
- The organization never commits—nor shuts it down.

Why it's harmful

- Wastes time and money.
- Confuses staff about whether AI is "real" or not.
- Prevents you from getting enough usage data to improve.

How to fix it

- Set **clear success and failure criteria** for pilots:
  - Timeframe (e.g., 90 days)
  - Metrics (triage time, usage, satisfaction)
- At the end, decide:
  - Scale it
  - Adjust and re-test
  - Or shut it down
- Communicate decisions clearly.

3.5. Anti-Pattern 5 – "Alert Washing with AI"

What it looks like

- You use AI primarily to **auto-close or suppress** alerts to reduce numbers.
- No strong justification or monitoring of what's being suppressed.
- "Look, alert volume is down!" becomes the main success metric.

Why it's harmful

- Real threats can be buried.
- Metrics look better while risk actually increases.
- Analysts might miss patterns that AI also misses.

How to fix it

- Require:
    - Multi-signal logic for suppression (not just one rule + AI guess).
    - Periodic sampling of suppressed alerts for quality.
- Track:
    - How many confirmed incidents originated from alert types currently suppressed.
- Focus AI triage on **prioritization**, not just aggressive suppression.

3.6. Anti-Pattern 6 – "Shadow AI & Shadow Automations"

What it looks like

- Individual engineers or teams:
    - Use unsanctioned AI scripts and automations
    - Connect to production systems without central oversight

Everyone is "experimenting," but:

- No shared guardrails
- No central logs
- No RACI

Why it's harmful

- Inconsistent behavior and unexpected side effects
- Hard to troubleshoot issues in incidents ("Who wrote this script?")
- Compliance and audit nightmares

How to fix it

- Create **official paths** for experiments:
    - Lab / non-prod environments
    - Documented scripts and runbooks
    - Review and promotion process to production
- Make it easier to do the **right thing** than the shadow thing.

3.7. Anti-Pattern 7 – "Ownerless AI"

What it looks like

- AI features exist, but:
    - No clear owner for quality and behavior
    - No one accountable for monitoring or improvement

Why it's harmful

- Problems go unnoticed or unresolved
- Models drift or become misaligned with current threats
- Feedback from analysts has nowhere to land

How to fix it

- Assign a named owner:
    - "AI-in-SOC product owner" or equivalent
- Define responsibilities:
    - Usage monitoring
    - Coordination with detection/automation
    - Roadmap and communication

3.8. Anti-Pattern 8 – "Humans Not in the Loop (Culturally)"

What it looks like

- Analysts feel:
    - They're not allowed to question AI
    - Decisions are "AI said so, end of story"
- Or they fear:
    - Using AI will be seen as laziness
    - Their own judgement doesn't matter

Why it's harmful

- Either:
  - Blind trust in AI → latent failures
  - Or refusal to use AI → wasted investment

How to fix it

- Train analysts explicitly:
  - "Your job is to **challenge** and **verify** AI, not worship it."
- Celebrate:
  - Cases where an analyst caught an AI mistake.
- Make AI usage part of:
  - Training
  - Playbooks
  - Performance conversations (as a tool, not a scorecard).

3.9. Anti-Pattern 9 – "No Kill Switch, No Rollback"

What it looks like

- You have automations and AI-driven actions, but:
  - No obvious way to stop them quickly
  - No simple rollback path

Why it's harmful

- When something goes wrong:
  - Outage lasts longer than necessary
  - Panic escalates
  - Leadership loses trust

How to fix it

- Implement:
  - Central toggles for each automation or playbook
  - Documented rollback steps for each action type
- Test:
  - Kill switch behavior in drills
  - "We press this and see X stop in logs, Y actions cease."

4. Patterns vs Anti-Patterns – Quick Comparison

Use this table as a quick sanity check:

Area	Good Pattern	Anti-Pattern
Rollout Approach	Suggest-first, then small autonomy in low-risk areas	Big-bang auto-remediation everywhere
Data Strategy	Fix key telemetry & context before relying on AI	"AI will cope with bad/incomplete data"
Architecture	Decisions in AI, actions in SOAR with guardrails	AI directly calls enforcement APIs
Governance	Clear AI owners, autonomy levels, guardrails	Ownerless AI, fuzzy rules, no documented boundaries
Culture	Analysts challenge AI, feedback loops in place	Blind trust or total rejection of AI
Metrics	Measure triage time, MTTA, quality, usage	"We reduced alert count" as the only metric
Multi-Tenant	Tenant-aware prompts, per-tenant policies	AI mixing context across tenants/BUs
Testing	Shadow mode, replay, simulations before enabling autonomy	Turning on autonomy straight in production
Response to Issues	Kill switch, rollback, PIR including AI aspects	Ad-hoc scrambling, no lessons incorporated

5. A Self-Check for Your AI-in-SOC Program

You can use this 10-question self-check with your team. Answer honestly, Yes/No:

1. Do we have **named owners** for AI in the SOC (product/feature ownership)?
2. Do we run AI first in **suggest-only modes** before letting it influence automations?
3. Can we **turn off** each major AI-driven automation or feature quickly and safely?
4. Do we track at least **3–5 metrics** showing AI's impact (time, quality, risk)?
5. Are autonomy levels and guardrails **documented per playbook**, not just in someone's head?
6. Do analysts have a **clear way to give feedback** when AI is wrong or confusing?
7. Do we do **shadow mode / replay** testing before enabling autonomy for a new scenario?
8. Is our **core telemetry** (identity, EDR, cloud, critical assets) reasonably complete and monitored?
9. Do risk/compliance know where AI is used and how we control it?
10. Have we explicitly decided on **use cases AI will not handle** (for now or ever)?

Rough interpretation:

- 8–10 "Yes" → You're mostly following good patterns; now focus on refining.
- 5–7 "Yes" → You're on the way, but some important anti-patterns may be forming.
- ≤4 "Yes" → Treat this as a warning—slow down autonomy, focus on foundations and governance.

Key Takeaways from Chapter 17

AI in the SOC is not about being clever—it's about being **deliberate**.

- Choose patterns that are repeatable and explainable.
- Hunt for anti-patterns early and fix them before they harden into habits.
- Use these patterns as shared language:
    - "We're trying to move from 'Big Bang Automation' to 'Suggest First, Then Automate'."
    - "We want 'Decisions in AI, Actions in SOAR,' not another magic box."

In the next chapters and appendices, you'll have checklists, worksheets, and templates to help embed these patterns into your roadmap, your tooling decisions, and your daily operations.

Chapter 18 – Ethics, Bias & Human Impact of AI in Security Operations

When most people hear "ethics in AI," they think of self-driving cars or social media algorithms. But AI in the SOC is just as ethically loaded—just in quieter, less obvious ways.

- We process **sensitive logs about people's digital lives**.
- We flag certain users as "risky" and others as "normal."
- We decide when to **monitor, contain, or disrupt** systems people rely on.
- We may automate actions that impact **jobs, access, or trust**.

This chapter is about making sure your AI-augmented SOC:

Reduces risk without quietly eroding privacy, fairness, and trust.

We'll cover:

1. Why ethics and human impact matter in the SOC
2. Bias in data, detections, and AI decisions
3. Privacy, monitoring, and responsible use of employee data
4. Explainability, accountability, and the "who is responsible?" question
5. Human impact on analysts: wellbeing, skills, and culture
6. Handling AI errors and AI-related incidents ethically
7. Practical principles and checklists for ethical AI in the SOC

Use this as a **guardrail overlay** on everything else in the book.

1. Why Ethics & Human Impact Matter in the SOC

It's tempting to think:

"We're security. We defend the business. Ethics is someone else's department."

But security operations already sit at a sensitive crossroads:

- You see **more about people's behavior** than almost any other function.
- You hold tools that can **limit access, monitor activity, and disrupt workflows**.
- You're under pressure to move fast—and now AI can accelerate you further.

Add AI and you magnify both sides:

- Done well:
    - You detect threats earlier, reduce breaches, and protect people and customers.
- Done badly:

- You over-monitor, mislabel employees as threats, or let opaque systems quietly steer decisions.

Ethics in AI for the SOC boils down to three big questions:

1. **Are we fair?**
   - Are we systematically treating some users, locations, or behaviors as riskier in unjustified ways?
2. **Are we respectful of privacy and dignity?**
   - Do we log and analyze only what we need?
   - Are we transparent about monitoring?
3. **Are we accountable?**
   - When AI is wrong—or harmful—can we explain and correct it?
   - Is there a named human responsibility?

Keep those questions in mind as we unpack the details.

2. Bias in Data, Detections & AI Decisions

Bias in AI isn't just an abstract academic concern. In a SOC, it can show up as:

- Certain users or regions getting more scrutiny than others
- Legitimate behavior being constantly flagged for particular teams
- Missed detection for rare but critical patterns because the model learned from "normal" logs

2.1. Where Bias Comes From

Bias often creeps in from:

1. **Biased data**
   - Historical logs reflect past decisions, which may themselves be biased.
   - Example: If past investigations focused heavily on certain geos or teams, training data will overrepresent those groups as "suspicious."
2. **Skewed feedback loops**
   - If analysts are more likely to escalate incidents for certain users or environments, models will learn those associations.
3. **Detection content and rules**
   - Rules designed with a narrow mental model ("bad logins from Country X") may become encoded in training sets.
4. **Missing context**
   - Lack of accurate asset criticality, role, business function leads models to use weaker proxies (IP ranges, login times, geolocation).

2.2. How Bias Shows Up in Practice

Concrete signs of bias:

- **Alert patterns**
    - A small subset of users or teams generates a disproportionate share of "suspicious" alerts, with very few confirmed incidents.
- **Investigation outcomes**
    - Certain categories of alerts almost never become confirmed incidents but consume a lot of time for specific groups.
- **Model behavior**
    - Anomaly models flag normal activity for night-shift teams, remote workers, or specific geographies simply because training data skewed toward 9–5, HQ-based work.

2.3. Mitigating Bias in AI-Driven SOC Workflows

You can't eliminate bias completely—but you can **actively manage it**.

1. **Diversify training and evaluation data**
    - Use data from:
        - Different regions, business units, and time periods.
    - When evaluating model performance, inspect breakdowns:
        - By region, department, user role, time-of-day.
2. **Introduce explicit guardrails against obvious proxies**
    - Avoid rules or models that rely solely on sensitive proxies like:
        - Country alone
        - Language alone
        - Work schedule alone
    - Use **stronger signals**:
        - Device posture
        - Unusual combination of actions
        - Known bad infrastructure / TTPs
3. **Use bias checks as part of model review**
    - When reviewing new AI features or detections, ask:
        - "Who is most impacted by this logic?"
        - "Does this disproportionately target a group with no evidence of higher risk?"
4. **Empower analysts to report perceived bias**
    - Give them a way to say:
        - "This model constantly flags remote workers in Region X; it seems off."
    - Include these reports in periodic model reviews.
5. **Monitor outcomes, not just alerts**
    - Focus on **confirmed incidents**, not just where alerts are generated.
    - If a group is constantly flagged but almost never confirmed malicious, that's a signal.

An ethical SOC doesn't pretend bias doesn't exist—it **hunts for it** and corrects it.

3. Privacy, Monitoring & Responsible Use of Employee Data

Security operations need data.
Ethical operations ask: **"How much data do we actually need—and how do we use it responsibly?"**

3.1. What's at Stake

SOC data often includes:

- Authentication logs (where, when, from which device)
- Device usage patterns
- Email metadata and sometimes content
- Web requests and URLs
- Application access logs

This can reveal:

- Working hours and locations
- Relationships and collaboration patterns
- Personal browsing or communication (even when not security-relevant)

With AI, the risk is that:

- It becomes easier to **aggregate, search, and interpret** that data at scale.
- Logs originally collected for security get repurposed for **productivity monitoring, HR decisions, or micro-management.**

3.2. Principles for Privacy-Respecting SOC AI

1. **Purpose limitation**
   - Use logs and AI analysis **only for security purposes**, unless there is a clearly documented and legally compliant reason otherwise.
   - Resist the temptation to turn SOC data into a "monitor everything about employees" system.
2. **Data minimization**
   - Collect and retain **only what you need** for security.
   - For AI, consider:
     - Masking or tokenizing user IDs before sending data to external AI services.
     - Removing message/body content where metadata is sufficient.
3. **Access control & least privilege**
   - Not every analyst needs access to raw content or full history.

- o Use role-based access:
  - Tier 1 may see summary + key indicators.
  - Tier 2 or IR lead may see deeper content as needed.
4. **Transparency (internally)**
   - o Within legal and policy boundaries, be clear with employees about:
     - What is monitored and why
     - How AI is used in security
     - What is **not** allowed (e.g., using SOC data for performance scoring)
5. **Retention policies**
   - o Align log and AI data retention with:
     - Security needs
     - Regulatory requirements
   - o Periodically purge or anonymize data that's no longer needed.

3.3. AI Assistants & Privacy

For LLM-style AI assistants, pay extra attention to:

- **What's sent to the model**
  - o Avoid sending full email contents or sensitive data unless necessary.
  - o Pre-filter or scrub inputs where possible.
- **How prompts are constructed**
  - o Don't accidentally leak unrelated context into a prompt for convenience.
- **Where the model runs**
  - o Internal vs external, region, data residency, and whether prompts/responses are logged or used for training.

Ethical practice is not "never use AI," but **"use AI with a clear boundary around security purpose and minimal data."**

4. Explainability & Accountability: Who Is Responsible?

When AI is involved in SOC decisions, a key ethical question emerges:

If the AI is wrong, who is responsible?

The answer must never be "no one."

4.1. Human Responsibility Doesn't Go Away

Regardless of sophistication:

- **Humans remain accountable** for:
  - o Choosing where to apply AI
  - o Setting autonomy levels

- o Reviewing and approving major actions
- o Designing and maintaining guardrails

If an AI-driven containment action takes down a business-critical system, the post-incident question is not "Which model did this?" but:

- Who approved that level of autonomy?
- Were guardrails adequate?
- Were we monitoring behavior appropriately?

4.2. Explainability in the SOC Context

You don't always need full mathematical interpretability—but you do need operational explainability:

- "Why did this alert get such a high risk score?"
- "Why did this account get flagged as risky?"
- "Why did this playbook decide to auto-isolate this host?"

Practical approaches:

1. **Reason codes & feature contributions**
   - o Even approximate explanations help:
     - "High risk due to: unusual geography, new device, failed MFA, CTI match."
2. **Traceable decisions**
   - o Link AI decisions back to:
     - Underlying alerts
     - Raw events
     - CTI entries
3. **Visible workflow history**
   - o Case/ticket timelines should show:
     - "AI assistant suggested X at time Y"
     - "Analyst accepted/rejected suggestion"
     - "Automation executed action under conditions Z"

Explainability isn't just for "AI fairness"—it's crucial for **incident reviews, audits, and building analyst trust.**

4.3. AI as "Advisor," Not "Authority"

Ethically, you want AI to:

- Provide **advice and context**, not act as an unquestionable authority.
- Encourage the mindset:

"AI said this, but does that make sense given what I know?"

You can reinforce this culturally and technically:

- UI patterns that show AI output as "suggested" not "final."
- Training that teaches analysts to:
  - Ask AI "why?" and "what's missing?"
  - Seek corroborating evidence.

Accountability remains with **human teams and leadership**. AI is a powerful tool—but still a tool.

5. Human Impact on Analysts: Wellbeing, Skills & Culture

We've talked about AI ethics toward **end users and the business**.
But there is another group we must treat ethically: **the SOC team itself.**

5.1. Risk: Burnout by Acceleration

AI can cut both ways:

- It can reduce repetitive toil…
- Or it can create **expectations of even more throughput**, making burnout worse.

Signals of unhealthy impact:

- Analysts feel pressured to handle **more alerts than ever**, just because AI "speeds things up."
- Little time is given for learning, reflection, and improving detections/playbooks.
- AI outputs are used to **micromanage or score individual analysts** ("Why did you disagree with the AI 15 times this week?").

5.2. Designing for a Healthy Analyst Experience

Ethically, your goal is:

Use AI to improve the quality of analyst work, not just the quantity.

Practical steps:

1. **Reinvest time savings**
   - When AI reduces triage time, explicitly allocate some of that time to:
     - Learning
     - Threat hunting
     - Improving content and processes
2. **Avoid "AI as surveillance" on staff**

- o Don't weaponize AI logs to nitpick individual analysts.
- o Focus on team-level metrics and improvement, not blame.
3. **Involve analysts in AI design**
    - o Ask them:
        - "Where does AI genuinely help you?"
        - "Where does it get in the way?"
    - o Give them a say in:
        - Prompt design
        - UI flow
        - Which tasks should/shouldn't be automated
4. **Train and upskill**
    - o Provide training not just on "how to use the tool," but:
        - How to think about AI as a partner
        - How to challenge and correct it
        - How to build prompts and workflows
5. **Recognize and reward "AI literacy"**
    - o Treat analysts who get good at using AI as **leaders and multipliers**, not just "those who took shortcuts."

5.3. Career Impact & Skills Evolution

AI will change SOC roles, but not in a purely subtractive way:

- Tier 1 roles may become:
    - o More about judging context and less about clicking the same buttons.
- New skill sets become valuable:
    - o Prompt design
    - o Workflow thinking
    - o Understanding model behavior and limitations

Ethically, leadership should:

- Communicate a **path forward**:
    - o "We're going to use AI to remove grunt work and give you more interesting problems."
- Provide opportunities:
    - o Training, internal projects, cross-functional work
- Be honest:
    - o Some tasks will be automated, but **domain expertise and judgment remain critical**.

6. Handling AI Errors & AI-Related Incidents Ethically

No matter how careful you are, AI will eventually:

- Misclassify something important
- Miss a pattern
- Over-prioritize noise
- Trigger or recommend a problematic action

The ethical difference is **how you respond**.

6.1. Treat AI Failures as First-Class Incidents

You should have a concept of an **"AI-related incident"**, e.g.:

- An AI-driven automation causes business disruption.
- AI advice leads to a serious misjudgment in investigation.
- AI assistant leaks inappropriate or sensitive information in its output.

When these happen:

1. **Log and classify them explicitly**
    - Don't just call it "tool behavior."
    - Record that AI was involved in the causal chain.
2. **Perform a proper post-incident review** that asks:
    - Was AI used correctly?
    - Were autonomy levels appropriate?
    - Did guardrails and monitoring function as intended?
    - Were humans sufficiently skeptical / informed?
3. **Adjust controls and training**
    - Improve guardrails, prompts, autonomy settings.
    - Update training and documentation.
4. **Be transparent with stakeholders** (within legal and regulatory bounds)
    - Acknowledge that AI was part of the issue.
    - Show the steps taken to prevent recurrence.

6.2. Fair Treatment of Individuals

When AI mistakes involve people:

- A user erroneously flagged as high-risk
- An employee's activity misinterpreted as malicious
- An individual's account auto-disabled incorrectly

Ethics demands:

1. **Prompt correction**
    - Restore legitimate access quickly.
    - Apologize where appropriate.
2. **Clear path of redress**
    - Give impacted individuals a way to raise concerns and get explanations.

- o Avoid the "computer said so" brush-off.
3. **Learning, not blaming**
    - o Don't blame the individual for being in the wrong place in the logs.
    - o Fix rules, models, and processes that led to the misclassification.

7. Practical Principles & Checklists for Ethical AI in the SOC

To make all of this operational, you can lean on a few **simple principles** and **practical checks**.

7.1. Five Ethical Principles for AI in the SOC

1. **Purpose-Bound**
    - o Use AI and security data **only** for security and clearly related risk management objectives.
2. **Proportionate**
    - o Match the **intrusiveness** of monitoring and automation to the level of risk.
3. **Transparent & Explainable**
    - o Document where AI is used and be able to explain major decisions and actions.
4. **Human-Centered**
    - o Keep humans in the loop for high-impact decisions.
    - o Design AI to **augment**, not diminish, human expertise and dignity.
5. **Accountable & Correctable**
    - o Assign ownership.
    - o Make it possible to challenge, correct, and improve AI behavior.

7.2. Quick Ethical Readiness Checklist

You can use this as a mini-audit once or twice a year.

Policy & Governance

- We have a documented **AI-in-SOC policy** that covers use cases, autonomy, and data usage.
- We have defined **who owns** AI behavior and improvement in the SOC.
- We have criteria and workflow for **AI-related incidents**.

Bias & Fairness

- We periodically check AI outputs and detections for **bias patterns** (by region, team, role, etc.).
- Analysts have a way to report "this feels biased/unfair."
- We avoid rules and models relying solely on sensitive proxies like location or schedule without strong justification.

Privacy & Data Use

- We only collect and retain SOC data that is justified for security.
- We have controls for masking/tokenizing sensitive fields when using external AI services.
- We have internal guidance on what SOC data **must not** be used for (e.g., general employee monitoring).

Explainability & Accountability

- For key AI decisions (scores, flags, actions), we can provide at least a **high-level explanation**.
- AI outputs and automation actions are **logged and auditable**.
- In post-incident reviews, we explicitly identify and analyze AI's role where relevant.

Human Impact & Culture

- AI is introduced as a **helper**, not a threat, in communications and training.
- Analysts receive training on:
    - How to use the AI assistant
    - How to challenge its outputs
- We monitor for burnout and don't simply use AI to ratchet up volume expectations.

7.3. Questions to Ask Before Turning on a New AI Use Case

Before deploying a new AI capability, ask:

1. **What problem is this solving, and is AI the right tool?**
2. **What data will this use?**
    - Is it necessary and proportionate?
    - Any sensitive fields we should mask?
3. **Who might this disproportionately impact?**
    - Certain users, BUs, regions?
    - Are we okay with that based on real risk, not stereotypes?
4. **What autonomy level are we granting?**
    - Suggest-only?
    - Human approval required?
    - Conditional auto?
5. **What guardrails and kill switches are in place?**
    - Preconditions?
    - Rate limits?
    - Rollback steps?
6. **How will we detect and respond if this behaves badly?**
    - Metrics?
    - Logs?

- AI-incident workflows?
7. **Who is responsible for monitoring and improving this capability over time?**

If you can answer these clearly and write them down, you're already far ahead of most organizations in ethical readiness.

Key Takeaways from Chapter 18

Ethics, bias, and human impact are not a separate "nice to have" add-on to AI in the SOC. They are:

- Essential for **trust**, internally and externally
- The foundation for **regulatory defensibility**
- The difference between AI that helps people and AI that quietly harms them

The good news: you don't need a brand-new ethical framework for security.
You need to:

- Extend your existing **security, privacy, and governance principles**
- Make space for **human concerns and perspectives** in AI decisions
- Treat AI like any powerful tool—useful, but needing **controls and care**

In the next chapter, we'll look ahead to the **next 3–5 years** of AI-driven security operations—and explore which parts of this story are likely to change dramatically, and which parts (like ethics and human judgment) are going to remain permanent fixtures.

Chapter 19 – The Next 3–5 Years: The Future of AI-Driven Security Operations

Trying to forecast anything in security for more than 6 months is usually a bad joke. But for AI in security operations, we can say a few things with confidence:

- Some trends are already **locked in**.
- Some risks are already **visible**.
- And some fundamentals will **not** change, no matter how clever the models get.

Think of this chapter as:

A pragmatic "how this probably plays out" guide, so you can steer—not just react.

We'll cover:

1. What **won't change** in AI-driven SOCs
2. How tools and platforms are likely to **converge**
3. The realistic trajectory of **autonomy levels**
4. The future **operating model** for security operations
5. How **regulation and assurance** will evolve
6. What happens to **skills and careers**
7. How this plays out for **different types of organizations**
8. "No-regret moves" you can make today

1. What Won't Change

Before predicting the new, anchor on the **constants**. Three things are very unlikely to change in the next 3–5 years.

1.1. You Still Need Good Telemetry

You will still need:

- Identity logs (IdP, VPN, SSO)
- Endpoint/EDR data
- Cloud control plane and workload logs
- Network/edge telemetry
- Asset and user context

No model can detect what it cannot see. AI may help fill gaps and correlate signals, but:

Garbage in → sophisticated garbage out.

Investments in logging, normalization, and enrichment will remain foundational—AI simply multiplies the return.

1.2. Human Judgment Still Decides Risk

In 3–5 years, AI will still:

- Misinterpret ambiguous situations
- Lack organizational context (politics, business priorities, risk appetite)
- Fail to fully understand **consequences** beyond the technical domain

Humans will still be needed to decide:

- Is this really an incident, or an expected-but-weird change?
- Is it acceptable to take this system down right now?
- Which investigation paths are worth the time?
- What do we tell executives, regulators, and customers?

AI will get better at **suggesting** and **explaining**, but:

The responsibility for risk decisions will still sit with people whose names are on org charts.

1.3. Governance & Documentation Will Still Matter

Boards, regulators, customers, and auditors will still ask:

- "What controls do you have?"
- "How do you know your tools are working?"
- "Who is accountable for this system's behavior?"

AI won't remove the need for:

- Policies and standards
- Runbooks and playbooks
- Post-incident reviews
- Metrics and reporting

If anything, AI will **increase** the demand for clear documentation of:

- Where AI is used
- What it's allowed to do
- How it's monitored and tested

2. Tooling & Architecture: From Silos to Security Data Fabrics

Today, many environments still look like a zoo:

- SIEM over here
- EDR console over there
- SOAR somewhere else
- Separate UEBA, threat intel platform, cloud security tools…

In the next 3–5 years, expect increasing **convergence**.

2.1. From SIEM + XDR + UEBA + SOAR → Integrated Platforms

You'll see more:

- Platforms that **combine**:
    - Log storage
    - Detection content
    - UEBA/behavior models
    - AI-assisted search
    - Case management
    - Automation/orchestration
- Native AI assistants embedded into those consoles as a primary interface.

That doesn't mean "one mega-vendor for everything" for everyone, but:

- The boundary between SIEM, XDR, UEBA, and SOAR will blur.
- "Ask the system in natural language" will be standard, not special.

You'll still likely have a few major components:

- A central **security data platform** (or a small number of them)
- One or more **enforcement planes** (EDR, firewalls, IAM, cloud platforms)
- One or more **AI assistants** that sit on top and help humans navigate it all

2.2. Security Data Fabrics & Open Schemas

We're already seeing the move to:

- Shared schemas (like ECS/OCSF-style mappings)
- Log pipelines that feed:
    - SIEM/XDR
    - Data lakes

- AI workloads

In 3–5 years:

- It will be more normal to talk about a **"security data fabric"** than "our SIEM."
- Data will be:
  - Stored once (or at least fewer times)
  - Queried by multiple engines (detections, AI, BI, threat hunting)

You'll still have to care about:

- Cost vs fidelity (not everything can be hot & detailed forever)
- Data locality and residency
- Governance over who can run which queries and models

But trendline: fewer silos, more shared data layers.

2.3. AI Everywhere, Not Just One "AI Product"

The idea of a single **monolithic "AI for security" product** will fade. Instead:

- Every relevant tool will have AI features:
  - AI for detection tuning in SIEM/XDR
  - AI for automated containment logic review in SOAR
  - AI in EDR to refine behaviors and prioritize cases
  - AI in CTI platforms to cluster and summarize
  - AI in cloud security to highlight misconfigurations and attack paths

You'll likely also maintain:

- One or two **cross-cutting AI assistants**:
  - That can see across tools
  - That know your environment
  - That analysts talk to throughout their workflow

But it's AI **as a layer**, not AI **as a standalone box**.

---

3. The Realistic Trajectory of Autonomy

Marketing loves the idea of "fully autonomous SOCs." Reality will be more nuanced.

Use the autonomy levels we defined earlier:

- **Level 0** – AI suggests; humans act
- **Level 1** – AI suggests; humans approve actions in the tool
- **Level 2** – AI/automation acts automatically in bounded, low-risk scenarios
- **Level 3+** – Broad autonomy with limited human oversight (unlikely in SOCs anytime soon)

3.1. Where We Are Now

Most organizations are somewhere between:

- **Level 0** for AI assistants (summaries, suggestions, queries), and
- **Level 1** for many automations (playbooks that require human approvals)

A smaller subset has:

- **Level 2** autonomy in tightly scoped scenarios (e.g., isolating commodity malware on non-critical endpoints).

3.2. Where We're Likely to Be in 3–5 Years

For most organizations:

- **Level 0** will be everywhere:
    - AI used routinely for triage, investigations, reporting, CTI, and hunting.
- **Level 1** will be normal for many incident types:
    - Human-in-loop approvals with AI-generated context and recommended actions as the standard view.
- **Level 2** will expand—but carefully:
    - Common candidates:
        - Auto-quarantine of clearly malicious emails
        - Auto-isolation of certain endpoint classes
        - Auto-enforcement of simple IAM hygiene rules (e.g., disabling unused accounts after defined patterns)
    - Still heavily constrained by:
        - Asset criticality
        - Environment (dev vs prod vs OT)
        - Tenant risk appetite
- **Level 3+** will remain rare:
    - Maybe in **test environments**, or
    - Very specific, low-impact domains where the downside is minimal.

The key shift:

We'll see *more* Level 2 automation in *more* organizations—but *narrow*, *uncoupled*, and *heavily guarded*, not "AI runs the SOC".

3.3. Playbook Fragments as Autonomous Units

Instead of "this whole incident is autonomous," we'll more likely see:

- Specific **steps** within a playbook being autonomous:
    - "If conditions A, B, C are true, perform step 3 automatically."
    - Everything else remains suggest-only or human-approved.

This granular autonomy allows you to:

- Dial up/down autonomy **per step** and **per use case**, instead of making a single big leap.

4. The Future Operating Model: SOC as Product & Platform

Expect the SOC to increasingly behave like:

A **product team** that delivers "security operations capabilities" to the business.

4.1. SOC as Product

You'll see SOCs:

- Define clear **"services"**:
    - Alert triage
    - Incident response
    - Threat hunting
    - Exposure management / attack surface monitoring
    - AI-augmented assistance
- Set **SLOs** (Service Level Objectives) for those services:
    - MTTA / MTTR targets
    - Coverage levels for key assets and TTPs
- Treat:
    - Detections
    - Playbooks
    - AI "skills" and prompts
        …as **product features** with owners, backlogs, and roadmaps.

4.2. Security Platform Teams

Many organizations will establish a **security platform team** that:

- Manages:
  - The security data fabric
  - Shared automation / SOAR engine
  - AI assistants and integrations
- Provides:
  - Self-service capabilities for detection engineering, hunting, and reporting
- Works with:
  - SOC
  - DevOps / SRE
  - Cloud and app teams

This mirrors the broader platform engineering trend in IT:

- Build shared, well-governed **platforms** instead of one-off scripts and point-to-point integrations.

4.3. Collaboration with IT, SRE & DevOps

AI-driven SOCs will need closer collaboration with:

- **IT operations and SRE**, because:
  - Incidents increasingly cross performance, reliability, and security boundaries.
  - Some automations (e.g., scaling down services, changing configs) overlap with SRE responsibilities.
- **DevOps / App teams**, because:
  - Cloud-native threats live at app and pipeline layers.
  - AI can help find risky configurations, but only app teams can safely change them at scale.

We can expect to see more:

- Shared on-call rotations for cross-domain incidents
- Joint incident handling runbooks (security + reliability + app)
- Shared use of AI assistants across these roles

5. Regulation, Assurance & "AI Risk Management"

Regulators and auditors are not ignoring AI in security. Over 3–5 years, expect:

- More explicit **guidelines** around AI use in critical functions
- Increased scrutiny over **model governance** and **data usage**

5.1. What Regulators Are Likely to Ask

Regulatory expectations may not be identical across sectors, but patterns will look like:

- **Transparency**
    - Where do you use AI in operations?
    - Are humans in the loop for high-impact decisions?
- **Model risk management**
    - How do you validate and test your models?
    - How do you detect and handle model drift or failures?
- **Data governance**
    - What data do you feed to AI systems?
    - How do you protect privacy and comply with residency rules?
- **Incident reporting**
    - Did AI contribute to the cause, spread, or delayed detection of an incident?
    - How did you adjust controls afterwards?

5.2. Internal Assurance & Second Lines of Defense

Your internal risk and audit teams will likely:

- Develop **control libraries** with explicit AI sections
- Include AI-enabled SOC controls in:
    - Internal audits
    - Risk assessments
    - Model risk frameworks

If you're ahead of the curve:

- You'll already have:
    - AI-in-SOC policies
    - Documented autonomy levels
    - AI incident definitions
    - Logs and metrics that make review straightforward

If you're behind:

- You'll scramble to retrofit governance and documentation onto systems already in production.

6. Skills & Careers: What Changes, What Becomes Valuable

AI will reshape skills, but not by removing the need for humans. It will shift **what's valuable**.

6.1. Skills That Rise in Value

Expect higher demand for people who can:

1. **Think in systems and workflows**
    - Understand how detections, data, automations, and AI components fit together.
    - Design robust playbooks and guardrails.
2. **Work fluently with data**
    - Query security data fabrics
    - Understand schemas and context
    - Interpret model outputs and metrics
3. **Collaborate with AI effectively**
    - Ask good questions
    - Spot hallucinations and gaps
    - Refine prompts and task patterns
4. **Communicate risk clearly**
    - Explain AI-assisted findings to:
        - Engineers
        - Executives
        - Auditors and regulators
5. **Build and improve content**
    - Detections, hunts, playbooks, report templates, AI "skills"

"AI literacy" will become as fundamental as "can read logs" is today.

6.2. Roles That Will Become Commonplace

You'll likely see more explicit roles like:

- **AI-in-SOC Product Owner**
    - Owns use cases, roadmap, and metrics for AI capabilities.
- **Security Automation / Orchestration Engineer**
    - Designs and maintains playbooks and guardrails.
- **Security Data Engineer**
    - Owns pipelines, schemas, data quality, and observability.
- **Hybrid Analyst / Detection Engineer**
    - Splits time between investigations and improving content & automations.

Traditional SOC labels (Tier 1/2/3) may blur into:

- **Triager / Investigator**
- **Responder / Coordinator**
- **Engineer / Builder**

The core: people who **understand threats, systems, and workflows** and are comfortable working side-by-side with AI.

6.3. What Won't Be Automated Away

In 3–5 years, highly unlikely to be replaced:

- Deep **incident command** and cross-stakeholder coordination
- **Root cause analysis** that involves business and human context
- Long-term **threat modeling and architecture decisions**
- **Negotiation and communication** with leadership, regulators, and customers
- Organizational and political navigation (who to involve, when, and how)

AI can support these—but **not own them**.

7. How This Plays Out for Different Types of Organizations

The future won't be uniform. A few archetypes:

7.1. Large Enterprises

- Likely to have:
    - Security data platforms
    - Multiple AI-augmented tools
    - Formal AI governance and model risk practices
- Focus:
    - Integration and rationalization of tools
    - Balancing autonomy with regulatory expectations
    - Building internal platform & product capabilities

7.2. MSSPs & MDR Providers

- AI will be essential to:
    - Scale to more tenants without linear headcount growth
    - Provide higher-value services (hunts, advisory, reporting)
- Focus:
    - Strong **multi-tenant isolation** and per-tenant policies
    - Highly standardized playbooks with AI-assisted customization
    - Differentiation on **explainability and transparency** for clients

7.3. Mid-Market & Traditional Organizations

- Likely to rely more on:
    - Vendor-embedded AI
    - Managed services
    - Cloud-native security platforms
- Focus:
    - Picking vendors with usable AI features and sane guardrails
    - Avoiding over-tooling and complexity
    - Developing a few **internal champions** who know how to use AI features effectively

7.4. Cloud-Native & "SOC of Few" Teams

- Will lean heavily on:
    - Cloud provider logs and platforms
    - Integrated AI assistants for investigations and config analysis
- Focus:
    - Building a **lean but sharp** detection and response capability
    - Using AI to compensate for small team size
    - Automating as much low-risk toil as possible

For all of these, the **principles** in earlier chapters still apply; the tools and depth differ.

---

8. "No-Regret Moves" You Can Make Today

Given all this, what can you do now that will **age well** no matter how the exact future unfolds?

8.1. Invest in Data Quality & Context

- Get critical logs in: identity, EDR, cloud, edge.
- Clean up:
    - Asset inventories
    - User/role data
    - Environment tags

This makes **every** future tool and AI capability more valuable.

8.2. Standardize Playbooks & Processes

- Document and refine your top 5–10 incident workflows.

- Normalize:
    - Ticket fields
    - Severity and priority definitions
    - Escalation paths

AI loves structure. So do humans.

8.3. Introduce AI in Low-Risk, High-Annoyance Areas

- Incident summaries
- Report drafting
- CTI digesting
- Timeline generation

This builds confidence and skills without risking outages.

8.4. Define Autonomy Levels & Guardrails Now

- Even if you're not using much autonomy yet, define:
    - What Level 0, 1, 2 mean for you
    - Where autonomy is never acceptable
    - How kill switches and rollback work

You'll be ready when the organization wants to **"turn it up"**.

8.5. Build AI Literacy Across Roles

- Train analysts, engineers, and leaders on:
    - What AI can and can't do
    - How to ask good questions
    - How to challenge and verify AI output

Make "working with AI" a **normal part of professional development**, not a niche hobby.

8.6. Start Measuring AI's Impact Early

- Track:
    - Time to triage
    - Time for investigations
    - AI usage

- Override rates

Even crude numbers beat anecdotes—and will help you justify future choices.

8.7. Formalize AI Governance

- Draft an AI-in-SOC policy.
- Assign an AI-in-SOC owner.
- Define AI-related incidents and review processes.

This will impress both executives and regulators—and save you time later.

Key Takeaways from Chapter 19

Ethics, bias, and human impact are not a separate "nice to have" add-on to AI in the SOC. They are:

- Essential for **trust**, internally and externally
- The foundation for **regulatory defensibility**
- The difference between AI that helps people and AI that quietly harms them

The good news: you don't need a brand-new ethical framework for security.
You need to:

- Extend your existing **security, privacy, and governance principles**
- Make space for **human concerns and perspectives** in AI decisions
- Treat AI like any powerful tool—useful, but needing **controls and care**

In the next chapter, we'll look ahead to the **next 3–5 years** of AI-driven security operations—and explore which parts of this story are likely to change dramatically, and which parts (like ethics and human judgment) are going to remain permanent fixtures.

Chapter 20 – Your 90-Day, 1-Year and 3-Year Plan

By now, you've seen the concepts, architectures, guardrails, case studies, and role guides. This chapter answers the practical question:

"OK, what exactly do we do next?"

We'll turn everything into a **time-boxed, realistic plan**:

- First **90 days** – Foundations & safe early wins
- First **12 months** – Scale AI assistance & selective automation
- **3-year horizon** – Mature, metrics-driven, AI-augmented security operations

You can adapt this plan whether you're:

- A large enterprise SOC
- An MSSP
- A mid-market team
- Or a "SOC of few" trying to punch above your weight

Use it as a **template**, not a prison. Adjust scope, depth, and tooling to your reality.

1. Principles for Your Roadmap

Before we timebox, three guiding principles:

1. **Value first, autonomy second**
   - Don't chase "self-driving SOC" as a goal.
   - Focus first on clear value: less toil, better triage, faster investigations, clearer reporting.
2. **Small slices, not big bangs**
   - Deliver in thin vertical slices:
     - One use case
     - One data path
     - One set of runbooks
   - Validate, then expand.
3. **Guardrails and metrics from day one**
   - Decide early how far AI is allowed to go, and how you'll measure success.
   - It's easier to relax guardrails than to bolt them on after a scare.

Keep those in mind as you read the timelines.

2. Your First 90 Days – Foundations & Safe Wins

Goal:
Establish **data, guardrails, and a pilot set of AI-assisted workflows** that deliver real value with minimal risk.

Think of this phase as **"get oriented, instrumented, and credible."**

2.1. Weeks 1–2: Baseline & Alignment

Objectives:

- Understand current state
- Align leadership and SOC on goals
- Capture baselines for later ROI

Key actions:

1. **Baseline the SOC**
   - Gather 30–90 days of metrics (from Chapter 11):
     - Alerts per day
     - MTTA / MTTR for key incident types
     - Average time per triage and investigation (even via sampling)
     - Rough analyst time split (triage vs investigations vs improvement)
2. **Identify top 3–5 pain points**
   - Typically:
     - Alert overload
     - Slow investigations
     - Reporting & documentation toil
     - CTI → actions gap
3. **Set initial AI goals**
   - Examples:
     - "Reduce time-to-first-triage by 30% on high-value alerts."
     - "Decrease time spent on incident report drafting by 50%."
     - "Turn CTI into hunts within 24–48 hours."
4. **Agree on risk appetite & red lines**
   - Decide, in principle:
     - No Level 2 autonomy on critical systems in the first year.
     - No AI-driven changes in OT / safety-critical environments.
     - AI use cases start in **suggest-only** domains.

Deliverable:
A short **AI-in-SOC vision memo**: 1–2 pages summarizing goals, guardrail philosophy, and initial focus areas.

2.2. Weeks 2–4: Data & Tooling Readiness

Objectives:

- Ensure AI has something meaningful to work with
- Map what AI will sit on top of

Key actions:

1. **Confirm critical telemetry is available** (at least for pilot scope)
    - Identity (IdP, VPN, SSO)
    - EDR on key endpoints
    - Cloud logs (control plane, auth, relevant apps)
    - SIEM or central log platform where AI can "see" data
2. **Fix obvious data gaps for the pilot**
    - Onboard missing critical assets into SIEM or XDR
    - Add or correct asset criticality tags where possible
    - Ensure basic user/role context is available
3. **Decide your initial AI tooling**
    - AI assistant (vendor-native or external)
    - Where AI will be invoked:
        - SIEM/XDR console
        - SOAR/case management
        - CTI platform
        - Reporting workflows
4. **Inventory existing automation**
    - List playbooks and scripts:
        - Which are manual?
        - Which require human approval?
        - Which, if any, are already auto?

Deliverable:
A **pilot scope document**: list of data sources, tools, and workflows where AI will be used first.

2.3. Weeks 4–8: Pilot AI in Safe Workflows

Objectives:

- Introduce AI assistance where risk is low & annoyance is high
- Start getting measurable improvements & feedback

Focus on **Level 0 (suggest-only)** use cases:

1. **Incident & alert summarization**

- Integrate AI assistant to:
  - Summarize alerts with context in 3–5 bullet points
  - Summarize full incidents for handover and closure
2. **Investigation helpers**
   - Allow analysts to ask:
     - "Show me the relevant events for this user/host in last 24–72 hours."
     - "Explain this pattern in simple terms."
     - "Suggest 3 next investigative steps."
3. **Reporting & documentation**
   - Use AI to:
     - Draft incident reports that analysts refine
     - Create simple executive summaries
     - Help maintain KB articles and playbooks
4. **CTI → hunts**
   - Feed CTI reports into AI to:
     - Summarize threats in your context
     - Propose hunt ideas and detection candidates

Parallel work:

- Define a **basic prompt library** for SOC users (Appendix A).
- Run short **enablement sessions**:
  - Show how to use the assistant
  - Show examples of "good prompts" and "bad prompts"

Deliverable:

- AI assistant live in at least **one key analyst workflow**.
- Documented list of **early wins and frustrations**.

2.4. Weeks 8–12: Measure, Tune, and Decide Next Steps

Objectives:

- Prove value
- Fix obvious issues
- Decide where to expand next

Key actions:

1. **Compare metrics vs baseline**
   - Has time per triage or report drafting changed?
   - Are analysts using the AI assistant regularly?
   - Where are override rates or "AI got this wrong" reports highest?

2. **Collect structured feedback from analysts**
   - What do they use AI for most?
   - Where do they avoid it?
   - Where did AI hallucinate or miss context?
3. **Refine prompts, workflows, and guardrails**
   - Adjust prompt templates to reduce confusion.
   - Improve data coverage for frequently missing context.
   - Tune where the AI is surfaced in the UI.
4. **Decide on 1–2 candidates for early Level 1 or Level 2 automation**
   - Focusing on:
     - Repetitive, low-risk playbooks
     - Highly structured workflows (e.g., commodity malware on non-critical endpoints, low-risk phishing follow-ups)

Deliverable:
A **90-day review** with:

- Before/after metrics
- Lessons learned
- Recommendations for next 12 months

---

3. Your 12-Month Plan – Scale AI Assistance & Selective Automation

Goal:
Move from **pilot novelty** to **embedded capability** across core SOC workflows, with **carefully chosen automation** and solid governance.

Think of this phase as **"operationalize AI and lay foundations for autonomy."**

3.1. Months 4–6: Expand AI Assistance Across the SOC

Objectives:

- Make AI assistant a normal part of day-to-day SOC work
- Extend coverage to more workflows

Key actions:

1. **Roll out AI assistance to more roles**
   - Tier 1 analysts, Tier 2/IR, threat hunters, CTI, SOC managers.
   - Provide role-specific prompt patterns:
     - Triage prompts for Tier 1
     - Timeline & hypothesis prompts for IR

- Hunt generation for threat hunters
- Digest & action prompts for CTI

2. **Standardize on AI-assisted case handling**
   o Encourage a common pattern:
     - AI-drafted summary → analyst validates & edits → stored in ticket.
   o Use AI to propose incident categorization and severities (human-confirmed).

3. **Integrate AI into knowledge workflows**
   o Use AI to help:
     - Create & maintain runbooks
     - Tag and organize knowledge base entries
     - Extract lessons and recommended improvements from past incidents

4. **Start building an AI feedback loop**
   o Log where analysts:
     - Override AI severity
     - Correct AI misclassification
     - Explicitly rate AI suggestions as helpful/unhelpful

3.2. Months 4–9: Build Guardrails & Governance into Concrete Practice

Objectives:

- Move from "policy on paper" to **guardrails in tooling**
- Prepare for safe autonomy in selected areas

Key actions:

1. **Implement autonomy levels across playbooks**
   o For each playbook, decide:
     - Which steps are manual only
     - Which are AI-suggested/human-approved
     - Which might become Level 2 (auto within guardrails)

2. **Add technical guardrails**
   o Precondition checks for automations:
     - Asset tags (critical vs non-critical)
     - Environment (prod vs dev)
     - Tenant / BU (with per-tenant policies)
   o Rate limits:
     - "No more than N similar actions in 30 minutes."
   o Kill switches and rollback procedures.

3. **Enhance logging and explainability**
   o Ensure all AI recommendations and automated actions are:
     - Logged with context
     - Traceable in case timelines
   o Ensure you can answer:

- "Why did this action occur?"
- "What did AI suggest, and what did the human approve?"

4. **Align with risk/compliance**
   - Walk risk and audit teams through:
     - AI-in-SOC policy
     - Autonomy levels
     - Logging and review processes
   - Incorporate AI into internal controls and risk registers.

3.3. Months 6–12: Introduce Carefully Bounded Level 2 Automation

Objectives:

- Let AI + automation handle very specific, low-risk tasks end-to-end
- Prove that your guardrail model works

Candidate use cases:

- Auto-isolating **non-critical endpoints** for commodity malware detections with:
  - High detection confidence
  - Corroborating signals
  - Strict rate limits
- Auto-enforcing **simple hygiene rules**, such as:
  - Forcing password reset or MFA enrollment after certain well-understood patterns
  - Disabling stale privileged accounts after defined conditions

Key actions:

1. **Select 1–3 automation candidates** with clear boundaries
2. **Run in shadow mode**
   - See what would have been auto-executed but don't execute yet.
   - Check for false positives and scaling issues.
3. **Enable Level 2 with strong guardrails**
   - Start in a limited scope:
     - A single environment
     - A subset of endpoints
     - A pilot group of tenants
4. **Monitor and review frequently**
   - Weekly or bi-weekly reviews:
     - Number of auto-actions
     - False positives / rollbacks
     - Near-misses or weird behaviors
5. **Treat any issues as "AI-related incidents"**
   - Run PIRs and adjust guardrails, not just "fix the bug and move on."

3.4. End of Year 1: Where You Should Be

By the end of Year 1, a healthy AI-in-SOC program will have:

- AI assistants widely used for:
    o Summaries, investigations, CTI digestion, reporting
- Clear **AI-in-SOC policy**, autonomy levels, and guardrails documented
- A few **well-run Level 2 automations** in narrow, low-risk domains
- Baseline metrics showing:
    o Improved triage and report times
    o Stable or improved MTTA and MTTR for key incident types
- Established **governance and audit** story:
    o Where AI is used
    o How it's controlled
    o How incidents involving AI are handled

You're not "fully autonomous"—but you've moved from **experimenting** to **operating**.

4. Your 3-Year Horizon – Mature, Metrics-Driven, AI-Augmented SOC

Goal:
Achieve a sustainable, **platform-oriented, AI-augmented SOC** where:

- AI assistance is deeply embedded
- Selective autonomy is safely expanded
- Metrics and governance are robust
- People's roles have evolved, not vanished

Think of this as **"AI as a normal part of how you do security, not a special project."**

4.1. By Year 2: Consolidation & Platform Thinking

Objectives:

- Reduce fragmentation
- Treat AI and automation as part of a **security platform**

Key actions:

1. **Rationalize tooling**
    o Avoid overlapping tools with redundant AI features.
    o Consolidate onto:

- A security data fabric / SIEM/XDR platform
- A central SOAR / automation control plane
- 1–2 primary AI assistants with deep integrations

2. **Build a security platform team** (if size permits)
   - Responsible for:
     - Data pipelines and schemas
     - AI integrations and prompt/skill libraries
     - Automation frameworks and guardrails
   - Serving multiple consumers:
     - SOC, SecEng, SRE, DevOps, risk

3. **Expand AI coverage to more use cases**
   - Cloud security posture & attack path analysis
   - Exposure management and prioritization
   - Support for red/purple team exercises (AI to simulate adversary viewpoints)

4. **Mature metrics & reporting**
   - Establish regular, board-ready metrics:
     - Time saved
     - Incident outcomes
     - Coverage of key TTPs and assets
     - AI performance and error trends

4.2. By Year 3: Deep Integration & Continuous Improvement

Objectives:

- AI-driven security operations become **continuous, adaptive, and collaborative**

Key actions:

1. **Integrate AI across security, IT, and SRE workflows**
   - Shared incidents where:
     - Performance, reliability, and security events are investigated together
   - AI assistant that:
     - Can answer questions for security + SRE + DevOps teams
     - Has access (with guardrails) to relevant data in all domains

2. **Extend Level 2 autonomy to more mature use cases**
   - Additional controls:
     - Dynamic risk scoring for assets and identities
     - Tiered responses depending on residual risk and environment
   - Always with:
     - Clear justifications
     - Ongoing reviews
     - Hard boundaries for Level 3+ autonomy in critical areas

3. **Continuous content & model improvement cycles**
   - Regular cadence (monthly/quarterly):
     - Review detection performance

- Review automation performance
- Review AI suggestion quality
    - Use feedback and incidents to:
        - Retire weak rules
        - Add new detections
        - Retrain or adjust models and prompts
4. **Institutionalize AI literacy**
    - New-hire training includes:
        - AI tools and workflows
        - Ethical and governance expectations
    - Role descriptions explicitly mention:
        - Working with AI assistants
        - Owning improvements based on AI usage data

4.3. What "Good" Looks Like at 3 Years

A mature AI-in-SOC program at 3 years might look like:

- **Operational**
    - Analysts treat AI assistants as standard tools, like the SIEM.
    - Triage and investigations consistently use AI for context and summarization.
- **Measured**
    - Clear trends:
        - Reduced triage time
        - Better coverage for critical threats
        - Fewer missed or late critical incidents
- **Guarded**
    - Automation is:
        - Limited to well-understood scenarios
        - Always within clear guardrails
        - Monitored via metrics and kill switches
- **Governed**
    - Risk, compliance, and audit have:
        - Visibility into AI behavior
        - Documented controls and incident procedures
- **Human-centered**
    - Analysts report:
        - Less mindless toil
        - More time on higher-value work
    - Career paths reflect:
        - Hybrid skills (analysis + engineering + AI literacy)

You may still have plenty to improve—but you've built a **living system** that can absorb new AI capabilities without chaos.

5. A Simple Roadmap Table You Can Adapt

Use this as a starting template (tweak months as needed):

Timeframe	Focus Area	Key Outcomes
0–30 days	Baseline & vision	Metrics baseline, AI objectives, risk appetite defined
30–60 days	Data & pilot setup	Critical data ready, AI assistant integrated in 1–2 workflows
60–90 days	Pilot & measurement	Early wins in triage/reporting, 90-day review & next-step plan
3–6 months	Scale AI assistance	AI used across SOC roles; prompt library; usage metrics
4–9 months	Guardrails & governance	Autonomy levels, guardrails, logging, AI-in-SOC policy applied
6–12 months	Bounded Level 2 auto	1–3 safe auto use cases; monitored; PIRs for issues
Year 2	Platform & integration	Security data fabric, central SOAR, consolidated AI assistants
Year 3	Maturity & expansion	Continuous improvement loops, broader but guarded autonomy

6. Turning This Chapter into Action Tomorrow

If you read this chapter and think, "Where do I even begin?", here's a **one-page starter**:

Tomorrow / This Week:

- Pick 1–2 **safe AI use cases** (incident summaries, CTI digestion).
- Define your **autonomy vocabulary** (Level 0/1/2).
- Ask your SOC lead or team:
    - "What's the most boring, repetitive security task we do today?"

This Month:

- Integrate AI into that task as a helper.
- Baseline a few metrics.
- Capture successes and failures honestly.

This Quarter:

- Decide what to scale, what to rework, what to drop.
- Write down your **90-day → 1-year → 3-year goals** in your own language.
- Socialize them with SOC, engineering, and risk.

From there, the rest of this book becomes your **playbook**:

- Chapters 4–8 → Architecture and roles
- Chapters 9–10 → Governance & guardrails
- Chapters 11–12 → Metrics & buying decisions
- Chapters 14–19 → Stories, patterns, ethics, and human impact
- Appendices → Prompts, policies, runbooks, checklists, and worksheets

The future of AI-driven security operations isn't about doing everything at once.
It's about **taking the next right step**, with eyes open, guardrails in place, and a roadmap that you control—instead of one that happens to you.

Appendix A – Example Prompts for Common SOC Workflows

This appendix is meant to be **copy–paste practical**.

You can drop these prompts straight into your AI assistant (ChatGPT, internal LLM, etc.), adapt them to your tools, and then refine them over time based on what works best for your team.

Where you see UPPERCASE placeholders, replace them with your own content, IDs, or links.

1. A1. How to Use These Prompts

Tip 1 – Add context up front

AI works best when it knows your role and goal. Example:

"You are helping me as a Tier 2 SOC analyst working in an enterprise environment with SIEM, EDR, and SOAR. Be concise and operationally focused."

Tip 2 – Paste data, don't just reference it

Where possible, paste relevant alert payloads, log snippets, or case notes directly into the prompt (or link to them if your AI assistant is integrated with your systems).

Tip 3 – Always ask for "next steps"

Even if you're asking for a summary, include something like:

"…and list the top 3 recommended next steps."

2. A2. Alert Triage & Enrichment Prompts

2.1. Initial Alert Understanding

2.1.1. Prompt – Quick alert summary (Tier 1)

I'm a Tier 1 SOC analyst. Summarize this alert in 3–5 bullet points, focusing on:

- What happened

- Which user/host/resource is involved
- Why this might be important
- Whether this looks like a likely true positive or false positive based on the data alone

ALERT PAYLOAD:

PASTE_ALERT_JSON_OR_FIELDS_HERE

2.1.2. Prompt – Severity sanity-check

Given this alert:

PASTE_ALERT_HERE

1. Explain in plain language what the alert means.
2. Assess whether the assigned severity (LOW/MEDIUM/HIGH/CRITICAL) seems appropriate given the evidence.
3. If you would change the severity, say what you would change it to and why.

2.2. Context & Enrichment Requests

2.2.1. Prompt – Enrichment checklist for an alert

I have this security alert:

PASTE_ALERT_HERE

Suggest a focused enrichment checklist for a Tier 1 analyst.
Divide it into:

- User context to pull
- Host/asset context to pull
- Network/CTI context to pull
- Past incident history to check

Keep it under 10 items total and mark which ones are **must-have** vs **nice-to-have**.

2.2.2. Prompt – Consolidated enrichment summary

I've collected this enrichment data for an alert:

ALERT:

ALERT_FIELDS_HERE

USER CONTEXT:

USER_ENRICHMENT_HERE

HOST/ASSET CONTEXT:

HOST_ENRICHMENT_HERE

THREAT INTEL:

CTI_SNIPPETS_HERE

1. Summarize the combined picture in plain language.
2. State how suspicious this looks (Low / Medium / High) and why.
3. Suggest the top 3 immediate actions a Tier 1 analyst should take next.

2.3. Prioritization & Queue Management

2.3.1. Prompt – Relative priority of multiple alerts

I have these 3 alerts waiting in the queue:

ALERT 1:

ALERT_1_HERE

ALERT 2:

ALERT_2_HERE

ALERT 3:

ALERT_3_HERE

For each alert:

- Explain in 2–3 sentences what it is about.
- Rate its risk as Low/Medium/High/Critical based on the data only.
- Then, rank the 3 alerts in the order they should be worked and explain why.

2.3.2. Prompt – Mapping alerts to episodes/incidents

I have these alerts that may be related:

PASTE_LIST_OF_ALERTS_OR_IDS_HERE

Based on their descriptions and any common fields:

1. Propose how you would group them into incidents/episodes.
2. For each proposed incident, give it a short title (e.g., "Suspicious admin login from new country followed by lateral movement") and a one-paragraph summary.
3. For each incident, suggest a priority (Low/Medium/High/Critical).

3. A3. Investigation & Timeline Prompts

3.1. Building a Timeline

3.1.1. Prompt – Turn raw events into a timeline

Turn the following events into a clear, chronological investigation timeline. For each step, include:

- Timestamp
- Entity (user/host/system)
- Short description
- Why this step might matter for the investigation

EVENTS:

PASTE_LOG_LINES_OR_EVENT_LIST_HERE

3.1.2. Prompt – Highlight key milestones in a timeline

Given this investigation timeline:

PASTE_TIMELINE_HERE

Identify and label:

- Likely initial access
- Possible privilege escalation
- Possible lateral movement
- Possible data exfiltration or impact

If any of these phases are missing or unclear, say so and suggest which additional data you would request.

3.2. Hypothesis Generation

3.2.1. Prompt – "What might be happening?"

Based on the following evidence:

PASTE_EVENTS_AND_ENRICHMENT_HERE

1. List 3–5 plausible hypotheses for what might be happening (e.g., false positive, misconfiguration, real attacker activity, compromised account).
2. For each hypothesis, list the top 3 additional checks or data points that would help confirm or refute it.

3.2.2. Prompt – Next investigative steps

I'm investigating this incident:

PASTE_INCIDENT_SUMMARY_AND_KEY_EVENTS_HERE

Assume I am a Tier 2 analyst with access to SIEM, EDR, IAM, and network logs. Suggest a prioritized list of **next 5–10 investigative steps**, grouped into:

- Must do immediately
- Nice to have if time allows

For each step, specify which tool/log source to use and what to look for.

3.3. Root Cause & Containment

3.3.1. Prompt – Draft root-cause options

Here is the current evidence and timeline for an incident:

PASTE_TIMELINE_AND_KEY_FINDINGS_HERE

Suggest 2–3 possible root-cause explanations, each in 3–5 sentences.
For each explanation, list:

- Evidence that supports it
- Missing evidence we'd need to gather
- Whether it's likely (High/Medium/Low) given what we know now.

3.3.2. Prompt – Containment options with pros/cons

For this incident:

PASTE_INCIDENT_SUMMARY_HERE

Propose 3 containment options. For each option:

- Describe the actions (e.g., isolate host X, disable user Y, block IP Z).
- List pros (e.g., speed, risk reduction).
- List cons (e.g., user impact, potential service disruption).

End with a recommendation for which containment option is most balanced for a typical enterprise environment and why.

---

4. A4. Threat Hunting Prompts
4.1. Hunt Design from an Idea or TTP
4.1.1. Prompt – Turn a TTP into a hunt plan

I want to hunt for this TTP in our environment:

TTP DESCRIPTION:

PASTE_TTP_OR_TECHNIQUE_DESCRIPTION_HERE

Help me design a hunt, including:

- Hypothesis statement
- Data sources needed (SIEM logs, EDR, IAM, etc.)
- 3–5 example queries or patterns to look for
- Indicators or behaviors that would increase confidence that the TTP is present
- Any likely false positive patterns and how to filter them out

4.1.2. Prompt – From CTI report to hunt tasks

Here is a chunk from a CTI report:

PASTE_CTI_SNIPPET_HERE

Convert this into a practical hunt plan for our SOC.
Include:

- Key behaviors and tools used by the actor
- 5–10 concrete things we can search for in our logs
- Suggested search windows (time range)
- Priority of the hunts (High/Medium/Low) and why.

4.2. Hunt Execution Assistance

4.2.1. Prompt – Generate SIEM queries from natural language

I'm using SIEM QUERY_LANGUAGE_HERE.

Write queries that:

1. Find all successful logins to privileged accounts from new countries in the last 7 days.
2. Find endpoints that executed PowerShell with suspicious flags (e.g., encoding, downloading) in the last 24 hours.

For each query, add 1–2 comments explaining what it does and how to tweak it.

4.2.2. Prompt – Hunt result triage help

I ran this hunt and got these results:

PASTE_SAMPLE_RESULTS_OR_SUMMARY_HERE

Help me:

1. Identify which results look most suspicious and why.
2. Suggest a short list of follow-up checks for the top 3 suspicious rows.
3. Suggest filters or refinements to narrow future hunts and reduce noise.

4.3. Hunt Documentation

4.3.1. Prompt – Document a completed hunt

We executed this hunt:

PASTE_HUNT_DESCRIPTION_AND_KEY_STEPS_HERE

And we observed these results:

PASTE_RESULTS_SUMMARY_HERE

Draft a hunt report with the following sections:

- Objective
- Scope and data sources
- Method / queries used
- Findings (including any suspicious patterns or confirmed benign results)
- Gaps or limitations of the hunt
- Recommendations for detections, controls, or future hunts

Keep it concise and structured for our internal wiki.

5. A5. CTI & Deception Prompts

5.1. CTI Digest & Relevance

5.1.1. Prompt – CTI technical + exec summary

This is a threat intel report:

PASTE_CTI_REPORT_OR_EXCERPT_HERE

Produce:

1. A short technical summary for detection engineers (1–2 paragraphs).
2. A short non-technical summary for executives (1 paragraph).
3. A bullet list of TTPs, mapped to MITRE ATT&CK where possible.
4. A bullet list of recommendations for our SOC (hunts, detections, controls).

5.1.2. Prompt – Relevance scoring for our environment

Assume our environment is:

- Industry: OUR_INDUSTRY
- Region: OUR_REGION
- Key technologies: LIST_KEY_STACK (e.g., AZURE, AWS, M365, OKTA, etc.)

Given this CTI excerpt:

PASTE_CTI_SNIPPET_HERE

1. Rate the relevance of this threat to our environment as Low/Medium/High and explain why.

2. List the 5 most actionable items we should consider (e.g., new detections, hunts, hardening steps).

5.2. Honeypot / Deception Analysis

5.2.1. Prompt – Summarize attacker activity on honeypot

Here are logs or a summary from a honeypot session:

PASTE_HONEYPOT_SESSION_LOGS_OR_SUMMARY_HERE

1. Summarize what the attacker attempted to do, step by step.
2. Identify any tools or techniques you can infer (e.g., brute force, web shell deployment, credential harvesting).
3. Suggest which of these behaviors we should try to detect in our production environment and how (high level).

5.2.2. Prompt – From honeypot logs to TTPs

Consider this set of honeypot interactions:

PASTE_LOGS_HERE

Map the observed behaviors to likely MITRE ATT&CK techniques, with a short explanation for each mapping.
Then list 3–5 candidate detection ideas we could deploy in our SIEM/EDR based on these observations.

6. A6. Playbooks, Runbooks & Automation Prompts

6.1. Drafting Playbooks

6.1.1. Prompt – Build a playbook from case history

Here are notes from several past incidents of the same type:

PASTE_TICKET_NOTES_OR_SUMMARIES_HERE

Based on these, draft a standardized playbook for this incident type with:

- Scope / when this playbook applies
- Objectives
- Step-by-step flow (including decision points)

- Roles involved (Tier 1, Tier 2, IR, etc.)
- Candidate steps for automation vs. those that must stay manual

Keep it structured and concise so we can paste it into our internal runbook wiki.

6.1.2. Prompt – Simplify an existing playbook

Simplify this existing playbook so that a new Tier 1 analyst can follow it under time pressure.
Remove redundant detail but keep all critical safety steps:

PASTE_PLAYBOOK_TEXT_HERE

6.2. Automation Design Help

6.2.1. Prompt – Automation candidates from a playbook

Given this playbook:

PASTE_PLAYBOOK_HERE

Identify:

- Steps that are strong candidates for full automation.
- Steps that should be semi-automated (AI/SOAR suggests, human approves).
- Steps that should remain fully manual.

For each automated step, describe the inputs needed and the systems to integrate with (e.g., SIEM, EDR, IAM, firewall).

6.2.2. Prompt – Risk review for a proposed automation

We are considering this automated workflow:

DESCRIBE_AUTOMATION_HERE

Perform a risk review and answer:

- What are the main technical and operational risks?
- What guardrails and conditions should we enforce (e.g., asset tags, risk thresholds, environment limits)?
- What logging and monitoring do we need to detect if this automation misbehaves?

Summarize in 5–10 bullet points suitable for a change advisory board (CAB) discussion.

7. A7. Reporting & Communication Prompts

7.1. Incident Reporting

7.1.1. Prompt – Technical incident summary

Draft a technical incident summary for our SOC knowledge base with the following sections:

- Summary
- Detection & triage
- Investigation & findings
- Root cause
- Containment & recovery
- Lessons learned

Use this information:

PASTE_CASE_NOTES_TIMELINE_AND_KEY_FINDINGS_HERE

7.1.2. Prompt – Executive-facing incident summary

Using the same incident data:

PASTE_SUMMARY_OR_KEY_POINTS_HERE

Create a 1–2 paragraph summary suitable for non-technical executives. Focus on:

- What happened
- Business impact
- Whether data was exposed or not
- How we responded
- Whether any follow-up actions are required from the business

7.2. MSSP / Customer Communication

7.2.1. Prompt – Client incident notification (MSSP)

We are an MSSP. Write a clear, professional incident notification email to a client based on this data:

PASTE_INCIDENT_DETAILS_HERE

The email should include:

- Brief description of the incident
- Timeframe
- Impact as currently understood
- Actions we have taken
- Recommended actions for the client
- Next steps and how we will keep them informed

Keep it neutral, factual, and avoid overly technical jargon.

7.2.2. Prompt – Monthly SOC report highlights

Using these notes and metrics from the past month:

PASTE_METRICS_AND_KEY_EVENTS_HERE

Draft a "Highlights" section for a monthly SOC report to stakeholders, including:

- 3–5 key incidents handled
- Any notable trends (e.g., increased phishing volume, new TTPs)
- Improvements made (detections, automations, processes)
- Planned focus areas for next month

8. A8. Governance, Risk & Audit Prompts

8.1. AI Use Case Documentation

8.1.1. Prompt – Document an AI capability for auditors

We have this AI capability in the SOC:

DESCRIBE_AI_USE_CASE_HERE

Create a documentation summary suitable for auditors with sections:

- Purpose and scope
- Data inputs and outputs
- How decisions are used (suggest-only, semi-auto, conditional auto)
- Key controls and guardrails
- Monitoring and performance metrics
- Change management (how updates to this AI are tested and approved)

8.2. AI Failure / Incident Documentation

8.2.1. Prompt – AI-related incident summary

An AI-assisted triage system contributed to this issue:

DESCRIBE_AI_FAILURE_OR_INCIDENT_HERE

Draft a concise summary for our incident register, including:

- What the AI system was supposed to do
- What went wrong
- How we detected it
- Impact on security/operations
- Immediate fixes applied
- Longer-term improvements planned

8.3. Policy Drafting

8.3.1. Prompt – Draft SOC AI usage policy

Help me draft a 1–2 page "AI Usage in the SOC" policy that covers:

- Approved use cases for AI (triage, summarization, AI assistant, etc.)
- Prohibited use cases (e.g., making final legal decisions, modifying certain critical controls)
- Data handling rules (which data can be sent to which AI systems)
- Human-in-the-loop requirements for high-impact actions
- Logging, monitoring, and audit requirements for AI components

Aim the policy at a mixed audience of SOC staff, security leadership, and risk/compliance teams.

9. A9. Training & Coaching Prompts

9.1. Coaching New Analysts

9.1.1. Prompt – Explain an alert type to a junior analyst

Explain this alert type to a new Tier 1 analyst:

PASTE_ALERT_TYPE_DESCRIPTION_OR_EXAMPLE_HERE

Cover:

- What it means technically
- Why it matters from a security perspective
- Common false positive causes
- Basic triage steps they should follow

Keep it simple, with clear bullet points.

9.1.2. Prompt – Practice scenarios for juniors

Generate 3 practice scenarios for a new Tier 1 analyst focusing on:

- Suspicious login
- Endpoint malware
- Phishing email

For each scenario, provide:

- A short description of the situation
- What evidence/logs they would see
- 3–5 questions they should ask themselves
- 3–5 actions they should try

9.2. Post-Incident Training

9.2.1. Prompt – Turn an incident into a training case

Turn this real incident into a training exercise for the SOC:

PASTE_INCIDENT_SUMMARY_AND_KEY_EVENTS_HERE

Output:

- A short narrative scenario for trainees
- A list of artifacts they will receive (alerts, logs, enrichment)
- 5–10 questions to guide their analysis
- An answer key with expected observations and decisions

Next Steps

You can extend this appendix over time with your own **organization-specific prompts**—for your tools, your naming conventions, and your common incident types. The key pattern is always the same:

1. Be explicit about your role and goal.
2. Provide concrete data or examples.
3. Ask for both **analysis** and **next steps**.
4. Feed back what works into your internal wiki, so your team shares and improves these prompts together.

Appendix B – AI-in-SOC Policy & Guideline Snippets

This appendix gives you **copy–paste text blocks** you can adapt into your own policies, standards, and procedures.

Use placeholders like:

- <ORG_NAME> – your organization
- <SOC_NAME> – your SOC / Cyber Defence Center
- <AI_SYSTEM_NAME> – specific AI component (e.g., "Triage Engine", "SOC AI assistant")

1. B1. How to Use These Snippets

- Treat them as **building blocks**, not finished legal text.
- Mix & match into:
    - SOC AI Policy
    - SOC Runbook / SOPs
    - Change management docs
    - Vendor requirements

You can also turn parts of these into **briefing material** for leadership, auditors, or regulators.

2. B2. Purpose & Scope Snippets

2.1. B2.1 – AI-in-SOC Policy Purpose

The purpose of this policy is to define how <ORG_NAME> uses artificial intelligence (AI) and machine learning (ML) capabilities within <SOC_NAME> to improve detection, investigation, and response, while maintaining appropriate control, accountability, and compliance with applicable laws and regulations.

2.2. B2.2 – Scope

This policy applies to:

- All AI and ML capabilities used in or by <SOC_NAME>, whether developed internally or provided by third parties.
- All employees, contractors, and service providers who use, configure, or manage AI-enabled tools in security operations.

- All environments in scope for <SOC_NAME>, including on-premises, cloud, and hybrid environments, unless explicitly excluded by other governance documents.

2.3. B2.3 – Policy Objectives

<ORG_NAME> will:

1. Use AI to reduce noise, accelerate investigations, and improve detection quality.
2. Ensure AI systems remain transparent, monitored, and aligned with <ORG_NAME>'s risk appetite.
3. Maintain human accountability for all security decisions and high-impact actions.
4. Protect personal and sensitive data used by AI systems in accordance with data protection and privacy requirements.
5. Provide auditors, regulators, customers, and internal stakeholders with clear explanations of how AI is used in security operations.

3. B3. Definitions Snippets

3.1. B3.1 – Key Terms

- **AI / Artificial Intelligence:** Any system that performs tasks such as classification, pattern recognition, anomaly detection, natural language processing, or decision support based on statistical or machine learning methods.
- **ML / Machine Learning Model:** A model trained on data to recognize patterns and make predictions, including but not limited to anomaly detectors, clustering models, and risk scoring models.
- **LLM / Large Language Model:** A model trained on text data that can generate or summarize text and assist with tasks such as investigation assistance and report drafting.
- **AI Capability / Use Case:** A specific application of AI within <SOC_NAME> (e.g., alert triage scoring, AI assistant for investigations, automated containment recommendations).
- **Autonomy Level:** The degree to which an AI capability can act without direct human approval (see B5).
- **AI Incident:** Any event in which an AI capability behaves incorrectly or unexpectedly in a way that could affect detection, response, availability, security posture, or compliance.

4. B4. Roles & Responsibilities Snippets

4.1. B4.1 – CISO / Head of Security Operations

- Owns the overall risk associated with AI use in <SOC_NAME>.
- Approves AI-related risk appetite, autonomy levels, and major AI use cases.
- Ensures AI governance is integrated into existing security governance.

4.2. B4.2 – SOC Product Owner / SOC Lead

- Owns the roadmap for AI capabilities within <SOC_NAME>.
- Prioritizes AI use cases based on risk reduction, operational efficiency, and business value.
- Coordinates with AI/ML engineers, automation engineers, detection engineers, and stakeholders (e.g., privacy, legal).

4.3. B4.3 – AI / ML Engineer (Security)

- Designs, trains, tunes, and evaluates AI/ML models used in <SOC_NAME>.
- Monitors model performance and drift, and proposes updates or retraining when needed.
- Documents model assumptions, limitations, and dependencies.
- Collaborates with detection engineers and analysts to incorporate feedback and ground truth.

4.4. B4.4 – Automation / SOAR Engineer

- Designs and maintains SOAR workflows and automations that consume AI outputs.
- Ensures automations respect autonomy levels and guardrails defined in this policy.
- Implements robust logging, error handling, and rollback mechanisms for all automated actions.

4.5. B4.5 – Detection Engineer

- Translates CTI, deception insights, and incident lessons into detection rules and content.
- Validates and refines AI-generated detections and logic.
- Provides labelled examples and feedback to improve model performance.

4.6. B4.6 – SOC Analysts & Threat Hunters

- Use AI tools as decision support and AI assistants, not as unquestionable authorities.
- Provide explicit feedback when AI outputs are incorrect, incomplete, or misleading.
- Escalate any suspected AI misbehavior as potential AI incidents.
- Participate in testing and validating AI-assisted workflows.

4.7. B4.7 – Data Protection / Privacy Officer

- Reviews data flows to and from AI systems, especially where personal or regulated data is processed.
- Ensures AI use aligns with privacy laws, data protection standards, and internal policies.
- Reviews AI use cases that involve PII, customer data, or regulated environments.

5. B5. AI Use Case Classification & Autonomy Levels

5.1. B5.1 – Use Case Categories

AI use cases in <SOC_NAME> are categorized as follows:

- **Category A – Decision Support:** AI provides recommendations, scores, or summaries, but does not directly perform actions (e.g., alert risk scoring, investigation AI assistant, incident summarization).
- **Category B – Semi-Automated Actions:** AI proposes specific actions which must be explicitly approved by a human analyst before execution (e.g., "quarantine endpoint X", "disable account Y").
- **Category C – Conditional Autonomous Actions:** AI is permitted to automatically execute certain predefined actions when strict conditions and guardrails are met (e.g., auto-quarantine of non-critical endpoints for confirmed commodity malware).

5.2. B5.2 – Autonomy Level Statement

Each AI capability shall be assigned an **Autonomy Level** as part of its design:

- **Level 0 – Suggest Only:** AI can never directly change systems; it provides information and recommendations only.
- **Level 1 – Human-in-the-Loop:** AI can prepare actions, tickets, or workflow steps, but a human must approve all changes to security controls or business systems.
- **Level 2 – Conditional Autonomy:** AI may execute certain actions automatically, within a documented scope and under documented conditions, with full logging and post-hoc review.

No AI capability in <SOC_NAME> may operate beyond Level 2 without explicit approval from the CISO and a documented risk assessment.

5.3. B5.3 – Approval Requirement Snippet

High-impact actions (e.g., disabling privileged accounts, blocking core network segments, modifying critical firewall rules, affecting safety-critical OT systems) shall **always** require human approval, regardless of AI confidence or model output.

6. B6. Data Handling & Privacy Snippets

6.1. B6.1 – Data Minimization

AI capabilities shall only receive the minimum necessary data required to perform their function. Use of full packet captures, email content, file contents, or other rich payloads shall be limited and justified, and where possible replaced by metadata or tokens.

6.2. B6.2 – Data Classification & AI Access

AI systems shall be granted access to data according to <ORG_NAME>'s data classification scheme:

- Public / Internal data may be used with minimal restrictions.
- Confidential data may be used where necessary, with appropriate controls.
- Highly confidential or regulated data (e.g., PII, PHI, PCI, contractual customer data) shall only be processed by AI systems explicitly approved for such data, with documented privacy and security controls.

Access to AI systems and their outputs shall respect <ORG_NAME>'s role-based access control (RBAC) model.

6.3. B6.3 – External / Cloud AI Services

When using external or cloud-based AI services:

- Logs and data sent to the service must be **pseudonymized or tokenized** where practical (e.g., replace usernames, email addresses, and IPs with unique tokens).
- Contracts must specify that data is used **only** to provide the service and not for unrelated model training, unless explicitly agreed and documented.
- Data residency and cross-border transfer requirements must be documented and adhered to for each service.

7. B7. Model Governance & Lifecycle Snippets

7.1. B7.1 – AI Use Case Lifecycle

Each AI capability in <SOC_NAME> shall follow a documented lifecycle:

1. **Proposal:** Define purpose, scope, inputs/outputs, autonomy level, and expected benefits.
2. **Risk & Privacy Review:** Assess data usage, regulatory impact, and risk profile.

3. **Design & Implementation:** Build or integrate the AI system, including guardrails and logging.
4. **Testing & Shadow Mode:** Validate on historical and/or parallel data before impacting production decisions.
5. **Production Deployment:** Enable in production under defined controls.
6. **Monitoring & Tuning:** Continuously measure performance, drift, and analyst feedback.
7. **Change Management & Retirement:** Manage updates and retirement through <ORG_NAME>'s standard change processes.

7.2. B7.2 – Performance Monitoring

For each AI capability, <SOC_NAME> shall define and monitor performance metrics appropriate to the use case, such as:

- True positive / false positive / false negative rates
- Average risk score for known incidents vs. benign events
- Analyst override rate (how often human analysts disagree with AI)
- Time saved per incident or alert

Significant performance degradation or unexplained behavior shall trigger investigation and possible rollback or retraining.

7.3. B7.3 – Testing & Shadow Mode

Before an AI capability influences production decisions or automations, it shall operate in **shadow mode** or suggestion mode for a defined period.
During this period:

- AI outputs are recorded and compared with human decisions.
- Model behavior on historical confirmed incidents is evaluated.
- Any high-risk anomalies are analyzed before enabling live impact.

8. B8. Automation Guardrails Snippets

8.1. B8.1 – Guardrail Principles

All automations that consume AI outputs shall:

- Be **explicitly documented** (inputs, logic, actions, conditions).
- Include **hard safety limits**, such as asset tags, environment filters (e.g., non-production only), or criticality thresholds.
- Log all actions with sufficient detail for later reconstruction and audit.
- Provide a clear mechanism for **immediate suspension** or **rollback** in case of misbehavior.

8.2. B8.2 – Safe Domains for Early Autonomy

<ORG_NAME> will prioritize conditional autonomy in lower-risk domains first, such as:

- Auto-closing clearly benign alerts after sufficient evidence is gathered.
- Auto-quarantining low-value endpoints for confirmed commodity malware.
- Auto-blocking known malicious IPs/domains from vetted threat feeds.

Autonomy in high-risk domains (e.g., privileged identity, core network changes, OT) will only be considered after extended evaluation and executive approval.

8.3. B8.3 – Human Override

Analysts must always be able to:

- Override AI recommendations.
- Cancel or roll back automated actions where feasible.
- Escalate concerns about automation behavior without fear of blame for questioning AI outputs.

9. B9. Third-Party / Vendor AI Snippets

9.1. B9.1 – Vendor AI Assessment

AI features provided by vendors (e.g., in SIEM, EDR, XDR, SOAR, cloud platforms) shall be assessed according to this policy. At minimum, <ORG_NAME> shall obtain:

- A functional description of what the AI feature does and how it is triggered.
- Information about data used (types, location, retention, and use for training).
- High-level documentation of testing, update practices, and safeguards.
- Any configuration options that affect autonomy, sensitivity, or impact.

9.2. B9.2 – Contractual Requirements

Contracts and data processing agreements with vendors providing AI capabilities shall, where applicable:

- Specify data usage and limitations (e.g., no secondary use for unrelated model training without consent).
- Address data residency, encryption, and access controls.
- Define obligations to notify <ORG_NAME> of significant AI changes, regressions, or AI-related incidents.

- Include rights for <ORG_NAME> to request documentation for audits and regulators.

10. B10. AI Incident Handling & Logging Snippets

10.1. B10.1 – AI Incident Definition

An AI-related incident is any event where:

- AI contributed to missed or delayed detection of a real security incident.
- AI-driven or AI-triggered automations caused or materially worsened a security or availability issue.
- AI systems processed data in violation of defined data handling rules.
- AI outputs were significantly misleading or incorrect in a way that could affect security decisions.

10.2. B10.2 – AI Incident Response

AI incidents shall be handled using <ORG_NAME>'s standard incident management process, with the following additions:

- Identify which AI capability and version were involved.
- Collect input data, configuration, and logs of AI outputs and resulting actions.
- Determine whether the root cause was data quality, model design, threshold configuration, workflow design, or misuse.
- Consider temporary rollback or downgrade of autonomy until root cause is understood.
- Document corrective actions to data, model, configuration, workflow, and training.

10.3. B10.3 – Logging Requirements

All AI capabilities that influence security decisions or actions must:

- Log their inputs (at least at a summarized or reference level).
- Log their outputs (scores, recommendations, generated actions).
- Log which downstream actions were triggered (manual or automated), with timestamps.

These logs must be retained in accordance with <ORG_NAME>'s logging and audit retention policies.

11. B11. Training & Culture Snippets

11.1. B11.1 – Analyst Training

<ORG_NAME> shall provide training to SOC analysts, detection engineers, and automation engineers on:

- The role and limitations of AI in <SOC_NAME>.
- How to effectively use AI assistants and AI tools (including good prompt practices).
- How to verify and challenge AI outputs.
- How to recognize and report AI-related issues or incidents.

11.2. B11.2 – Culture of Questioning AI

<ORG_NAME> expects and encourages staff to question AI outputs.

- Analysts shall not be penalized for overriding or challenging AI decisions when they have reasonable grounds.
- Patterns of disagreement between humans and AI should drive investigation and improvement, not blame.
- Leadership shall reinforce that AI is a **tool**, not an authority.

12. B12. Example: One-Page "AI in SOC" Policy Summary

You can use this as an **executive-friendly summary** at the front of your detailed policy.

1. Purpose
<ORG_NAME> uses AI within <SOC_NAME> to reduce noise, accelerate investigations, and improve detection quality, while maintaining human accountability, regulatory compliance, and appropriate control.

2. Where We Use AI
We use AI for:

- Alert triage and risk scoring (decision support).
- Analyst AI assistants (summarization, query assistance, enrichment guidance).
- Drafting incident reports and playbooks.
- Supporting pre-emptive defense (CTI processing, deception analysis).

We may use AI to trigger or propose containment and remediation actions, subject to defined guardrails.

3. Autonomy & Human Oversight

- AI in <SOC_NAME> operates primarily at **Level 0 (suggest only)** and **Level 1 (human-in-the-loop)**.
- In limited, well-defined domains, some capabilities operate at **Level 2 (conditional autonomy)**, with scope and conditions documented.
- High-impact changes (e.g., privileged identity, core networks, safety-critical systems, regulatory communications) always require human approval.

4. Data & Privacy

- AI systems receive the minimum necessary data, with preference for metadata and pseudonymization.
- Use of personal and regulated data in AI is reviewed by the Data Protection/Privacy Officer.
- External AI services must comply with <ORG_NAME>'s data handling, residency, and security requirements.

5. Governance & Monitoring

- Each AI capability has a named owner, documented scope, and autonomy level.
- All AI models and workflows are tested in "shadow mode" before impacting production.
- We monitor AI performance and analyst overrides and adjust models and policies accordingly.

6. Incidents & Accountability

- AI-related failures are treated as incidents, investigated, and used to improve systems.
- People remain accountable for approving high-impact actions and for the overall security posture; AI does not replace human responsibility.

7. Culture & Training

- Staff are trained to use AI as a teammate, not an oracle.
- Challenging or overriding AI decisions is encouraged where warranted.
- Lessons learned about AI performance feed back into models, workflows, and training.

Next Steps

You can now weave these snippets into your **SOC handbook, security policies**, and **operational standards**, customizing wording and detail to fit your environment, regulatory context, and existing governance frameworks.

Appendix C – Sample Runbooks & Report Templates

This appendix gives you **ready-to-use, AI-aware runbooks and report templates** you can adapt to your environment.

- The **runbooks** show how to blend traditional SOC steps with AI/AI assistant and automation.
- The **report templates** give you consistent, reusable formats for documentation.

Use them as starting points for your internal wiki / SOAR / knowledge base.

1. C1. How to Use This Appendix

- Treat these as **reference patterns**, not gospel.
- For each runbook:
  - Swap in your tools (e.g., "SIEM" → "Splunk", "EDR" → "Defender for Endpoint").
  - Adjust automation levels to your risk appetite.
  - Add tenant/customer-specific steps if you're an MSSP.

Where you see placeholders:

- <ORG_NAME> – your organization
- <SOC_NAME> – your SOC / Cyber Defense Center
- <TOOL_NAME> – your SIEM/EDR/SOAR/etc.

2. C2. Generic Incident Runbook Template

Use this template when drafting your own runbooks.

2.1. C2.1 Runbook Header

- **Runbook ID:** RB-XXX
- **Title:** <Incident type> Response
- **Version / Date:** vX.Y – YYYY-MM-DD
- **Owner:** <Team/Role>
- **Autonomy Level:**
  - Default: Level 0 (suggest only) / Level 1 (human-in-loop) / Level 2 (conditional auto)

2.2. C2.2 Scope & Preconditions

- **Scope – This runbook applies to:**
  - Incident type(s):

- o   Example alerts/detections:
- o   In-scope environments:
- **Out of scope (handled by other runbooks):**
  - o   e.g., full domain-wide ransomware, large-scale data breach.
- **Preconditions:**
  - o   Required logs/sensors:
    - ▪   Identity, Endpoint, Network, Cloud, etc.
  - o   Required tools:
    - ▪   SIEM, EDR, IAM, SOAR, Ticketing, Mail gateway, etc.

2.3. C2.3 Roles & Responsibilities

- **Tier 1 Analyst:** Initial triage, enrichment, documentation.
- **Tier 2 / IR Analyst:** Deep investigation, containment decision.
- **SOC Lead / Incident Commander:** Major decisions, coordination, comms.
- **Automation / SOAR Engineer:** Support for automation failures, edge cases.

2.4. C2.4 High-Level Flow

1. Detect & validate alert.
2. Enrich & assess risk.
3. Decide: True Positive (TP) vs False Positive (FP) vs "Needs more data."
4. Contain & mitigate (if TP).
5. Eradicate & recover.
6. Document, close, and feed lessons back into detections and AI models.

2.5. C2.5 Step Table (Pattern)

Use a table like this; you'll see concrete examples next.

Step	Description	Who	AI / Automation Use	Notes / Decision Points
1	Validate alert	T1	AI assistant summary	...
2	Enrich user/host	T1	Auto-enrichment via SOAR	...
3	Risk assessment	T1/T2	AI triage score	...
...	...	...	...	...

2.6. C2.6 Exit Criteria

Incident can be closed when:

- Root cause identified or at least well-supported hypothesis.

- Containment and recovery actions completed or handed off.
- Relevant tickets updated and reports drafted.
- Detection content / playbooks updated if needed.

3. C3. Runbook #1 – Suspicious User Login (Potential Account Compromise)

3.1. C3.1 Header

- **Runbook ID:** RB-IDENT-001
- **Title:** Suspicious User Login / Possible Account Compromise
- **Version / Date:** v1.0 – YYYY-MM-DD
- **Owner:** Identity & Access Security Team
- **Autonomy Level:**
    - Level 0/1 for decisions about disabling users
    - Level 1/2 for purely investigative enrichment

3.2. C3.2 Scope

- **Applies to:**
    - Alerts about unusual or impossible travel logins
    - Logins from new countries/devices
    - Multiple failed logins followed by success
    - Login anomalies from IdP / IAM / VPN / SSO tools
- **Out of scope:**
    - Confirmed business email compromise with financial fraud indicators (use dedicated BEC runbook).

3.3. C3.3 Step Table

#	Step	Role	AI / Automation Use	Notes
1	Receive & validate alert	T1	AI assistant: "Summarize this alert, why does it matter, likely FP/TP?"	Quickly understand context. If clearly broken test alert or known false pattern, mark as FP and close with reason.
2	Auto-enrichment	SOAR / T1	SOAR pulls: user attributes (role, dept, privileges), device info, geo-IP, known devices, recent logins	If enrichment fails, investigate data pipeline health before proceeding.
3	Risk scoring	AI triage / T1	AI triage engine scores alert based on: user privilege, geo, device reputation, history, CTI	T1 reviews score (e.g., Low/Med/High/Critical). Overrides allowed with reasoning field.
4	Check recent activity	T1	AI assistant: "Summarize last 24–72h of login activity for this user across all sources."	Look for: multiple locations, new devices, odd times.
5	User contact attempt	T1 / T2	AI assistant: "Draft short email/IM script to ask user to confirm activity, no links."	If business process allows, call user via known corporate phone. Never use contact details from the suspicious session.
6	Decision: Suspected compromise?	T2	AI suggestion: "Based on evidence, does this pattern match normal behavior or likely compromise?"	T2 must decide: (a) No compromise, (b) Unclear – monitor, (c) Likely compromise – proceed to containment.

Augmented Security Operations

#	Step	Role	AI / Automation Use	Notes
7	Containment: disable & reset	T2 / IAM	Optional: SOAR pre-populates actions; human must approve for privileged users	Actions: force sign-out, require password reset, reset sessions, revoke tokens, remove active sessions/MFA devices as per policy.
8	Session / scope analysis	T2	AI assistant: "Generate a timeline of key actions for this user from TIME_A to TIME_B."	Check for: mailbox rule changes, MFA changes, access to sensitive apps, unusual downloads.
9	Eradication & recovery	T2	—	Implement password/MFA reset, educate user, restore any misconfigurations.
10	Documentation & closure	T1/T2	AI assistant: draft incident summary; analyst verifies	Ensure incident tagged, IOCs captured, detection rules reviewed.

3.4. C3.4 Exit Criteria

- Account confirmed safe (user verified activity or containment done).
- Any malicious sessions terminated, tokens revoked.
- MFA and password reset where necessary.
- Lessons learned captured (e.g., new TTP, detection gap).

4. C4. Runbook #2 – Phishing Email Reported by User

4.1. C4.1 Header

- **Runbook ID:** RB-MAIL-001
- **Title:** Reported Phishing Email Investigation & Response
- **Owner:** Email Security / SOC
- **Autonomy Level:**
    - Level 2 possible for auto-quarantine of clearly malicious emails (depending on org policy).

4.2. C4.2 Scope

- **Applies to:**
    - Users reporting suspicious emails via button / ticket / forward.
    - Mail gateway phishing detections needing human review.
- **Excludes:**
    - Confirmed BEC or large campaign events (use advanced playbook).

4.3. C4.3 Step Table

#	Step	Role	AI / Automation Use	Notes
1	Ingest user report / alert	T1	AI assistant: "Summarize this email content and headers. Is this likely phishing?"	Include headers, body, links, attachments (sanitized).
2	Auto-analysis of indicators	SOAR / T1	Integrations: URL sandbox, attachment sandbox, threat intel, domain age/IP rep	SOAR can trigger sandboxes; AI summarizes sandbox results.

#	Step	Role	AI / Automation Use	Notes
3	Classification	T1/T2	AI assistant: "Classify this email as benign, spam, or phishing. Explain briefly."	T2 makes final decision. AI is advisory only.
4	Search for similar emails	T1	AI assistant: "Generate search query for all recipients of similar emails in last 7 days."	Use mail logs to find affected users.
5	Bulk actions	T2 / SOAR	SOAR can auto-move matching emails to quarantine/junk; AI suggests list	Level 2 autonomy may allow auto-quarantine for known bad indicators. Human approval required for ambiguous cases.
6	Check for clicks / credential reuse	T2	AI assistant: "Summarize which users clicked links or opened attachments from this campaign."	Cross-reference web proxy, DNS, EDR, IAM logs.
7	Containment	T2	—	Actions may include: reset passwords for users who submitted creds, block domains/URLs, update mail gateway rules.
8	User communication	T1/T2	AI assistant: draft:	

- Thank-you message to reporting user
- Awareness notice to affected users (if needed) | Ensure no direct links to suspicious sites in messages. |
  | 9 | **Update detections** | Detection Eng. | AI assistant: "Draft pattern/rule for mail gateway/SIEM to detect similar emails." | Validate, test, and deploy rules. |
  | 10 | **Documentation & closure** | T1 | AI assistant: draft incident summary & campaign description | Capture IOCs, distribution list, and effective controls. |

4.4. C4.4 Exit Criteria

- Malicious emails removed or mitigated.
- Users who interacted with the phishing email evaluated and remediated.
- Detection rules updated where needed.

5. C5. Runbook #3 – Endpoint Malware Alert (Single Host, Non-Critical)

5.1. C5.1 Header

- **Runbook ID:** RB-ENDP-001
- **Title:** Endpoint Malware Detection on Non-Critical Host
- **Owner:** Endpoint Security Team
- **Autonomy Level:**
  - Level 2 allowed for automatic isolation of non-critical endpoints with high-confidence malware alerts.

5.2. C5.2 Scope

- **Applies to:**

- o EDR detections with malicious verdict for commodity malware on normal user devices.
- **Excludes:**
    - o Critical servers, domain controllers, OT systems (separate runbooks).
    - o Ransomware or lateral movement patterns (see ransomware runbook).

5.3. C5.3 Step Table

#	Step	Role	AI / Automation Use	Notes
1	Receive EDR alert	T1	AI assistant: "Explain this alert and detection logic in simple terms."	Understand type (malware, PUA, script, macro).
2	Check host criticality & tagging	SOAR / T1	Automation fetches host tags, criticality, owner	If host tagged as critical → follow critical host procedure (no auto-isolation).
3	Auto-isolation decision	AI triage / SOAR	Policy: if non-critical, detection confidence high, known malware → auto-isolate	Human notified; can override/undo via defined process.
4	Malware details & scope	T1/T2	AI assistant: "Summarize file/path, process tree, persistence mechanisms, and known TTPs."	Helps quickly understand severity and impact.
5	Check for lateral activity	T2	AI assistant: "Generate queries to find related activity from this host/user in SIEM and EDR."	Look for remote connections, use of admin tools, unusual SMB/RDP.
6	Containment actions	T2	SOAR can orchestrate: maintain/isolate host, block hash, update AV signatures	Ensure no autonomous host wipes; follow org policy.
7	Eradication	IT / T2	—	Clean or reimage host per standard; ensure no persistence.
8	User interaction	T1	AI assistant: draft user comms (simple note: machine under maintenance, minimal tech detail)	Coordinate with IT/helpdesk.
9	Update detections / lessons	Det. Eng.	AI assistant: "What generic patterns could detect similar malware earlier?"	Create or refine detection content.
10	Documentation & closure	T1	AI assistant: draft technical case summary	Include notes on whether auto-isolation worked well.

5.4. C5.4 Exit Criteria

- Host remediated (cleaned/reimaged).
- No signs of lateral movement or persistence.
- Blocking controls in place (hash/signature, URL/domain, etc.).

6. C6. Runbook #4 – Early-Stage Ransomware on Single Endpoint

6.1. C6.1 Header

- **Runbook ID:** RB-RANS-001
- **Title:** Suspected Ransomware Activity on Single Endpoint
- **Owner:** Incident Response Team
- **Autonomy Level:**
    - o Level 1–2 for rapid isolation of non-critical endpoints.
    - o Level 0–1 for any actions involving file deletion, backups, or servers.

6.2. C6.2 Scope

- **Applies to:**
    - EDR/AV alerts for ransomware-like behavior (suspicious encryption, shadow copy deletion).
    - File server or endpoint logs with sudden spike in file modifications from single host.
- **Excludes:**
    - Confirmed multi-endpoint or domain-wide outbreak (use major incident runbook).

6.3. C6.3 Step Table

#	Step	Role	AI / Automation Use	Notes
1	Confirm alert type	T1	AI assistant: "Explain why this alert suggests ransomware (what behaviors?)."	Understand detection logic & context.
2	Immediate isolation decision	T1/T2	AI triage: if host non-critical + strong ransomware signals → recommend immediate isolation	Human may approve auto-isolation; log decision. For critical hosts, escalate to IR lead before isolating.
3	Snapshot key info	SOAR / T2	Automation collects: running processes, network connections, recent events, user, map of accessed shares	Ensure snapshot before any further impact or reboot if possible.
4	Assess blast radius	T2	AI assistant: "Summarize which file shares and servers this host accessed in last X hours."	Check for: encryption patterns, impacted directories, other suspicious hosts.
5	Check for other hosts	T2	AI assistant: "Generate SIEM queries to find similar patterns on other endpoints/servers."	Look for EDR alerts, file event anomalies, process behaviors.
6	Containment	IR Lead / T2	—	May include: keeping host isolated, blocking C2 domains, disabling suspect user accounts (if compromise suspected).
7	Coordinate with IT / business	IR Lead	AI assistant: draft short internal comms for IT/business owner	Set expectation: possible data impact, ongoing investigation.
8	Eradication & forensic steps	IR / Forensics	—	Preserve key artefacts, consider full disk image if needed. Remove malware, reimage host, restore from backups as per policy.
9	Detection & control improvements	Det. Eng. / IR	AI assistant: help draft detection patterns & hardening steps (backups, segmentation, MFA, patching)	Feed lessons into pre-emptive defense program.
10	Documentation & PIR trigger	IR	AI assistant: draft technical report + PIR outline	For ransomware, trigger formal post-incident review.

6.4. C6.4 Exit Criteria

- Ransomware activity fully contained to initial host(s).
- Confirm no wider spread or persistence.
- Recovery verified and business impact documented.

7. C7. Technical Incident Report Template

Use this for **internal SOC documentation** in your wiki/ticket system.

7.1. C7.1 Header

- **Incident ID:** INC-XXXX
- **Title:** <Short descriptive title>
- **Severity:** Low / Medium / High / Critical
- **Status:** Open / Contained / Resolved / Closed
- **Date/Time Detected:**
- **Date/Time Resolved:**
- **Detection Source(s):** SIEM / EDR / User report / CTI / Deception / Other
- **Owner / Incident Commander:**

7.2. C7.2 Summary

3–6 sentences: what happened, how it was detected, what systems/users were involved, current status.

7.3. C7.3 Environment & Scope

- **Impacted users/accounts:**
- **Impacted hosts/endpoints:**
- **Impacted applications/services:**
- **Impacted data (if any):**

7.4. C7.4 Detection & Triage

- **Initial alert(s):**
  - Alert IDs, rules, detection names, timestamps.
- **AI involvement:**
  - Was AI used for triage (risk scoring, grouping)? How did it influence prioritization?
- **Initial triage actions:**
  - Key checks, enrichment steps, quick decisions.

7.5. C7.5 Investigation

- **Key questions investigated:**
  - e.g., "Was the account compromised?", "Did malware spread laterally?"
- **Timeline (high level):**
  - YYYY-MM-DD HH:MM – <Event>
  - …
- **Findings:**
  - User/host behavior analysis.

- TTPs identified (map to MITRE if you use it).
- Evidence of lateral movement / privilege escalation / exfiltration (if any).
- **Use of AI/AI assistant during investigation:**
  - Query assistance? Timeline drafts? Hypothesis suggestions?

7.6. C7.6 Root Cause & Contributing Factors

- **Likely root cause:**
  - e.g., Phishing link clicked and credentials entered, unpatched system exploited, misconfiguration exposed service, etc.
- **Contributing factors:**
  - Gaps in patching, missing control, user training, detection blind spots, process failures.
- **Confidence level:** High / Medium / Low (explain any uncertainty).

7.7. C7.7 Containment, Eradication & Recovery

- **Containment actions:**
  - Host isolation, account disable, blocking rules, mail removal, etc.
- **Eradication:**
  - Malware removed, persistence deleted, backdoors closed.
- **Recovery:**
  - Systems restored, access re-enabled, data restored from backup where necessary.
- **Residual risk:**
  - Any uncertainty about remaining compromise.

7.8. C7.8 Impact Assessment

- **Business impact:**
  - Downtime, degraded service, manual workarounds, user disruption.
- **Data impact:**
  - Data accessed/modified/exfiltrated? Type and sensitivity.
- **Regulatory/contractual impact:**
  - Notification requirements, reportable event assessment.

7.9. C7.9 Lessons Learned & Improvements

- **What worked well:**
  - Controls, detections, processes, team behavior.
- **What did not work well / needs improvement:**
  - Detection gaps, noisy rules, communication issues, tool limitations.
- **Improvements implemented / planned:**
  - Detections, playbooks, controls, training.
- **AI-related improvements:**
  - Model/triage rule updates, new AI assistant patterns, automation tuning.

7.10.   C7.10 Attachments & References

- Links to SIEM queries, dashboards, ticket(s), forensic reports, CTI references.

8. C8. Executive Incident Summary Template

Use this for **management / non-technical stakeholders**. Often 1 page.

8.1. C8.1 Basic Details

- **Incident ID:**
- **Title:**
- **Severity:** Low / Medium / High / Critical
- **Status:** Contained / Resolved / Monitoring
- **Date(s):** Detection date, incident window.

8.2. C8.2 What Happened (Plain Language)

1–2 short paragraphs:

- What was detected (e.g., suspicious login, malware on endpoint, phishing campaign).
- How it was discovered (e.g., automated detection, user report).
- Which part of the organization was affected.

8.3. C8.3 Impact

- **Systems / services impacted:**
  - e.g., "Single user laptop", "File share for Team X", "No production impact."
- **Data impact:**
  - "No evidence of data exfiltration."
  - or: "Limited access to internal documents in SharePoint site Y."
- **Business disruption:**
  - "No downtime." / "Minor disruption for N users." / "Service X unavailable for Y hours."

8.4. C8.4 Response

- **Key actions taken:**
  - Bullet list: isolations, blocks, resets, restores.
- **Timeline highlights:**

- o Detection time.
- o Containment time.
- o Recovery time.

8.5. C8.5 Risk & Next Steps

- **Residual risk:**
  - o "We consider the immediate risk contained, and we are monitoring for recurrence."
- **Follow-up actions:**
  - o e.g., user training, control hardening, new detection rules, third-party coordination.
- **Support requested from business:**
  - o e.g., assisting with process changes, supporting rollout of MFA, allowing maintenance windows.

9. C9. MSSP / Multi-Tenant Customer Report Template

For service providers reporting to clients.

9.1. C9.1 Monthly/Quarterly SOC Report – Structure

1. **Cover Page**
   - o Client name
   - o Reporting period
   - o SOC contact info
2. **Executive Summary**
   - o Overall security posture summary
   - o Top events/incidents
   - o Key improvements
3. **Key Metrics**
   - o Total alerts processed
   - o Incidents by severity
   - o Mean time to detect / respond
   - o Top use cases / detections triggered
4. **Significant Incidents**
   - o Short summaries (use exec summary template)
5. **Trends & Observations**
   - o Attack trends, campaign activity, repeated issues
6. **Detection & Control Changes**
   - o New rules, tuning, automations relevant to the client
7. **Recommendations**
   - o Technical and procedural actions for client

9.2. C9.2 Example Section Text

Executive Summary (Client-Facing)

During the period <DATE_RANGE>, <SOC_NAME> monitored your environment 24/7 and processed <N> security alerts.

We identified <X> high-severity and <Y> medium-severity incidents. All high-severity incidents were contained without confirmed data exfiltration or significant business disruption.

The most common threat patterns involved phishing attempts against users and commodity malware detections on user endpoints. We continued to see automated scanning and vulnerable service probing, which were successfully blocked by existing controls.

Significant Incident Summary (Per Incident)

- **Incident ID & Title**
- **Date Range**
- **What Happened:** 2–3 sentences.
- **Impact:** systems/data; whether business disruption occurred.
- **Actions Taken by <SOC_NAME>:** bullets.
- **Recommended Client Actions:** bullets (e.g., enable MFA for more users, patch systems, review user training).

10. C10. Post-Incident Review (PIR) Template

For structured after-action reviews.

10.1. C10.1 Basic Info

- **Incident ID & Title:**
- **Date of PIR Meeting:**
- **Participants:**
- **Facilitator:**

10.2. C10.2 Objectives

- Understand what happened and why.
- Identify what worked / what didn't.
- Capture improvements for technology, process, people, and AI.

10.3. C10.3 What Happened

- Short recap of the incident (from technical report).
- Key dates and milestones.

10.4. C10.4 What Worked Well

- Detections that fired correctly.
- Effective decisions or containment actions.
- Tools or playbooks that helped.
- AI and automation aspects that added clear value.

10.5. C10.5 What Didn't Work / Pain Points

- Missed or delayed signals.
- Communication gaps.
- Process confusion.
- Tool / integration problems.
- AI misfires, misleading summaries, or unhelpful suggestions.

10.6. C10.6 Improvements & Action Items

For each improvement:

- **Area:** Detection / Automation / Playbooks / Training / AI Models / Governance / Other
- **Description:**
- **Owner:**
- **Priority:** High / Medium / Low
- **Target Date:**

10.7. C10.7 AI-Specific Reflection (Optional Section)

- **Did AI help in this incident? How?**
- **Where did AI hinder or mislead?**
- **Should we adjust:**
    - AI triage thresholds?
    - AI assistant prompts?
    - Automation guardrails?

This appendix should give you enough structure to:

- Stand up **concrete, AI-aware runbooks** for your core SOC use cases.
- Standardize **incident reporting** for internal, executive, and customer audiences.
- Run **consistent post-incident reviews** that feed back into your AI models, detections, and playbooks.

Customize aggressively—these are meant to be **practical scaffolding**, not rigid templates.

Augmented Security Operations

Appendix D – SOC Maturity & Readiness Checklists

This appendix gives you **structured checklists** you can use to:

- Assess your current SOC maturity
- Check readiness for AI augmentation and automation
- Identify concrete gaps to feed into your roadmap

You can turn these into:

- Spreadsheets
- Internal wiki pages
- Self-assessment forms (with scores 1–5 per item)

Where you see 1–5, you can score:

- **1** = Not true at all
- **2** = Partially true / ad-hoc
- **3** = Mostly true in some areas
- **4** = Largely true across the SOC
- **5** = Fully true, documented, and consistently applied

1. D1. High-Level SOC Maturity Checklist

Use this to get a **quick view** of where you are today across core dimensions.

You can average each section to map roughly onto the maturity levels from Chapter 11:

- 1–2 = Level 0–1 (Fragmented / Instrumented)
- 3 = Level 2 (Augmented candidate)
- 4 = Level 2–3 (Ready for Semi-Autonomous)
- 5 = Level 3–4 (Selectively Autonomous capable)

1.1. D1.1 Strategy & Governance

Score each 1–5:

1. We have a **documented SOC mission and scope** (what we protect, what "good" looks like).
2. Our **risk appetite** for detection and response (including false positives/negatives) is understood and communicated.
3. We have a **SOC roadmap** or improvement plan updated at least annually.
4. We have **clear roles and responsibilities** (SOC org chart, RACI for major workflows).

5. We have documented **incident severity classifications** and corresponding response expectations (SLAs / SLOs).

Average Strategy & Governance score: ___ / 5

1.2. D1.2 Data & Visibility

1. Key **identity logs** (IdP, AD/LDAP, SSO, VPN) are reliably ingested into SIEM/XDR.
2. Key **endpoint telemetry** (EDR/AV/OS logs) is ingested and searchable.
3. Key **network/edge logs** (firewalls, proxies, WAF, VPN, DNS) are ingested and searchable.
4. Key **cloud & SaaS logs** (e.g., M365, Azure/AWS/GCP, Okta, Salesforce, critical SaaS) are ingested.
5. **Crown jewels** (critical apps, databases, OT) have defined telemetry and visibility.
6. We monitor **data quality** (ingestion failures, parsing errors, gaps).
7. We monitor **coverage** (e.g., % of endpoints reporting, % of critical apps onboarded).

Average Data & Visibility score: ___ / 5

1.3. D1.3 Detection & Response

1. We have a **documented catalog of detection rules/use cases** (not just vendor defaults).
2. We track **detection performance** (TP/FP rates or at least representative samples).
3. We have **documented playbooks** for top 5–10 incident types.
4. We use **case management** (tickets/incidents) with consistent fields and status flows.
5. We measure basic response metrics (e.g., MTTA, MTTD, MTTR).
6. We review and tune **noisy or low-value alerts** regularly.

Average Detection & Response score: ___ / 5

1.4. D1.4 People & Operating Model

1. We have sufficient **analyst coverage** for our operating hours (24/7 or follow-the-sun if applicable).
2. Analysts have **clear career paths** (e.g., T1 → T2 → IR / detection / automation).
3. We invest in **training and skill development** for analysts (technical skills + tools).
4. We have **detection/content engineering** capacity (not just "everyone does everything ad-hoc").
5. The SOC **collaborates** with IT, cloud, DevOps, and business units during incidents.

Average People & Operating Model score: ___ / 5

1.5. D1.5 Tooling, SOAR & Automation

1. We have a **central SIEM/XDR** that analysts primarily use (not just a dozen consoles).
2. We have at least **basic SOAR / orchestration** or scripting for repetitive tasks.
3. SOAR / automation is used for **enrichment** (e.g., CTI lookups, user/asset lookups).
4. Some **low-risk workflows** are already partially automated (e.g., ticket creation, user notifications).
5. We have **logging and audit trails** for automations (what they did, when, and on what).

Average Tooling & Automation score: ___ / 5

Overall SOC Maturity Insight

- Strategy & Governance: ___
- Data & Visibility: ___
- Detection & Response: ___
- People & Operating Model: ___
- Tooling & Automation: ___

This gives you a **baseline** before you add AI-specific readiness.

2. D2. AI Readiness Checklist (Pre-Autonomous SOC)

This checklist focuses specifically on **whether your SOC is ready to benefit from AI** (triage, AI assistants, automation) without chaos.

Use it **per environment** if needed (e.g., corporate IT vs OT).

2.1. D2.1 Data & Telemetry Readiness for AI

1. We can reliably extract **representative samples of alerts** and associated logs (e.g., last 3–6 months) for training and testing AI.
2. Our main log sources use a **consistent schema** or mapping (e.g., normalized fields).
3. We can join logs with **user and asset context** (e.g., user role, asset criticality).
4. We can provide **labels** (True Positive / False Positive / Benign / Suspicious) for at least a subset of historical incidents.
5. Ingestion latency is acceptable for AI-assisted triage (e.g., minutes, not hours).

Average AI Data Readiness score: ___ / 5

2.2. D2.2 Process & Playbook Readiness

1. We have **repeatable processes** (playbooks) for our most common alert types.
2. We understand and can articulate **current triage criteria** (how analysts decide severity/priority).
3. We log **investigation outcomes** consistently (e.g., confirmed incident type, root cause).
4. We track **remediation outcomes** (what worked, what didn't) in a way that AI can learn from.
5. We have a **change management process** for detection rules, playbooks, and workflows.

Average AI Process Readiness score: ___ / 5

2.3. D2.3 Governance & Risk for AI

1. We have a **draft or formal policy** describing AI usage in the SOC (even if simple).
2. We have an **AI use case approval process** (someone must sign off on new AI capabilities).
3. We have identified at least one **AI owner / champion** (e.g., SOC product owner, AI engineer).
4. We have a way to **log and review AI outputs** (scores, recommendations, actions).
5. We have criteria for what constitutes an **AI-related incident** (and will treat it as such).

Average AI Governance score: ___ / 5

2.4. D2.4 People & Culture Readiness

1. Analysts are **aware of AI/AI assistant tools** and why we're considering them.
2. There is **no strong fear or resistance** ("AI will definitely replace us") dominating the culture.
3. Analysts are **encouraged to question tools** and raise concerns, not blindly follow them.
4. We are prepared to provide **training** on how to work with AI (prompting, validation, feedback).
5. Leadership is willing to give analysts **time to experiment** and refine AI workflows.

Average AI Culture Readiness score: ___ / 5

2.5. D2.5 Technology & Integration Readiness

1. Our SIEM/XDR/SOAR tools can **integrate with AI services** (via APIs, connectors, or built-in features).
2. We can provide **sandbox/test environments** for new AI capabilities (not only production).
3. We have **monitoring for the AI infrastructure** itself (availability, errors, performance).

4. We can configure **RBAC and logging** for AI usage (who used what, when).
5. We have at least **initial POCs or experiments** with AI-based triage, AI assistant, or response (even if small).

Average AI Tech Integration score: ___ / 5

AI Readiness Snapshot

- AI Data Readiness: ___
- AI Process Readiness: ___
- AI Governance: ___
- AI Culture: ___
- AI Tech Integration: ___

If most scores are **1–2**, focus on **foundations** before pushing AI into production triage or actions.
If you're at **3+**, you can safely experiment with **Level 0–1 (suggest / human-in-loop)**.
If you're at **4+**, you can consider **limited Level 2 (conditional auto)** in low-risk domains.

3. D3. SOC "Autonomy Readiness" Checklist

This checklist is for when you're considering **actual automated actions** driven or informed by AI (Level 2).

3.1. D3.1 Policy & Guardrails

1. We have **explicitly documented which actions may be automated** (e.g., isolate non-critical endpoints, revoke risky tokens).
2. High-impact actions (e.g., disabling privileged accounts, changing core firewall rules) are **explicitly excluded** from full autonomy.
3. Every automated workflow has a **documented scope and preconditions** (what must be true before it runs).
4. There is a **published list of Level 2 automations** and their owners.
5. We have a **kill switch** or easy method to suspend specific automations if they misbehave.

Average Policy & Guardrails score: ___ / 5

3.2. D3.2 Logging, Monitoring & Control

1. All automations log **inputs, decisions, and actions** with timestamps.
2. We regularly **review automation logs** (e.g., monthly) for anomalies and unintended behavior.

3. Analysts can **easily see** whether an action was automatic or manually triggered.
4. We measure **override/rollback frequency** (how often humans undo automated actions).
5. We have a process to **update or roll back automation logic** quickly if new information emerges.

Average Logging & Monitoring score: ___ / 5

3.3. D3.3 Testing & Validation

1. New automations are **tested with synthetic / historical data** before going live.
2. We use **shadow mode** or dry run for new AI-driven decisions before allowing them to act.
3. For each automation, we have defined **success criteria and failure scenarios**.
4. We periodically **re-test automations** after major infrastructure or tool changes.
5. We have at least one **documented case** where we identified and fixed a problem with automation through testing—not after a major incident.

Average Testing & Validation score: ___ / 5

3.4. D3.4 Impact & Risk Awareness

1. For each automation, we understand the **business impact** if it triggers in error (e.g., short user disruption vs major outage).
2. We have **business owners** for critical systems who know what automations exist around them.
3. We can explain to leadership **where we allow autonomy and why**.
4. We have run **tabletop exercises** that include AI/automation behavior (e.g., "What if it isolates 50 hosts incorrectly?").
5. We have defined **escalation paths** if automation impacts critical services or VIP users.

Average Impact & Risk Awareness score: ___ / 5

Autonomy Readiness Insight
If all subsections are ≥3, you can consider Level 2 autonomy for **low-risk, well-understood** scenarios.
If any are ≤2, focus on governance and control first.

4. D4. AI-in-SOC Maturity Grid (Condensed)

You can use this as a **single-page view** for leadership.

Rate each row 1–5 and then mark which column best matches your reality.

Dimension	1–2: Level 0–1	3: Level 2	4: Level 2–3	5: Level 3–4
Data & Visibility	Fragmented logs, gaps, no consistency	Key sources in SIEM, basic normalization	Coverage for main domains + health monitoring	Rich, high-quality telemetry with strong context & monitoring
Playbooks & Process	Mostly ad-hoc, tribal knowledge	Basic playbooks for common incidents	Playbooks used daily; updated regularly	Playbooks integrated with SIEM/SOAR and AI; continuous improvement
AI Usage	Little or only vendor-default AI	AI assistants / small experiments used by some analysts	AI-assisted triage in production (no auto actions)	AI is integral for triage, hunting, reporting; selective autonomy in low-risk areas
Automation	Almost none	Automation for enrichment & ticketing	Some semi-auto responses (human approval)	Conditional autonomy for select low-risk actions with strong guardrails
Governance & Risk	No AI policies, informal risk handling	Initial AI policy; some oversight	Defined AI use case lifecycle and metrics	Mature AI governance; AI failures treated systematically as incidents
People & Culture	"Alert factory" mindset, little time to improve	Recognition of need to reduce toil; early upskilling	Analysts use AI/AI assistant as normal; question tools openly	SOC thinks in systems; continuous feedback into AI, detections, and process

You can attach your **average score per row** to one of the columns to describe where you are and where you want to go.

5. D5. Quick "Go / No-Go" Gate for AI Triage & AI assistant

Use this 10-question checklist when deciding: "Are we ready to roll out AI triage and AI assistant beyond a small pilot?"

Answer **Yes/No**:

1. We can **reliably fetch historical alerts + logs** for testing AI.
2. We have **at least some labelled incidents** (TP/FP) for major alert types.
3. Our analysts already use **consistent fields** in incident tickets (type, cause, outcome).
4. We have **playbooks** for the incident types we want AI to support.
5. We have **documented AI use cases** (triage, AI assistant) with clear boundaries.
6. We have at least a **draft AI policy** and understand our data/privacy constraints.
7. We have a way to **monitor AI performance** (e.g., compare AI scores vs actual incident outcomes).
8. Analysts have been **briefed about AI**, its role, and their right to challenge it.
9. We can run AI in **suggest-only mode** without changing production triage logic immediately.
10. We have a **named owner** for the AI capability who will watch it and improve it.

- **8–10 Yes:** Strong candidate for broader AI triage/AI assistant rollout.
- **5–7 Yes:** Proceed with small, tightly scoped pilots; fix gaps before scaling.
- **≤4 Yes:** Focus on foundations first; broader AI in triage is premature.

6. D6. Quick "Go / No-Go" Gate for Level 2 Autonomy

Similarly, use this when deciding if a **specific automation** can move from human-approved to conditional auto.

For the **one** playbook/automation in question, answer Yes/No:

1. The **incident type is well-understood** and repetitive.
2. The **action is low-impact** if triggered incorrectly (e.g., minor user inconvenience, not major outage).
3. The automation has ** clear preconditions** (what must be true before it fires).
4. We have at least **30–50 past cases** of this incident type to validate the logic.
5. We have run the automation in **semi-auto mode** with humans approving for a period.
6. We have **zero or very few serious overrides** ("this would have been harmful").
7. The automation is **fully logged** (inputs, decisions, actions).
8. We have a **simple kill-switch** (off switch) for this automation.
9. Business/asset owners for affected systems have been **informed and agree**.
10. We have updated **documentation and runbooks** to reflect the new autonomy level.

- **9–10 Yes:** Reasonable to move to Level 2 autonomy (conditional, still monitored).
- **7–8 Yes:** Consider limited/autonomous scope only (e.g., specific host group); monitor closely.
- **≤6 Yes:** Keep at Level 1 (human approval) and refine before autonomy.

7. D7. Turning Checklists into a Practical Plan

Once you've filled in these checklists:

1. **Highlight all items scored 1–2**
   - These are **foundational gaps**.
   - Prioritize fixes before deploying complex AI or autonomy in that area.
2. **Highlight items scored 3**
   - These are **"ready but immature"** areas.
   - Good places to pilot AI in **Level 0–1** (AI assistant, suggest-only triage).
3. **Highlight items scored 4–5**
   - These are candidates for:
     - Scaling AI assistant usage
     - Introducing Level 2 autonomy (carefully)
     - More advanced pre-emptive use (CTI, deception, hunting loops)
4. Build a **3–6 month action list**:

- o 3–5 high-priority improvements for:
    - Data & visibility
    - Processes & playbooks
    - People & training
    - AI use cases & governance
5. Review these checklists **every 6–12 months**
    - o Track your maturity movement per dimension.
    - o Celebrate progress (e.g., "We moved from average 2.3 to 3.5 in AI Governance").

These SOC maturity & readiness checklists are meant to be **living tools**.

Customize them, add your own domain-specific sections (OT, industrial, MSSP multi-tenant, etc.), and integrate them into:

- Internal assessments
- SOC road mapping workshops
- Budget and planning cycles
- Post-incident reviews ("Which checklist items would have helped us avoid this?")

The goal isn't a perfect score—it's **continuous, deliberate movement** toward a SOC that is:

- Better instrumented
- More efficient
- Safer and more effective with AI
- And ultimately capable of **selective autonomy** where it truly reduces risk.

Appendix E – Practical Checklists, Templates & Worksheets

This appendix is your **grab-and-go toolkit**.

Where the chapters explain *what* and *why*, Appendix E gives you **ready-made checklists and templates** you can:

- Print and put on the SOC wall
- Drop into Confluence / Notion / SharePoint
- Use in workshops and planning sessions
- Reuse for reviews, audits, and board updates

It's organized into:

1. Quick Checklists
2. Design Templates
3. Operational Worksheets
4. Review & Governance Helpers

Feel free to copy, remix, and adapt all of this to your own environment.

1. Quick Checklists

These are lightweight lists you can use as "pre-flight checks" before you deploy AI in the SOC, choose new use cases, or adjust autonomy.

1.1. AI Readiness Checklist (SOC-Level)

Use before you invest heavily in AI-in-SOC, or as a quarterly health check.

Data & Telemetry

- Critical identity logs (IdP, VPN, SSO) are ingested and searchable.
- EDR/endpoint telemetry is ingested for most endpoints, especially critical ones.
- Cloud control plane logs are enabled and ingested for key cloud providers.
- Network/edge/security appliance logs are ingested (firewalls, proxies, gateways).
- Key business applications produce usable security/audit logs.
- Asset inventory and CMDB are in reasonable shape for critical systems.
- User / role / HR context (e.g., department, privilege level) is available for enrichment.

Processes & Playbooks

- Top 5–10 incident types have basic **runbooks** (even if not fully automated).
- Ticket/case templates exist for incidents (fields are consistent and structured).
- Escalation thresholds and paths are documented.
- You have some notion of **severity** and **priority** consistently applied.

People & Culture

- SOC leadership supports using AI as **augmentation**, not replacement.
- At least 1–2 people can act as **champions** for AI-in-SOC.
- Analysts are open to trying new workflows (and giving honest feedback).
- There is no culture of "tool worship" (AI outputs can be questioned).

Governance & Risk

- A draft **AI-in-SOC policy** exists or is being written.
- Clear "red lines" exist (systems or actions where automation is never allowed).
- You can log and audit AI interactions and automated actions.
- Risk/compliance are aware of initial AI plans (even at a high level).

If you're missing many items above, focus your first 90 days on **foundations**, not fancy AI features.

1.2. AI Use Case Selection Checklist

Use this when deciding *which* AI use cases to pursue first.

For each candidate use case, ask:

Value

- Does this reduce significant **toil** (repetitive work) for the SOC?
- Does it help with a **real bottleneck** (e.g., triage, reporting, investigations)?
- Is the impact **measurable** (time saved, MTTA/MTTR, quality)?

Risk

- Can we start with **Level 0 or 1** (suggest-only / human-in-loop)?
- Does failure of this AI output have **limited impact** (no direct business outage)?
- Are there clear manual fallbacks if AI performs poorly?

Data & Feasibility

- Do we already have **sufficient data** for this use case?
- Is the data quality reasonable (few missing fields, consistent formats)?

- Can we integrate AI into the **places analysts already work** (SIEM, SOAR, ticketing)?

Adoption

- Will analysts actually use this, or is it "nice in theory"?
- Can we explain the feature and expected use in **10–15 minutes**?
- Can we pilot with a **small group** and expand later?

If a use case scores high on value, low-medium on risk, and medium-high on feasibility, it's a good candidate for your **first 90 days**.

1.3. Guardrails & Autonomy Checklist

Use whenever you design or review an automated / AI-influenced playbook.

For each playbook step:

Autonomy Level

- We have explicitly chosen:
    - Level 0 – Suggest-only (AI recommends, human acts)
    - Level 1 – Human-in-loop (AI/SOAR proposes, human approves)
    - Level 2 – Conditional autonomy (auto-action with guardrails)

Preconditions

- Asset scope is limited (e.g., only user endpoints, non-critical servers).
- Environment is clear (e.g., "never run in production DB cluster or OT").
- Detection / alert source is trusted and well-understood.
- Any required **tags/metadata** (criticality, tenant, environment) are available.

Rate & Blast Radius

- Rate limits set (e.g., "max N actions per X minutes").
- Actions are **idempotent** or safe to repeat (or explicitly controlled).
- There is a defined **rollback** step for each reversible action.

Logging & Audit

- Every auto-action is logged with:
    - Timestamp
    - Playbook name and version
    - Conditions met (inputs, scores)
    - Who/what triggered it (AI, rule, human)

- Logs are accessible for investigations and post-incident reviews.

Kill Switch

- There is a simple way to disable this playbook or its auto steps quickly.
- Operators know **who can flip the switch** and how.

If any of these are unclear or missing, **do not enable Level 2** for that step yet.

1.4. Ethics, Bias & Privacy Quick Check

Run this before enabling new AI behaviors that touch user data or access decisions.

- Are we using logs and data **only for security purposes**, not for general employee monitoring?
- Are we collecting/retaining the **minimum data** needed for this AI use case?
- Are we sending data to external AI services with:
    - Encryption in transit
    - Data minimization and/or masking
    - Clarity on whether data is used to train shared models
- Could this logic **disproportionately flag** a certain region, shift, role, or group?
- Do we have a way for analysts to say, "This looks biased or unfair"?
- Is there a way for impacted individuals (e.g., users misflagged) to get issues corrected?
- Is AI clearly positioned as **advisory**, with humans responsible for high-impact decisions?

If answers are mostly "no" or "not sure", pause and involve **risk/compliance/HR** before proceeding.

1.5. Metrics & ROI Checklist

Use when designing or reviewing an AI initiative.

- We have **baseline** numbers for the impacted workflow (before AI).
- We know **what to measure** after AI (e.g., time saved, MTTA, MTTR, error rates).
- We agree on:
    - Time period for measurement (e.g., 4–8 weeks).
    - Sample size (alerts/incidents/time window).
- We can distinguish:
    - "More cases handled because of AI" vs
    - "Same effort but with better quality/coverage."
- We have a **simple ROI story**:
    - Time saved x volume x cost

- o Plus qualitative benefits (clarity, analyst satisfaction, fewer escalations).
- Metrics will be reviewed at:
  - o 30-day and/or 90-day checkpoints.

2. Design Templates

These templates help you design AI use cases, playbooks, prompts, and policies in a structured way.

2.1. AI Use Case Design Canvas

Use this for each AI use case you want to design or pilot.

Use Case Name
(e.g., "AI-Assisted Alert Summaries for Identity Alerts")

1. Problem & Outcome

- Current pain / problem:
- Desired outcome (in one sentence):
- How we'll measure success (metrics):

2. Scope & Context

- Data sources involved:
- Incident / alert types in scope:
- Roles involved (Tier 1, Tier 2, IR, CTI, etc.):
- Tools where AI will appear (SIEM, SOAR, ticketing, separate console):

3. AI Function(s)

Tick all that apply and describe:

- Summarization (alerts/incidents) – How:
- Context gathering (related events, user/host history) – How:
- Recommendations (next steps, severity, playbooks) – How:
- Report drafting (IR, executive summaries) – How:
- Scoring/prioritization – How:
- Other – How:

4. Autonomy & Guardrails (Initial)

- Initial autonomy level:

- o Level 0 – Suggest-only
- o Level 1 – Human-in-loop
- o Level 2 – Conditional auto (later phase)
- Guardrails for this use case:
  - o Data limitations:
  - o Systems excluded:
  - o Actions excluded or require extra approval:

5. Inputs & Outputs

- Inputs to the AI:
  - o Fields, logs, context, timeline events, etc.
- Outputs from the AI:
  - o Format (bullets, JSON, fields in ticket):
  - o Where outputs are stored/visible:

6. Risks & Failure Modes

- What could go wrong if AI behaves poorly?
- How will we detect that it's going wrong (metrics, complaints, overrides)?
- Manual fallback plan:

7. Adoption Plan

- Who will use this first (pilot group)?
- Training required (docs, short session, examples):
- Feedback collection:
  - o Channel or form:
  - o Review cadence:

8. Go/No-Go Criteria

- Minimum quality expectations before we call it a success:
- Conditions where we'll roll back or pause the use case:

2.2. Playbook + Autonomy Template

A structured template for designing or refactoring a playbook with autonomy levels.

Playbook Name
(e.g., "Endpoint Malware on User Workstation – Standard Response")

Overview

- Playbook purpose:

- Applicable environments/tenants:
- Out of scope (systems, geos, special cases):

Step Table

Step #	Description	Autonomy (0/1/2)	Preconditions (if Level 1/2)	Rollback / Notes
1				
2				
3				
4				

Guardrails

- Asset tags required (e.g., endpoint = true, criticality != critical):
- Environments allowed (e.g., EU user endpoints only):
- Rate limit (e.g., max 5 isolations / 15 minutes):
- Additional approvals needed for certain steps:

Kill Switch & Ownership

- How to disable this playbook / auto steps quickly:
- Who owns this playbook (name, role):
- Who can approve changes to autonomy or guardrails:

2.3. Prompt Template Sheet

A simple way to standardize prompts for common SOC workflows.

For each common task, define:

Task Name: (e.g., "Alert Summary for Tier 1 Analyst")

Prompt Template:

Instruction to AI (role, style, goal)

Slots for variables (e.g., {{alert_json}}, {{user_context}})

Example

Task: Incident Summary for IR Handover

Prompt Template:

"You are helping an incident responder understand the current state of a case. Given the incident details, alert list, and key events below, produce:

- A 5–8 bullet summary of what happened (chronological)
- Current impact (users, systems, data)
- Actions taken so far
- 3–5 recommended next steps for the responder

Use only the data provided. Clearly mark anything that is speculative as 'possible/unconfirmed'."

Inputs:

- {{incident_description}}
- {{list_of_alerts}}
- {{timeline_events}}

Output Format:

- Markdown bullets stored in ticket field AI_summary

You can create similar templates for:

- Alert triage
- CTI → hunts suggestions
- Hunt query generation
- Executive-level incident summaries

2.4. AI-In-SOC Policy Skeleton (Mini Outline)

Use this as the starting outline for your own policy.

1. Purpose & Scope

- Why we are using AI in the SOC
- Systems and use cases in scope / out of scope

2. Definitions

- AI assistant, automation, autonomy levels, AI-related incident, etc.

3. Principles

- Purpose-bound, proportionate, human-in-loop, accountable, privacy-respecting

4. Approved AI Use Cases (High Level)

- Triage assistance
- Investigation assistance
- CTI summarization

- Reporting assistance
- Limited automation for low-risk scenarios

5. Autonomy Levels & Guardrails

- Definitions of Level 0/1/2
- Where Level 2 is allowed / not allowed
- Preconditions (asset tags, environments, tenants)
- Rate limits, kill switches

6. Data Usage & Privacy

- What data can/cannot be sent to AI services
- Data residency expectations
- Rules for external AI vendors (no training on our data without explicit approval, etc.)

7. Roles & Responsibilities

- SOC lead, automation/platform owner, AI-in-SOC owner, risk/compliance, etc.

8. AI-Related Incidents

- Definition
- Examples
- Required steps in post-incident review

9. Training & Awareness

- Expectations for analysts using AI
- Periodic refreshers and ethical consideration training

10. Review & Updates

- Policy review cadence (e.g., annually)
- Who can approve revisions

This skeleton pairs well with the more detailed policy snippets in **Appendix B**.

2.5. Incident Report Template (AI-Assisted)

Standard incident reporting with explicit places where AI can help.

1. Incident Overview

- Incident ID:
- Date/time detected:
- Date/time resolved (or current status):
- Reporter / source (alert, user, tool, etc.):

2. AI-Assisted Summary (Human-Verified)

AI-generated initial summary pasted here and edited by analyst.

- Final summary (3–8 bullets):

3. Scope & Impact

- Affected users/accounts:
- Affected systems/assets (with criticality):
- Data at risk / affected (if any):
- Business impact (if known):

4. Timeline

- Key events with timestamps:
    - …
    - …

(AI can help draft this from events; analyst verifies.)

5. Root Cause & Contributing Factors

- Root cause (if established):
- Contributing technical factors:
- Contributing process/organizational factors:

6. Detection & Response

- How it was detected (alert, model, manual, etc.):
- Time to detect (MTTD for this incident):
- Time to respond (MTTR for this incident):
- Response actions taken:

7. Role of AI & Automation

- AI/automation used in:
    - Detection / triage:
    - Investigation:
    - Containment / eradication:
    - Documentation:
- Issues encountered with AI/automation (if any):

8. Lessons Learned

- What worked well:
- What didn't work:
- Changes made or proposed:
    - Detections:
    - Playbooks/automation:
    - AI prompts/models:
    - Processes/training:

9. Approvals / Review

- Incident owner:
- Reviewed by (IR lead / SOC lead):
- Date of review:

3. Operational Worksheets

These help you keep track of AI use cases, experiments, and content.

3.1. AI Use Case Inventory Worksheet

Track all current and planned AI-in-SOC use cases.

ID	Use Case Name	Status (Idea/Pilot/Prod)	Primary Owner	Autonomy Level (0/1/2)	Notes / Next Step

3.2. AI Pilot Evaluation Worksheet

For each pilot, capture results in a structured way.

Pilot Name:
Duration:
Owner:

1. Objective (Restated)

2. Metrics (Before vs After)

Metric	Before (Baseline)	After (Pilot)	Comment
Avg triage time per alert			
Avg investigation time			
Incident volume handled			
MTTA / MTTR (if applicable)			

Metric	Before (Baseline)	After (Pilot)	Comment
Analyst satisfaction (0–10)			

3. Qualitative Feedback

- Analyst comments (what they liked / disliked):
- Issues with AI behavior:
- Data quality issues uncovered:

4. Decision

- Scale to more users / alert types
- Adjust and re-run pilot
- Do not proceed (explain why)

5. Follow-Up Tasks

- Detections / rules to adjust:
- Playbooks to update:
- Prompts to refine:
- Documentation / training updates:

3.3. Detection & Automation Improvement Log (AI-Driven)

Track improvements triggered by AI usage and feedback.

Date	Source (Incident / Feedback / AI Suggestion)	Area (Detection/Playbook/Prompt)	Change Made / Planned	Owner	Status (Planned/In Progress/Done)

This log demonstrates continuous improvement to management and auditors.

4. Review & Governance Helpers

Short forms and checklists to bake AI into your regular reviews and governance.

4.1. Quarterly AI-in-SOC Review Snapshot

Fill this out each quarter and share with leadership.

Quarter:
Prepared By:

1. Usage & Adoption

- Analysts using AI assistants regularly:
- % of qualifying incidents using AI for summaries:
- Top 3 most-used AI tasks:

2. Impact Metrics

- Avg time per triage (before vs now):
- Avg time for incident report drafting (before vs now):
- Any notable changes in MTTA/MTTR for specific incident types:

3. Autonomy & Guardrails

- of Level 0-only use cases:
- of Level 1 workflows:
- of Level 2 automations and their scope:

- Any changes to autonomy levels this quarter:

4. AI-Related Issues & Incidents

- AI-related incidents (if any):

- Brief description & actions taken:

5. Ethics, Bias & Privacy

- Any concerns raised by analysts or stakeholders:
- Any changes in data usage or external AI providers:

6. Roadmap Updates

- New use cases proposed:
- Use cases retired or paused:
- Big rocks for next quarter:

4.2. AI-Related Incident Addendum

Attach this to your standard PIR template when AI is involved.

1. AI Involvement

- Where was AI used in this incident?
    - Detection / triage:
    - Investigation:
    - Containment / remediation:
    - Documentation / reporting:

2. Did AI Contribute to Impact?

- Positive contributions (caught something faster, clearer context):
- Negative contributions (misclassification, delayed response, wrong action):

3. Controls & Guardrails

- Were autonomy levels and guardrails followed?
- Did any guardrail fail or prove inadequate?
- Was a kill switch or rollback used?

4. Lessons for AI & Automation

- Changes needed in prompts/models:
- Changes needed in guardrails/levels:
- Changes needed in policies/training:

4.3. New AI Feature Review Checklist

Run this whenever a vendor ships a new AI feature or you consider turning one on.

- What specific **use case** does this feature support?
- Does it overlap with anything we already have?
- What data will it consume and where will it run (region, tenancy)?
- What autonomy level does it introduce by default? Can we force Level 0/1?
- What guardrails does it provide? (preconditions, rate limits, kill switch)
- How transparent is it? (reason codes, logs, metrics)
- What could go wrong if it misbehaves?
- Who will own this feature internally once enabled?
- How will we measure whether it's helping?
- Do risk/compliance need to review this before we turn it on?

If you can't answer these, treat the feature as **"unsafe by default"** until clarified.

You can pair Appendix E with:

- **Appendix F** for buying and RFP decisions

- **Appendix G** for training and hands-on labs
- **Appendix H** for 90-day / 1-year / 3-year planning
- **Appendix B–D** for policies, runbooks, and maturity checklists

Taken together, these give you everything you need to go from **concept** to **structured, documented practice** for AI in your SOC.

Appendix F – AI Buyer's RFP Checklist & Vendor Questionnaire

This appendix gives you **copy-paste ready** content for RFPs, market scans, and vendor evaluations focused on **AI-enabled SOC tooling**.

You can use it to:

- Draft a **formal RFP**
- Run a **lighter-weight vendor questionnaire**
- Structure your **POC evaluation scorecards**

It's organized into:

1. How to use this appendix
2. RFP requirement checklist (by category)
3. Vendor questionnaire (ready-to-send question bank)
4. Example scoring & comparison template

1. How to Use This Appendix

1.1. Decide What You're Buying

You can apply this checklist to:

- A **SIEM/XDR** platform with AI features
- EDR / email / identity tools with embedded AI analytics
- A **SOAR / automation** platform with AI decisioning
- A **cross-tool AI assistant** for SOC analysts
- A **security data / analytics platform** with AI on top

You don't need every requirement for every product type. Mark each requirement as:

- **M** – Must Have
- **S** – Should Have (important but not mandatory)
- **C** – Could Have (nice to have)

…and adjust for your environment (enterprise, MSSP, small SOC, highly regulated, etc.).

2. RFP Requirement Checklist

Use this section to build the **"Requirements"** part of your RFP or vendor evaluation document.

2.1. Use Case Fit & Capabilities

These requirements ensure the vendor's AI features actually support your **SOC workflows**, not just generic "AI".

Checklist

- Tool supports AI-assisted **alert triage** (summarization, prioritization, grouping).
- Tool supports AI-assisted **investigations** (context gathering, timeline building, suggested next steps).
- Tool supports AI-assisted **threat hunting** (query generation, pattern suggestions) where applicable.
- Tool supports AI-assisted **reporting and documentation** (incident reports, executive summaries, KB drafts).
- Tool supports AI-enriched **CTI workflows** (summaries, action recommendations, detection/hunt ideas).
- AI capabilities are clearly mapped to SOC use cases (not just a generic "AI engine").

Example RFP wording

The proposed solution must clearly describe which AI-enabled capabilities are available and how they align to typical SOC workflows, including (as applicable): triage, investigation, threat hunting, CTI processing, reporting, and automation. The vendor must provide example use cases that closely resemble our environment (industry, size, technology stack).

2.2. Data & Integration

These requirements cover the **data foundation** that AI will rely on.

Checklist

- Supports ingestion of logs/events from our key platforms (identity, EDR, cloud, network, SaaS, etc.).
- Supports **normalization** into a clear schema (e.g., OCSF/ECS-like or vendor-defined with documentation).
- Supports **enrichment** with user and asset context (CMDB, HR systems, IAM, asset inventory).
- Integrates with existing **SIEM/XDR**, **SOAR**, and **ticketing/case** systems via APIs.
- Supports **search and analytics** across combined data sources used by AI models.
- Provides mechanisms for **data quality monitoring** (missing sources, parse failures, delays).

Example RFP wording

The solution must ingest and normalize telemetry from our core systems (identity, EDR, cloud control plane, network edge, and key applications). The vendor must describe supported data sources, normalization approach, and enrichment with user/asset context. The solution must expose APIs or connectors to integrate with our existing SIEM/XDR, SOAR, and case management systems.

2.3. Autonomy, Guardrails & Control

Make sure you can **control how far AI goes**, and where humans stay in the loop.

Checklist

- Supports **configurable autonomy levels**, such as:
    - Suggest-only (Level 0)
    - Human-in-loop approvals (Level 1)
    - Conditional automation with guardrails (Level 2)
- Provides a way to enforce **per-playbook/per-action** autonomy settings.
- Supports **preconditions** for automated actions (asset criticality, environment, tenant, time of day, etc.).
- Supports **rate limiting** of automated actions (e.g., max N actions per time window).
- Provides a **central kill switch** to disable specific AI features or automations.
- Provides **rollback capabilities** for automated actions where applicable (e.g., un-isolate endpoint).
- All AI-driven suggestions and actions are **logged and auditable** with sufficient detail.

Example RFP wording

The solution must support configurable autonomy levels, from "recommendation only" to "conditional automatic actions," with the ability to define guardrails (asset type, environment, time window, tenant, etc.). The vendor must describe how autonomy is configured, how actions can be rate-limited, and how kill switches and rollbacks are implemented.

2.4. Model Transparency & Performance

You need enough visibility into how AI behaves to **trust, tune, and defend it**.

Checklist

- Vendor can explain, at a high level, the **types of models** used (e.g., anomaly detection, supervised ML, rules + ML, LLMs).
- Solution provides **reason codes/explanations** for risk scores and classifications (e.g., "unusual location + new device + failed MFA").
- Solution exposes **metrics** for AI performance (TP/FP rates, precision/recall where appropriate).
- Supports **feedback loops** where analysts can:
    - Override AI decisions

- o Flag incorrect suggestions
- o Provide labels that feed into tuning or retraining
- Supports **safe model updates**:
  - o Ability to test new models or rules in shadow mode
  - o Option to delay or opt-out of certain model updates in critical environments

Example RFP wording

The vendor must describe how AI models are evaluated and monitored in production, including available performance metrics and feedback mechanisms. The solution should provide high-level explanations for AI-derived risk scores and decisions and allow us to validate model changes before they are fully enforced in our environment.

2.5. Security, Privacy & Data Usage

This ensures AI features align with your **security and privacy obligations**.

Checklist

- All customer data is **encrypted in transit and at rest**.
- The solution supports **data residency** requirements (regions, in-scope datacenters, etc.).
- Vendor clearly states whether customer data is used to **train shared/global models**.
- Customer can **opt out** of data being used to train models outside their own tenancy.
- Supports **masking/tokenization** of sensitive fields before AI processing.
- Provides documentation on **access controls** for AI features (who can see what).
- Provides relevant **security certifications / attestations** (e.g., SOC 2, ISO 27001, etc.).
- Logs all AI-related data accesses and actions for **audit**.

Example RFP wording

The vendor must provide details on data usage for AI features, including whether and how our data is used to train or improve models beyond our own tenancy, and any opt-out options. The solution must support encryption, access control, and logging aligned with our security and privacy requirements, and support regional data residency constraints where applicable.

2.6. Multi-Tenant & MSSP Readiness (if applicable)

Critical if you're an MSSP/MDR or a large multi-BU environment.

Checklist

- Supports **strong tenant isolation** for data and AI outputs.

- AI assistants can be constrained to **per-tenant context**.
- Supports **per-tenant policies**, thresholds, and autonomy levels.
- Supports **per-tenant reporting** and SLA views.
- Provides **efficient onboarding/offboarding** of tenants.
- Prevents cross-tenant leakage in logs, AI prompts, and responses.

Example RFP wording

For multi-tenant use, the solution must enforce strict logical isolation between tenants in both data and AI functionality. The vendor must demonstrate how AI assistants and automation respect tenant boundaries and how per-tenant policy, configuration, and reporting are implemented.

2.7. UX, Adoption & Training

AI that is hard to use won't be used.

Checklist

- AI features are available **within existing analyst consoles** (SIEM/XDR/SOAR/case tools), not just a separate portal.
- UI clearly distinguishes **AI suggestions** from confirmed facts/actions.
- Provides **role-based experiences** (Tier 1, Tier 2, IR, hunters, CTI, managers).
- Provides **prompt templates** or "skills" library for common tasks.
- Vendor offers **training and enablement** (docs, videos, workshops).
- Provides **usage metrics** (how often AI is used, by whom, for what).

Example RFP wording

The solution should integrate AI features directly into analysts' existing workflows, with clear distinction between AI suggestions and system-of-record data. The vendor should describe available training, documentation, and usage analytics for AI features to support adoption and continuous improvement.

2.8. Pricing & Licensing

Avoid surprises.

Checklist

- Clarify whether AI features are **bundled** or **separately licensed**.
- Clarify pricing drivers:
    - Number of users
    - Data volume
    - Number of AI queries or "tokens"
    - Number of tenants
- Clear **limits and rate caps** (e.g., API limits, request caps).

- Support for **pilot / phased rollout** pricing.
- Transparent 1–3 year **cost projection** based on your expected growth.

Example RFP wording

The vendor must provide transparent pricing information for AI capabilities, including licensing model, usage-based components, and any limits or overage fees. The response should include 1-, 2-, and 3-year cost estimates under realistic usage and growth assumptions.

2.9. Vendor Maturity & Roadmap

You want a partner, not a science experiment.

Checklist

- AI features are **generally available**, not just beta/preview, for production use.
- Evidence of **reference customers** using AI features in critical workflows.
- Vendor can show a **history of delivering** AI improvements in the last 12–24 months.
- Clear **roadmap** for AI features over the next 12–24 months.
- Process for **customer feedback** influencing roadmap.

Example RFP wording

The vendor must provide a summary of AI-related capabilities currently in production, reference deployments, and a roadmap for the next 12–24 months. The response should describe how customer feedback is collected and used to prioritize AI feature development.

3. Vendor Questionnaire (Ready-to-Use Question Bank)

This section is a **question bank** you can drop into an RFP or send as a standalone questionnaire. Pick and choose what's relevant.

3.1. Use Cases & Capabilities

1. Which specific SOC workflows does your AI support today (triage, investigation, hunting, CTI, reporting, automation)? Please provide 3–5 concrete examples.
2. What are the most common use cases your current customers use your AI features for?
3. What can your AI not do (or not do well) today? Please describe known limitations.
4. How does your AI behave when it lacks sufficient data or context to make a confident recommendation?

3.2. Data & Integration

1. Which data sources do you natively integrate with (identity, EDR, cloud, email, network, etc.)? Please list key vendors and integration methods.
2. How do you handle data normalization and enrichment? Do you use a standard schema?
3. How do you enrich events with user and asset context? Which CMDB/asset/IAM systems are supported?
4. How does your AI correlate events across multiple data sources? What are typical latency and scale characteristics?
5. What data quality monitoring and alerting features exist (e.g., missing sources, parse failures, ingestion delays)?

3.3. Autonomy & Guardrails

1. Describe how your solution represents and configures different autonomy levels (e.g., suggest-only, human-in-loop, conditional auto).
2. How do we define guardrails for automated actions (asset scope, environment, tenant, time-of-day, rate limits)?
3. Can you demonstrate how to disable or "kill switch" a specific automation or AI-driven feature?
4. How is rollback handled for automated actions (e.g., un-isolating hosts, reverting IAM changes)?
5. How are AI recommendations and automated actions logged and made available for audit and post-incident review?

3.4. Model Transparency & Performance

1. What types of models are used for your key AI capabilities (detections, triage, scoring, assistants, etc.)?
2. How do you evaluate and monitor model performance in production (metrics, thresholds, alerts)?
3. How do you provide explanations for AI-driven decisions (e.g., risk scores, anomaly flags)? Please share examples.
4. How do analysts provide feedback on AI outputs (e.g., marking suggestions as incorrect, overriding decisions)? How is this feedback used?
5. How are model updates rolled out? Can customers test updates in shadow mode or opt out of certain changes in sensitive environments?

3.5. Security, Privacy & Data Usage

1. How is customer data protected (encryption, access control, tenant isolation) in the context of AI features?
2. Do you use customer data (logs, prompts, interactions) to train or improve models beyond that customer's tenancy? If so, how and under what controls?
3. Can customers opt out of their data being used to train global models? What are the implications?
4. Where is AI processing performed geographically? Please describe data residency options.
5. What options exist to mask, tokenize, or pseudonymize sensitive fields before AI processing?
6. Which security certifications or attestations do you hold that are relevant for AI-enabled services (e.g., SOC 2, ISO 27001)?

3.6. Multi-Tenant & MSSP

(Use if you're an MSSP or multi-tenant organization.)

1. How does your platform enforce tenant isolation for data and AI-derived insights?
2. How is tenant context passed into AI workflows (e.g., prompts, queries) to prevent cross-tenant data mixing?
3. Can we configure different policies, thresholds, and autonomy levels per tenant? Please provide examples.
4. How do you support MSSPs for onboarding/offboarding tenants at scale and managing per-tenant reporting and SLAs?
5. Do you have existing MSSP customers using your AI features? Can you provide anonymized examples or references?

3.7. UX, Adoption & Training

1. Where do analysts interact with AI features (which consoles, UIs, workflows)? Please provide screenshots or demos.
2. How do you distinguish AI suggestions from system-of-record data and human actions in the UI?
3. What training, documentation, and best-practice libraries (e.g., prompt templates) do you provide for SOC teams?
4. What usage analytics do you provide for AI features (by user, by team, by function)?
5. How have you seen organizations successfully drive adoption of your AI features, and what pitfalls should we avoid?

3.8. Pricing & Commercials

1. Are AI features included in your base product, or licensed separately? Please break down clearly.
2. How is AI usage metered (users, data volume, tokens, calls, tenants, etc.)?
3. What limits or rate caps apply to AI features, and what happens when they are exceeded?
4. Can you provide a 1-, 2-, and 3-year cost estimate based on our projected usage profile (data volumes, users, tenants)?
5. Do you offer a structured pilot or POC program with defined scope, success criteria, and pricing?

3.9. Vendor Maturity & Roadmap

1. Which AI capabilities are generally available today and approved for production use?
2. How many customers are using your AI capabilities in production SOC workflows? Please provide representative profiles (industry, size).
3. What significant AI-related improvements did you ship in the last 12–24 months?
4. What are your top AI roadmap priorities for the next 12–24 months?
5. How do you collect and prioritize customer feedback for AI features? Can customers participate in design partnerships or advisory boards?

4. Example Scoring & Comparison Template

Once you collect responses, you'll want a structured way to compare vendors.

You can use something like this (adapt or convert to a spreadsheet):

Dimensions (example)

- Use Case Fit
- Data & Integration
- Guardrails & Autonomy
- Transparency & Performance
- Security & Privacy
- Multi-Tenant / MSSP (if relevant)
- UX & Adoption
- Pricing & Commercials
- Vendor Maturity & Roadmap

Scoring Table (1–5 scale, with weights)

Dimension	Weight (%)	Vendor A	Vendor B	Vendor C	Notes
Use Case Fit	20%				
Data & Integration	15%				
Guardrails & Autonomy	15%				
Transparency & Performance	10%				
Security & Privacy	10%				
Multi-Tenant / MSSP	10%				
UX & Adoption	10%				
Pricing & Commercials	5%				
Vendor Maturity & Roadmap	5%				

You can then:

- Multiply each score by its weight
- Sum for a final score per vendor
- Combine with **qualitative notes** (e.g., culture fit, support experience, references)

Next Steps

- Treat this appendix as a **menu, not a script** — remove or adjust items that don't fit your context.
- The most important thing is **clarity**: vendors should understand exactly what you care about, so you can spot who truly aligns with your AI-in-SOC strategy.
- Reuse this checklist whenever you evaluate a new product or major AI feature; over time it becomes your **institutional memory** for good AI buying decisions.

You can pair this appendix with **Chapter 12 (AI Tooling Buyer's Guide)** and **Appendix E (Data & Use Case Design Worksheets)** to go from, "We need AI" to, "We know **exactly** what we're asking the market for—and how we'll decide."

Appendix G – Hands-On Labs & Exercises

This appendix turns the book into **something you can do**.

You'll find:

- Practical labs you can run in a **test** or **low-risk** environment
- Exercises for analysts, engineers, leaders, and risk teams
- Step-by-step tasks, expected outcomes, and reflection questions

Use these labs as:

- Internal workshops
- Training for new hires
- Small POCs before bigger investments

You don't need a specific vendor; just:

- A SIEM or log/search platform
- Some form of SOAR or automation engine (even basic)
- Access to an AI assistant that can see or be given data (securely)

1. How to Use This Appendix

For each lab you'll see:

- **Who it's for**
- **Prerequisites**
- **Objectives**
- **Steps**
- **Variations / extensions**
- **Debrief questions**

You don't have to run all labs. A good first path:

1. Lab 1 – AI-assisted alert summaries
2. Lab 2 – AI-assisted investigations
3. Lab 3 – CTI → hunts & detections
4. Lab 4 – Autonomy levels & playbooks
5. Lab 5 – Shadow-mode triage scoring
6. Lab 6 – Metrics & ROI mini-project
7. Lab 7 – Ethics, bias & privacy tabletop
8. Lab 8 – AI-related incident postmortem simulation

1.1. Lab 1 – AI-Assisted Alert Summarization

Who: Tier 1/2 analysts, SOC leads
Prereqs:

- Access to a SIEM or alert queue (real or test)
- AI assistant that can accept text or structured input
- Non-production or **sanitized** data for training

Objective:
Make AI summaries part of everyday triage, in a safe way.

Steps

1. **Pick 10–20 recent alerts**
   - Include:
     - A few true positives
     - A bunch of false positives
     - Some "weird but benign" cases
2. **Create a simple summary template**
   For each alert, you want the AI to produce something like:
   - What happened?
   - Who/what is impacted?
   - Why might this matter?
   - What should a Tier 1 analyst check next?
3. **Design your base prompt**

   Example (adapt to your tools):

   "You are helping a SOC analyst triage an alert. Given the alert details and enriched context, produce a 3–5 bullet summary:

   - What happened
   - Who/what is impacted (user, host, application)
   - Why this might matter
   - 2–3 suggested next steps for the analyst
   Avoid speculation; use only the data provided."
4. **Run alerts through the AI**
   For each alert:
   - Copy the alert fields + relevant context (prior events, user/asset info) into the prompt input.
   - Ask the AI to generate the summary.
5. **Have analysts manually review**
   - Analysts compare the AI summary vs:
     - Raw alert

- How they would describe it to a peer or lead

For each case, record:

- **Helpful?** (Y/N)
- **Accurate?** (Y/N)
- Needed corrections (missing context, overstatement, wrong conclusion)

6. **Iterate the prompt**
   - If AI over-speculates, add "If uncertain, state that explicitly and ask for more data."
   - If AI misses context, ensure you're passing in the right fields or add instructions ("Always mention environment and asset criticality when available").
7. **Define a standard "AI summary" section in tickets**
   - Decide where AI summaries will live in your case/ticket template.
   - Agree that **analysts must review and amend** AI summaries, not just paste them.

Variations / Extensions

- Add **severity suggestions**:
  - Ask the AI to propose a severity and a one-line justification.
- Try this on **different alert types**:
  - Identity anomalies
  - Endpoint malware
  - Cloud IAM changes
- Integrate directly into your tool:
  - If possible, embed the AI call into the alert view instead of copy/paste.

Debrief Questions

- When was the AI genuinely useful vs. noise?
- Did summaries help **less experienced analysts** more than senior ones?
- What information did AI frequently miss that you should enrich alerts with?
- What rules do you want to enforce? (e.g., "AI summary must never be stored without analyst review.")

1.2. Lab 2 – AI-Assisted Investigation Timelines

Who: Tier 2 / IR, hunters, SOC leads
Prereqs:

- Access to incident histories or grouped alerts
- Ability to export related events or views from SIEM/XDR
- AI assistant capable of handling multi-step input

Objective:
Use AI to build coherent **timelines** of activity faster, while keeping humans in charge of interpretation.

Steps

1. **Select 3–5 past incidents**
    - Ideally:
        - 1 account compromise
        - 1 endpoint malware case
        - 1 cloud misconfiguration / abuse case
2. **Pull raw event sequences**
For each incident:
    - Export key events (logins, process events, network connections, IAM changes) within a defined window.
    - Ensure timestamps are clear and consistent.
3. **Create an investigation timeline prompt**

    Example:

    "Given the following events (with timestamps), build a chronological timeline. For each step, include:

    - Time
    - Action taken
    - Actor (user, host, service)
    - What is known vs uncertain
    Then list 3–5 questions that still need answering."
4. **Feed events to the AI**
    - Paste in the event list (or a summarized version if very long).
    - Ask for the structured timeline.
5. **Compare to existing IR notes**
    - Compare AI's timeline to:
        - Your original incident doc, if one exists
        - Your memory, if the incident is recent
    - Note:
        - Missing steps
        - Wrong sequencing
        - Helpful or harmful "interpretations"
6. **Enforce "known vs guessed" discipline**
    - If AI blurs speculation with fact:
        - Update prompt: "Clearly mark any inference as 'possible/uncertain' and do **not** present it as fact."
7. **Integrate into your IR template**
    - Add a "Timeline (AI-initial – human verified)" section into your standard incident report.
    - Make it normal for IR to:

- Ask AI for a first draft
- Then correct and enrich it

Variations / Extensions

- Ask AI to:
  - Map events to **MITRE ATT&CK** techniques (where obvious).
  - Suggest **containment and eradication** steps based on the timeline.
- Run the lab with:
  - One junior and one senior analyst on the same case; compare how they use AI differently.

Debrief Questions

- Did AI save you meaningful time building timelines?
- Did it surface steps you might have overlooked?
- Where did it misinterpret events, and how can you prevent that?
- How comfortable would you be sharing AI-assisted timelines with leadership or regulators **after review**?

1.3. Lab 3 – CTI to Hunts & Detections

Who: CTI analysts, hunters, detection engineers
Prereqs:

- At least 1–3 public or internal CTI reports
- SIEM/EDR with hunt/detection capability
- AI assistant

Objective:
Practice turning **CTI narratives** into **hunts and detection ideas** with AI assistance, then validating them.

Steps

1. **Pick one CTI report**
   - Preferably:
     - A threat actor profile
     - A recent campaign write-up
     - A malware analysis with TTPs
2. **Prompt AI for a CTI summary**

   Example:

   "Summarize this CTI report for our SOC in 8–10 bullet points focused on:

- The main TTPs used
- The log sources where we might see them
- Any relevant IOCs (IPs, domains, hashes)
Don't exaggerate targeting; stick to the text."

3. **Ask AI to propose hunts**

Example:

"Based on this report and assuming we have identity, EDR, and cloud logs, propose 5–7 specific hunt ideas. For each:

- Data sources needed
- A rough query or filter logic (in generic pseudocode)
- What a positive hit would look like."

4. **Translate 1–2 hunts into real queries**
    - Pick the most promising ones.
    - Implement in your SIEM/EDR's query language.
    - Run them on a test or low-risk dataset first.
5. **Ask AI to suggest detection rules**

Example:

"Turn hunt #2 into a candidate detection rule. Specify:

- Logic
- Severity
- Enrichment needed
- Likely false positives
- Tuning ideas."

6. **Review rule quality**
    - Detection engineers review:
        - Logic correctness
        - Feasibility given your logs
        - False positive risk
7. **Decide what becomes permanent**
    - Some hunts → detection rules
    - Others remain **on-demand hunts**
    - Document decisions and rationale.

Variations / Extensions

- Use multiple CTI reports on the **same actor** and see if AI can consolidate TTPs.
- Ask AI to:
    - Generate a **short briefing** for leadership from the CTI report and your hunt results.

Debrief Questions

- Did AI help you move from report → hunts faster?
- Were the AI-suggested hunts realistic for your environment?
- What extra internal context does AI need (asset types, common workflows, industry specifics)?
- How will you make "CTI → hunts/detections with AI help" a **repeatable workflow**?

1.4. Lab 4 – Designing Autonomy Levels & Playbooks

Who: SOC leads, automation/SOAR engineers, IR leads, sometimes risk/compliance
Prereqs:

- SOAR or automation platform (or even a structured playbook document)
- At least 1 existing playbook (e.g., malware on endpoint, phishing report)

Objective:
Practice applying **Level 0–2 autonomy** and guardrails to a real workflow.

Steps

1. **Select one high-volume incident type**
   - Example:
     - Commodity malware on user workstation
     - Basic phishing emails
2. **Document current workflow**
   - List steps as they exist today:
     - Info gathering
     - Decisions
     - Actions (containment, comms, closure)
3. **Label each step with an autonomy level**
   For each step, decide:
   - Level 0 – AI may **suggest** next actions, human does them manually
   - Level 1 – AI/SOAR may **prepare** the action, but human must click approve
   - Level 2 – System may execute automatically if preconditions are met
4. **Define guardrails for any Level 2 steps**
   - Preconditions:
     - Asset must be tagged non-critical
     - Environment is "user endpoint" not "server/OT"
     - Detection must be from a short allow-listed rule set
   - Rate limits:
     - No more than X auto-isolations per 30 minutes
   - Logging:
     - All auto-actions must be logged with reason and context
5. **Update your playbook**
   - Add columns:

- Autonomy level
- Preconditions
- Rollback steps

6. **Implement in SOAR (or design how you would)**
    - For each step:
        - Configure manual/approval/auto
        - Encode preconditions as filters/conditions
    - Create or document a **kill switch** for this playbook.

7. **Walk through a tabletop run**
    - Simulate an incident:
        - Show which steps would be auto-run vs require approval.
    - Ask:
        - "Are we comfortable with this?"
        - "What could go wrong?"
        - "What do we monitor?"

Variations / Extensions

- Run this with **phishing** or **identity anomalies** instead.
- Include **risk/compliance** in the session to get their view.
- Add an AI assistant step:
    - For each decision step, AI proposes context and pros/cons of actions.

Debrief Questions

- Which steps were easy to classify as Level 2 and which were contentious?
- Did the exercise change your view of how "ready" you are for automation?
- What new guardrails (asset tags, environment labels, tenant policies) do you need?
- How will you document and communicate autonomy levels across the SOC?

1.5. Lab 5 – Shadow-Mode AI Triage Scoring

Who: SOC leads, detection engineers, data/platform teams
Prereqs:

- SIEM/XDR alerts
- Some way to store AI scores (even a spreadsheet)
- AI assistant or scoring logic

Objective:
Test AI-driven **alert risk scoring/triage** in shadow mode before it affects queues.

Steps

1. **Define a simple scoring scale**

- 0–100 risk score or categories:
  - Low / Medium / High / Critical
2. **Define scoring factors**
Examples:
   - Alert type and severity
   - Asset criticality
   - User role (privileged vs regular)
   - Presence of known bad indicators
   - Unusual behavior signals
3. **Design a scoring prompt**

   Example:

   "Given this alert and context (fields X, Y, Z), assign a risk score from 0–100 and a category (Low/Medium/High). Briefly explain the top 3 reasons."

4. **Run scoring in shadow mode**
   - For 1–4 weeks, take a sample of alerts daily (or all of them, if feasible).
   - For each alert:
     - Capture AI's score and explanation in a side system (spreadsheet, DB, etc.).
     - Do **not** change alert order or triage process yet.
5. **Compare AI scores with human decisions**
   - Did analysts treat high-scored alerts as more important?
   - Are there many cases where AI scores high but analysts close as benign?
   - Are there real incidents scored low by AI?
6. **Refine scoring logic**
   - Adjust prompts or feature weights.
   - Improve context (e.g., asset criticality data).
   - Potentially exclude certain rules from high scoring if they're noisy.
7. **Decide whether to experiment with AI-sorted queues**
   - Once correlation is acceptable, consider:
     - Letting AI score influence the **default sort order** for specific alert types only.

Variations / Extensions

- Run the same alerts through **two different scoring approaches** and compare.
- Use AI to propose **clusters** of related alerts (pseudo-incidents) and score at cluster level.

Debrief Questions

- When did AI scores clearly help?
- What types of alerts did AI struggle with?
- Did shadow mode reveal **data quality issues** (missing tags, user context)?

- What minimum accuracy/precision would you require before making AI scores visible to analysts?

1.6. Lab 6 – Metrics & ROI Mini-Project

Who: SOC leads, CISOs, platform owners, sometimes finance/risk
Prereqs:

- Access to case/incident/ticket data
- Baseline metrics (or ability to reconstruct them)

Objective:
Quantify where AI is helping (or not) and build a **simple ROI story**.

Steps

1. **Pick 2–3 AI use cases you've tried or plan to try**
   Examples:
   - Alert summarization
   - Incident report drafting
   - Investigation timelines
   - CTI summarization
2. **Define metrics for each**
   - Time saved per task (estimate or measure)
   - Change in MTTA/MTTR for affected incidents
   - Change in number of incidents handled or quality (fewer misses)
3. **Collect "before" data**
   - Pull:
     - Historical triage and investigation times
     - Past incident volumes and timings
   - If you don't have detailed data:
     - Sample a few cases and estimate effort.
4. **Collect "after" data** (post-AI)
   - For a month or two, measure:
     - How long tasks take **with** AI.
     - Whether volume/quality changed.
5. **Calculate rough ROI**
   - Example approach:
     - (Average minutes saved per task) x (number of tasks per month) x (analyst hourly cost)
   - Factor in:
     - Licenses or platform costs (ballpark)
6. **Create a simple 1-page ROI summary**
   - For each AI feature:
     - What it does

- Key metrics before vs after
- Rough time/cost benefit
- Qualitative feedback from analysts

Variations / Extensions

- Include **human factors**:
    - Survey analysts on perceived toil reduction.
- Align metrics explicitly to:
    - Risk reduction (e.g., faster response to identity incidents).

Debrief Questions

- Which AI use cases gave the clearest, defensible benefit?
- Did any use cases add complexity without clear gain?
- How can you use these metrics to:
    - Drive roadmap priorities
    - Communicate up to leadership

1.7. Lab 7 – Ethics, Bias & Privacy Tabletop

Who: SOC leads, analysts, CTI, HR, legal, risk/compliance
Prereqs:

- AI-in-SOC policy draft (even rough)
- At least a conceptual view of where AI is (or will be) used

Objective:
Stress-test your **ethical, fairness, and privacy** thinking with realistic scenarios.

Steps

1. **Prepare 3–4 scenarios**

    Examples:

    - **Scenario A – Biased Anomaly Model**
      An anomaly model flags a disproportionate number of alerts for employees in one region or on one type of contract, with almost no true incidents.
    - **Scenario B – Over-Monitoring**
      AI is used to correlate login, email, and web traffic to "identify insider threats"; HR wants access to the dashboard for performance monitoring.
    - **Scenario C – AI Misclassifies a User**
      AI risk scoring flags an executive as "high risk" due to unusual travel; their access is limited, causing business impact and reputational strain.

- o **Scenario D – Privacy & External AI**
  An AI assistant is configured to consume ticket text and raw logs; someone notices sensitive content (personal data, legal topics) in the prompts.
2. **Run the tabletop discussion**
   For each scenario, ask:
   - o Is this plausible in our environment?
   - o What would we do **today**?
   - o Who needs to be involved?
   - o What policies or guardrails do we need?
3. **Map to the Ethical Principles (from Chapter 17)**
   - o Purpose-bound
   - o Proportionate
   - o Transparent & explainable
   - o Human-centered
   - o Accountable & correctable
4. **Identify gaps**
   - o Missing policies or standards
   - o Missing technical controls (masking, role-based access)
   - o Missing escalation paths (for AI-related concerns)
5. **Turn findings into actions**
   - o Draft or update:
     - AI-in-SOC policy
     - Privacy guidance for log/AI data
     - Reviewer checklists for new AI features

Variations / Extensions

- Have each group role-play:
  - o SOC lead
  - o Affected employee
  - o Regulator/auditor
  - o HR or legal
- Run annually as an **"AI ethics fire drill."**

Debrief Questions

- Which ethical risks felt most real and urgent?
- Where do you lack technical or organizational controls?
- How can you embed ethical checks into **change and design processes** (not as an afterthought)?

1.8. Lab 8 – AI-Related Incident Postmortem Simulation

Who: SOC, IR, platform/automation, risk/compliance, sometimes leadership
Prereqs:

- Run Lab 4 (autonomy) first if possible
- Some form of post-incident review template

Objective:
Practice handling an incident where AI or automation **played a role in the impact**, not just in detection.

Steps

1. **Invent or adapt a realistic scenario**

    Example:

    - A detection logic update causes an EDR rule to misclassify a business-critical application component as malicious.
    - Your Level 2 automation isolates hosts automatically when this detection fires.
    - Over a few minutes, dozens of critical servers are isolated, causing a service outage.

2. **Run the incident simulation**
    - Simulate:
        - Alert storm
        - Auto-actions being executed
        - Escalations from IT / business

3. **Pause and conduct a mock post-incident review**
    Use questions like:
    - What happened? (timeline)
    - Where did AI or automation influence the outcome?
    - Which guardrails worked or failed?
    - How quickly did we detect the automation misbehavior?
    - How did we stop it (kill switch, rollback)?

4. **Assess your current capabilities**
    - Do you **have**:
        - Kill switches?
        - Rollbacks?
        - Logging that clearly shows AI involvement?

5. **Update your real PIR template**
    - Add explicit sections:
        - "AI or automation involvement"
        - "AI-related contributing causes"
        - "Changes to AI guardrails/usage as a result"

6. **Define follow-up work**
    - Technical:
        - Better testing before enabling auto-actions
        - Rate limits
    - Organizational:
        - Who can approve new Level 2 automations

- Communication expectations during an AI-related incident

Variations / Extensions

- Run a lighter scenario:
    - AI assistant hallucinating an incorrect explanation that misdirects an investigation.
- Include **communications**:
    - Draft a hypothetical note to executives:
        - Honest but calm explanation of AI involvement and fixes.

Debrief Questions

- How comfortable are you that your current automations can be stopped quickly?
- What changes to your procedures and controls feel non-negotiable after this exercise?
- How will you ensure **every future real incident** checks for AI/automation contributions?

Appendix H – 90-Day / 1-Year / 3-Year Action Worksheets

This appendix turns **Chapter 19** into fill-in templates you can print, share, or drop into a wiki.

You'll get:

1. A **Current State Snapshot** worksheet
2. A **90-Day Plan** worksheet
3. A **1-Year Plan** worksheet
4. A **3-Year Vision** worksheet
5. A **Roadmap & Backlog** worksheet
6. A **Stakeholder & Ownership** worksheet
7. A **Review & Retrospective** checklist for each horizon

You can use these:

- In internal workshops
- As living docs for your AI-in-SOC program
- For alignment between SOC, platform, risk, and leadership

1. Current State Snapshot Worksheet

Purpose: Capture where you are today before starting your 90-day plan.

Fill this out once, then update annually.

1.1. SOC Profile

Item	Notes / Values
Organization / Business Unit	
SOC Type (internal/MSSP/hybrid)	
Primary locations / time zones	
SOC hours (24×7, follow-the-sun, etc.)	
Number of analysts (Tier 1/2/3)	
Other roles (hunters, CTI, engineers, platform)	

1.2. Tooling & Data Overview

Area	Tools / Platforms in Use	Notes / Gaps
SIEM / XDR		
EDR / Endpoint		
Identity / IdP / SSO		
Cloud Security		

Area	Tools / Platforms in Use	Notes / Gaps
Email / Web Sec		
SOAR / Automation		
Case / Ticketing		
CTI Platform		
Data Lake / Data Fabric (if any)		

1.3. Telemetry Coverage Snapshot

Rate each **critical area** (0–5: 0 = none, 5 = excellent) and add notes.

Data Area	Coverage (0–5)	Notes (Gaps, Issues, Priorities)
Identity logs (IdP, VPN, SSO)		
Endpoint / EDR		
Cloud control plane		
Cloud workload logs		
Network / edge		
Email security events		
Key internal apps		
Asset inventory & CMDB		
User/role/HR context		

1.4. Current Metrics Baseline

(Use rough numbers if exact ones aren't available.)

Metric	Value / Range	Source / How Measured
Alerts per day (avg)		
Alerts per analyst per shift (avg)		
% alerts that become incidents (rough)		
MTTA (time to acknowledge) – critical alerts		
MTTD / time to confirm detection – key use cases		
MTTR – selected incident types		
Average time per alert triage		
Average time per investigation		
Time to draft incident report (significant incidents)		

1.5. AI Usage Today (If Any)

Question	Answer
Do you use any AI assistants for SOC work today?	Yes / No + which tools
Main AI use cases (if any)	
Any automation with AI-influenced decisions?	
Existing guardrails / policies for AI in SOC	
Biggest perceived **pain points** AI could help with	

2. 90-Day Plan Worksheet

Purpose: Turn the next 90 days into a focused, achievable plan.

Use this with Chapter 19 (first 90 days).

2.1. 90-Day Objectives (Top 3–5)

Write these as **outcome statements**, not tasks.

Examples:

- "Reduce average incident report drafting time by 30%."
- "Pilot AI summaries in triage for two alert types."

#	Objective (Outcome-focused)	Owner	Success Criteria (How we know)
1			
2			
3			
4			
5			

2.2. Initial AI Use Cases (90-Day Scope)

Pick **2–4 safe, low-risk** use cases.

Use Case	Description / Scope	Risk Level	Autonomy Level (0/1 only in 90 days)	Tools / Data Needed
AI-assisted alert summaries				
AI-assisted incident reports				
CTI summarization → actions				
Investigation timelines				

2.3. 90-Day Guardrail Decisions

Decide your **initial safety boundaries**.

Area	Decision / Policy Snippet	Notes / Follow-ups
Autonomy allowed	e.g., "Only Level 0 (suggest) in 90 days. No auto-actions."	
Critical systems red lines	e.g., "No AI-driven changes in OT, payments, core banking."	
Data not to send to AI	e.g., "No full email bodies; PII masked for external AI."	
Who can approve changes	e.g., "SOC lead + platform lead for any new AI integration."	

Area	Decision / Policy Snippet	Notes / Follow-ups
Kill switch expectation	e.g., "Each integration must define how to disable quickly."	

2.4. 90-Day Workplan (By Month)

Break down high-level activities.

Month 1 (Weeks 1–4)

- Baseline metrics and current state captured
- 90-day objectives agreed and signed-off
- Pilot use cases chosen
- Data & access for pilots validated
- AI-in-SOC **vision memo** drafted (1–2 pages)

Tasks / Notes:

-
-

Month 2 (Weeks 5–8)

- AI assistant configured / integrated for pilot use cases
- Analysts trained on prompts & usage for pilots
- Shadow usage started (no production decisions changed)
- Feedback collection mechanism created (form, tag, channel)

Tasks / Notes:

-
-

Month 3 (Weeks 9–12)

- Pilot usage at stable cadence (e.g., "used in 60% of qualifying alerts/incidents")
- Before/after metrics collected for pilot use cases
- 90-day review completed (what worked/what didn't)
- Draft of **1-Year Plan** started based on lessons learned

Tasks / Notes:

-
-

2.5. 90-Day Risks & Mitigations

Risk / Concern	Impact (H/M/L)	Likelihood (H/M/L)	Mitigation / Owner
Analysts don't adopt AI assistant			
AI output is confusing or misleading			
Integration takes longer than expected			
Data quality issues limit usefulness			
Leadership expects "magic" too quickly			

3. 1-Year Plan Worksheet

Purpose: Shape your first full year of AI-in-SOC into themes, milestones, and governance.

Use this after (or near the end of) your 90-day cycle.

3.1. 1-Year Themes (3–5)

Examples:

- "Make AI assistance standard in investigations and reporting."
- "Implement autonomy levels and guardrails in all major playbooks."
- "Introduce 2–3 narrow Level 2 automations."

Theme #	Theme (1-sentence headline)	Why it matters
1		
2		
3		
4		
5		

3.2. Year-1 Use Case Expansion Map

Think about expanding horizontally (more workflows) and vertically (more depth).

Use Case Area	Current Status (from 90 days)	Year-1 End State Target
Alert triage & summaries		e.g., "Used on 80% of critical alerts."
Investigations & timelines		
Incident reporting		
Threat hunting		
CTI → hunts/detections		
Automation for low-risk cases		e.g., "2–3 Level 2 playbooks in prod."
Metrics & dashboards		e.g., "AI KPIs visible in SOC dashboard."
AI governance & policy		

3.3. Year-1 Autonomy & Guardrail Roadmap

Define **what you'll allow** by the end of the first year.

Area / Playbook Type	Year-1 Target Autonomy Level	Guardrail Requirements	Owners
Commodity endpoint malware	Level 2 in narrow scope	Non-critical assets only; rate limits; rollback	SOC + Automation Lead
Standard phishing on user mailbox	Level 1–2	User notification; no deletion of mailbox	
Identity risk scoring suggestions	Level 0	Human review for account lock/disable	
Cloud misconfigurations	Level 0–1	Only suggest; changes via change mgmt	

3.4. Year-1 Governance & Policy Checklist

Mark what you will have **in place by end of Year 1**.

Item	Target Date	Status (Planned/In Progress/Done)
Formal AI-in-SOC policy approved		
Defined autonomy levels and examples documented		
AI usage logging & audit trail implemented		
AI-related incident classification & PIR process added		
AI ethics / privacy guidance for SOC data + AI prompts		
Regular (e.g., quarterly) AI feature review with risk/audit		

3.5. Year-1 Milestone Timeline (Quarterly)

Q1 (Months 1–3) – 90-Day Plan

- See Section 2 worksheet.

Q2 (Months 4–6) – Scale AI Assistance

- AI assistant available to Tier 1, Tier 2, IR, CTI
- Prompt library created per role
- AI summaries embedded in standard incident templates
- First AI usage metrics dashboard live

Q3 (Months 7–9) – Guardrails & Initial Automation

- Autonomy levels defined for top 5 playbooks
- Guardrails and kill switches implemented for those playbooks
- Shadow-mode evaluation of 1–3 candidate Level 2 automations
- First AI-related tabletop exercise run

Q4 (Months 10–12) – Bounded Level 2 Automations & Review

- 1–3 Level 2 automations live in production (narrow scope)
- Monitoring & rollback tested in exercises
- Year-1 metrics & ROI summary produced
- Draft 3-Year vision updated based on experience

Add your own tasks under each quarter.

4. 3-Year Vision Worksheet

Purpose: Articulate a pragmatic 3-year end state that guides decisions now.

4.1. 3-Year Vision Statement (1–2 Paragraphs)

Prompt:

"In three years, our SOC will be an AI-augmented, guardrail-driven operation where…"

Write your vision:

4.2. 3-Year Capability Targets

Rate where you want to be (0–5: 0 = none, 5 = mature).

Capability Area	Target (0–5)	High-Level Description of 3-Year State
Data quality & security data fabric		
AI assistance in triage & investigations		
Automation for low-risk incidents		
Automation for moderate-risk, narrow cases		
Metrics & ROI reporting		
AI governance & model risk management		
Integration with IT/SRE/DevOps workflows		
Analyst AI literacy & training		
Ethical / privacy controls for SOC AI		

4.3. 3-Year "Non-Negotiables"

List guardrails and principles that **must still hold** in 3 years.

Examples:

- "We will never allow uncontrolled Level 3 autonomy for high-impact actions."
- "Humans will always review major containment decisions."

#	Principle / Non-Negotiable
1	
2	
3	
4	

4.4. 3-Year "Big Rocks"

Identify **3–7 major initiatives** that will get you there.

Initiative / Big Rock	Rough Timing (Year 1/2/3)	Owner / Team
Consolidated security data platform / fabric		
Central SOAR & automation control plane		
SOC AI assistant & prompt/skill library		
Formal AI governance & risk framework		
Cross-team AI-enabled incident management (Sec + SRE + Dev)		

5. Roadmap & Backlog Worksheet

Purpose: Turn strategies into **trackable work items**.

You can convert this into a Kanban board (To-Do / Doing / Done).

5.1. Initiative Backlog

ID	Initiative / Work Item	Horizon (90d/1y/3y)	Owner	Status	Notes / Dependencies
				To-Do / Doing / Done	

5.2. AI Use Case Backlog

Use this for ideas you're not ready to implement yet.

| Use Case Idea | Potential Value (H/M/L) | Complexity (H/M/L) | Target Horizon | Notes / Prereqs |

6. Stakeholder & Ownership Worksheet

Purpose: Make it clear **who owns what** and who needs to be involved.

6.1. RACI for AI-in-SOC Program

R = Responsible, A = Accountable, C = Consulted, I = Informed

Activity / Area	CISO	SOC Lead	Det/Content Eng	SOAR/Platform	CTI Lead	Risk/Compliance	IT/Cloud/App	HR/Legal
Define AI-in-SOC vision & goals								
AI use case selection & prioritization								
Autonomy level decisions								
Guardrail & kill switch design								
AI tool selection / RFPs								
AI prompt/skill library maintenance								
Metrics & ROI reporting								
AI-related incident review								
Ethics & privacy oversight								

Fill in R/A/C/I for each cell.

6.2. Named Owners

Area / Capability	Primary Owner (Name & Role)	Backup / Delegate
AI-in-SOC overall program		
AI assistant configuration & prompts		

Area / Capability	Primary Owner (Name & Role)	Backup / Delegate
Automation & SOAR guardrails		
Data pipelines & schemas		
Metrics & dashboards		
AI governance / policy		
Ethics & privacy checks		

7. Review & Retrospective Checklists

Use these at the **end of 90 days, Year 1, and annually**.

7.1. 90-Day Review Checklist

- Did we hit our 90-day objectives (fully / partially / not at all)?
- What AI use cases clearly added value?
- What use cases were confusing or low value?
- Did we stay within our agreed guardrails?
- Any near misses or AI-related issues?
- What data quality problems surfaced?
- How did analysts feel about AI usage (qualitative feedback)?
- Which lessons change our Year-1 plan?

Document 3–5 key lessons and 3 concrete changes you'll make:

7.2. Year-1 Review Checklist

- AI assistant usage is now **normal** in core workflows (triage, investigations, reporting).
- AI-in-SOC policy is published and used.
- Autonomy levels & guardrails are documented for top playbooks.
- At least 1–3 Level 2 automations are live with monitoring & rollback.
- AI metrics (usage, time savings, impact) are visible on at least one SOC dashboard.
- Risk/compliance and audit understand where AI is used and how it's governed.
- At least one AI-related tabletop or incident review has been run.
- We have updated our 3-year vision based on what worked.

7.3. Annual "Health Check" Snapshot

Rate your AI-in-SOC program annually (0–5: 0 = nonexistent, 5 = mature & improving).

Area	Score (0–5)	Comment / Next Action
AI use case coverage		

Area	Score (0–5)	Comment / Next Action
Data readiness & quality		
Guardrails & autonomy control		
Metrics & ROI		
Governance & AI risk management		
Analyst adoption & AI literacy		
Ethics, bias, and privacy practices		

Use this to choose **the next 1–2 focus areas** for the coming year.

You can integrate these worksheets into:

- Your internal wiki or Confluence
- A shared spreadsheet/Notion board
- A quarterly planning deck for SOC leadership

The aim is simple:

Turn your 90-day, 1-year, and 3-year AI-in-SOC plans into **living documents** that keep you honest, aligned, and moving forward.

Appendix I – Glossary & Acronyms

This glossary collects the main terms, acronyms and concepts used throughout the book. It's written for practitioners, not academics: short, plain-language definitions you can use in planning, design, and day-to-day operations.

A

AI (Artificial Intelligence)
Algorithms and models that perform tasks that normally require human intelligence—such as pattern recognition, language understanding, summarization, or decision support. In this book, "AI" usually refers to ML models plus large language models (LLMs) used in security operations.

AI Assistant (Security Assistant)
An AI-powered helper (often LLM-based) that analysts interact with in natural language to summarize alerts, build timelines, suggest queries, draft reports, etc. It does not replace analysts; it provides suggestions and drafts that humans validate.

AI-in-SOC
Shorthand for all uses of AI inside Security Operations: triage, investigations, threat hunting, reporting, automation, and decision support, plus the governance, guardrails, and metrics around them.

Alert
A notification generated by a security tool (SIEM, XDR, EDR, email security, etc.) indicating potentially suspicious or malicious activity based on rules, signatures, behaviors, or models.

Alert Fatigue
When analysts face so many alerts—most of them low-value or false positives—that they become overloaded, miss important alerts, or disengage.

Anomaly Detection
A technique (often ML-based) for finding data points or behaviors that deviate from an established baseline of "normal" activity, such as unusual logins, traffic patterns, or process behavior.

Asset
Any system, device, application, account, or data store that the organization cares about protecting.

Asset Criticality
A rating of how important an asset is to the business (e.g., low, medium, high, mission-critical). Used heavily in prioritization, risk scoring, and guardrails for automation.

ATT&CK / MITRE ATT&CK
A publicly available knowledge base of adversary tactics, techniques, and procedures (TTPs) maintained by MITRE. Used to map detections, incidents, and hunts to a consistent threat model.

Autonomy Levels (Level 0 / 1 / 2 / 3)
A simple framework in this book for how "independent" AI and automation are allowed to be:

- **Level 0** – Suggest-only: AI recommends, humans do the work.
- **Level 1** – Human-in-loop: AI/automation prepares actions; humans must explicitly approve.
- **Level 2** – Conditional autonomy: Automation executes certain actions automatically when guardrails/preconditions are satisfied.
- **Level 3+** – Broad autonomy with limited oversight; generally considered too risky for most SOC scenarios in the near term.

Automation (Security Automation)
Scripts, playbooks, or workflows that execute actions (enrichment, containment, notifications, changes) automatically or semi-automatically, often via SOAR or orchestration tools.

B

Baseline (Behavioral Baseline)
The "normal" pattern of activity used for comparison in anomaly detection and behavior analytics—e.g., typical login locations, volumes, or processes for a user or host.

Behavior Analytics / UEBA (see "UEBA")
The analysis of user and entity behaviors over time to spot anomalies that may indicate compromise or misuse.

C

Case / Ticket
A record in a case management or ticketing tool that tracks the lifecycle of an alert or incident: context, actions taken, ownership, notes, and final disposition.

Cloud Control Plane
The management and configuration layer of cloud platforms (e.g., API calls, IAM changes, resource creation/deletion events). Critical for detecting cloud misuse and misconfigurations.

CTI (Cyber Threat Intelligence)
Information about threats and adversaries—indicators (IOCs), TTPs, infrastructure, motivations, and targeting. Can be internal, commercial, government, or open-source.

CTI → Hunts / Detections
The process of taking CTI and turning it into concrete hunts (queries, searches) and detection content (rules, analytics) for the SOC.

D

Data Fabric / Security Data Fabric
An architectural approach where security-relevant data from multiple sources is integrated and accessible in a consistent way, often via a central platform or data lake, so that SIEM, AI, and analytics can all use the same underlying data.

Data Lake / Security Data Lake
A large, centralized repository for raw or semi-structured security data (logs, events, telemetry). Often used for long-term retention, big-data analytics, and AI workloads.

Data Leakage / Data Exfiltration
Unauthorized or unintended transfer of data from an organization to an external destination, or to locations where it shouldn't be.

Data Minimization
Principle of collecting and processing only the data that is necessary for a specific purpose (e.g., security operations), especially relevant when feeding data into AI systems.

Data Residency
Requirements or constraints on where data must be stored and processed geographically (e.g., region, country, legal jurisdiction).

Detection Engineering
The practice of designing, implementing, testing, and maintaining detection logic (rules, signatures, analytics) that identify malicious or risky activity.

E

EDR (Endpoint Detection and Response)
A platform that monitors endpoint activity (processes, file changes, network connections, behaviors) to detect, investigate, and often respond to threats on endpoints (laptops, workstations, servers).

Enrichment
Adding external or contextual information to raw alerts/events (e.g., asset criticality, user role, geo, threat intel, vulnerability data) to improve triage, investigation, and AI decisioning.

Event
A single record or log entry describing something that happened (e.g., login success, process start, firewall allow/deny, API call). Alerts are often built from one or more events.

Exposure Management / Attack Surface Management
Processes and tools for discovering, prioritizing, and reducing exposed assets, vulnerabilities, and misconfigurations that attackers could exploit.

F

Feedback Loop (Human Feedback Loop)
The mechanism by which analyst decisions and corrections (e.g., "false positive", "AI suggestion wrong", "true positive") are fed back into detection tuning, AI model improvement, and playbook refinement.

G

Guardrails (AI Guardrails / Automation Guardrails)
Technical and procedural constraints around AI and automation—such as autonomy levels, preconditions (asset tags, environment), rate limits, approvals, and kill switches—that limit blast radius and enforce policy.

H

Hunt / Threat Hunt
A proactive, hypothesis-driven search for evidence of compromise or suspicious activity using available data (SIEM, EDR, cloud logs, etc.), rather than waiting for alerts.

Human-in-the-Loop
A design where AI/automation suggests or prepares actions, but a human must review, validate, and approve before they are executed.

I

IdP (Identity Provider)
A system that authenticates users and issues identity tokens or assertions (e.g., Azure AD, Okta). Core source of identity logs and signals.

Incident
A confirmed security event or series of events that has or is likely to have an impact on confidentiality, integrity, or availability. Typically escalated from one or more alerts.

Incident Response (IR)
The processes and activities used to detect, investigate, contain, eradicate, and recover from security incidents, plus communication and lessons learned.

IOC (Indicator of Compromise)
Evidence associated with malicious activity, such as IP addresses, domains, file hashes, registry keys, or artifacts that indicate compromise.

K

KPI (Key Performance Indicator)
A metric used to track operational performance (e.g., MTTA, MTTR, alerts per analyst, time per investigation).

KRI (Key Risk Indicator)
A metric that provides an early signal of increasing risk (e.g., number of high-risk incidents per quarter, coverage of critical assets, exposure trends).

Kill Switch
A mechanism to quickly disable specific AI features, automations, or playbooks, especially when they misbehave or contribute to an incident. Often implemented as a config flag or central control.

L

LLM (Large Language Model)
A type of AI model trained on large corpora of text to generate and understand natural language. Used for summaries, explanations, query generation, and code or playbook drafting.

Least Privilege
Security principle that users/systems should have the minimum access necessary to perform their tasks—applies equally to humans, automation, and AI services.

Log
A record of an event or message from a system or application (e.g., syslog entries, Windows event logs, API logs).

M

MDR (Managed Detection and Response)
A service where a third party (often an MSSP-type provider) delivers detection and response capabilities on behalf of a customer, often using their own platforms and analysts.

MSSP (Managed Security Service Provider)
An organization that provides managed security services (e.g., monitoring, detection, response, firewall management) for multiple customers (tenants), usually in a multi-tenant environment.

MTTA (Mean Time To Acknowledge)
Average time between an alert being generated and someone in the SOC acknowledging or picking it up for triage.

MTTD (Mean Time To Detect)
Average time between the start of an attack or incident and its detection/identification as such.

MTTR (Mean Time To Respond / Resolve)
Average time from detection (or alert acknowledgment) to containment, eradication, or resolution of the incident.

Multi-Tenant / Multi-Tenancy
An architecture where a single platform logically separates data and configuration for multiple customers, business units, or tenants. Crucial for MSSPs and large enterprises with strong segmentation requirements.

N

Noise (Alert Noise)
Low-value or irrelevant alerts/events that do not represent real risk and clutter analyst queues, making it harder to focus on what matters.

O

Onboarding (Tenant / Data Source Onboarding)
The process of integrating a new customer, business unit, or data source into the SOC's tooling and workflows, including log ingestion, normalization, enrichment, and playbook configuration.

P

Playbook (SOAR Playbook)
An orchestrated workflow, usually implemented in a SOAR/automation tool, that defines steps for responding to a particular incident type (e.g., enrich, contain, notify, document). May include manual and automated steps.

Post-Incident Review (PIR) / Postmortem
A structured analysis conducted after an incident (including AI-related incidents) to understand what happened, what worked, what didn't, and what changes are needed in detections, processes, guardrails, or tooling.

Prompt
The input text or structured instructions given to an AI assistant/LLM to perform a task (e.g., summarize this alert, generate a hunt query, propose a playbook step).

Prompt Engineering
The practice of designing and refining prompts to get consistent, useful outputs from AI models.

Prompt Template / Prompt Library
Reusable prompt patterns for common SOC tasks (e.g., "Summarize this incident for Tier 1", "Turn this CTI report into hunts"), often parameterized and shared across the team.

R

RACI (Responsible, Accountable, Consulted, Informed)
A matrix used to clarify roles and responsibilities for activities (e.g., who owns AI guardrails, who approves autonomy changes, who is informed about AI-related incidents).

Rate Limiting (for Automation)
Restricting the number of automated actions within a time window (e.g., "no more than 10 auto-isolations per 30 minutes") to reduce blast radius from misconfigurations or model errors.

Risk Appetite
The level and types of risk an organization is willing to accept to achieve its objectives, including how much operational risk it will tolerate from automation and AI-driven actions.

Runbook
Step-by-step instructions for handling a particular scenario or task, often more detailed and human-focused than a playbook. A runbook may be the blueprint that a playbook automates.

S

Scorecard (Vendor / Use-Case Scorecard)
A structured way to evaluate and compare tools or initiatives across dimensions (e.g., use-case fit, integration, guardrails, pricing), often including weighted scores and qualitative notes.

Security Operations (SecOps)
The overall function of monitoring, detecting, investigating, and responding to security threats, including processes, people, and technology.

SOC (Security Operations Center)
The team and function responsible for day-to-day security monitoring, detection, response, and sometimes threat hunting and CTI. Can be internal, outsourced, or hybrid.

SOC of One / SOC of Few
Informal term for very small teams (sometimes a single person) performing SOC functions, often with heavy reliance on automation and integrated tools.

SIEM (Security Information and Event Management)
A platform that collects, aggregates, normalizes, and stores logs/events from multiple sources and provides correlation, search, dashboards, and detection rules.

SLA (Service Level Agreement)
A formal agreement on service expectations (e.g., for MSSPs or between internal teams), such as response times, availability, and coverage.

SLO (Service Level Objective)
A specific measurable target for service performance (e.g., "90% of critical alerts acknowledged within 15 minutes").

SOAR (Security Orchestration, Automation and Response)
A category of tools focused on orchestrating and automating security workflows—enrichment, ticketing, containment actions, notifications, and documentation.

Shadow Mode (Shadow / Dry Run)
Running an AI/automation capability in "observation only" mode—producing scores or suggested actions without actually impacting queues or systems—so you can compare to human decisions and measure performance before enabling active use.

T

Telemetry
The stream of data (logs, events, metrics) from systems, applications, networks, and security tools, used for detection, investigation, and AI models.

Tenant (in Multi-Tenant Context)
A logically isolated environment for a particular customer, business unit, or group in a shared platform. Each tenant has its own data, configuration, and policies.

Threat Actor
An individual or group (criminal, insider, nation-state, etc.) that carries out malicious cyber activity.

Threat Model
A structured view of what you're defending against—adversaries, their capabilities, likely targets, and techniques—often used to prioritize detections and hunts.

Threat Hunting (see "Hunt")

TTP (Tactics, Techniques, and Procedures)
The methods used by adversaries:

- **Tactics** – high-level objectives (e.g., persistence, lateral movement)
- **Techniques** – more specific ways of achieving those objectives (e.g., Pass-the-Hash)
- **Procedures** – detailed, implementation-level steps or tools used in an environment.

Triage (Alert Triage)
The initial assessment of an alert to decide if it is a true positive, false positive, low priority, or needs escalation.

U

UEBA (User and Entity Behavior Analytics)
An analytics approach that models "normal" behavior for users and entities (hosts, applications, services) and detects anomalies that may indicate compromise or misuse. Often implemented as part of SIEM/XDR platforms.

Use Case
A concrete scenario where a tool or process provides value (e.g., "AI-assisted triage for identity alerts," "Automated isolation for commodity malware on non-critical endpoints").

W

Workflow
The sequence of steps, decisions, and actions taken to complete a SOC task (triage, investigation, reporting, containment). In this book, workflows are often encoded into playbooks, runbooks, and automation.

X

XDR (Extended Detection and Response)
A platform that aggregates and correlates telemetry from multiple layers (endpoint, network, identity, email, cloud), often with built-in analytics and response actions, to provide more integrated detection and response than standalone tools.

Miscellaneous Terms Used in the Book

AI-Related Incident
Any incident where AI or automation influenced the outcome—positively or negatively—including misclassification, over-aggressive actions, or failure to detect something.

Ethical AI in SOC
The responsible use of AI in operations, focusing on fairness, privacy, transparency, human impact, accountability, and avoiding misuse of monitoring data.

Pattern / Anti-Pattern (for AI-in-SOC)

- **Pattern** – A recurring design or practice that tends to work well (e.g., "Suggest First, Then Automate").
- **Anti-Pattern** – A recurring design or practice that tends to cause failure or harm (e.g., "Big Bang Automation", "Magic Box Vendor").

Security Platform Team
A team that provides shared security infrastructure—data pipelines, SOAR, AI assistants, integrations—as a platform for multiple security and IT teams.

You can extend this glossary with your own organization-specific terms (internal tool names, custom playbook labels, business unit acronyms) to make the book's concepts map directly onto your environment.

www.ingramcontent.com/pod-product-compliance
Lightning Source LLC
LaVergne TN
LVHW081547070526
838199LV00061B/4239